GRADUS

BOOK II

GRADUS

AN INTEGRATED APPROACH TO HARMONY, COUNTERPOINT, AND ANALYSIS

BOOK II

by Leo Kraft

PROFESSOR OF MUSIC, QUEENS COLLEGE OF THE CITY UNIVERSITY OF NEW YORK

W. W. Norton & Co., Inc., New York

to the memory of Paul Klapper

Copyright © 1976 by W. W. Norton & Company, Inc.

First Edition

Library of Congress Cataloging in Publication Data

Kraft, Leo.
  Gradus.

  Includes bibliographies.
  — —Music anthology.
  1. Music–Theory. 2. Music–Analysis, appreciation.
I. Title.
MT6.K877G7 Class suppl: MT6.K877G7Suppl. 781 75–40207
ISBN 0–393–09191–0 (Book II)

Book design by Hermann Strohbach

ISBN 0 393 09191 0

Printed in the United States of America

1 2 3 4 5 6 7 8 9

CONTENTS

PART NINE: ADVANCED CONTRAPUNTAL TECHNIQUES   3

   62   Florid Counterpoint   3
   63   Imitation   6
   64   Canon   8
   65   Short Pieces Based on Imitation   9

PART TEN: THE CHORALE   13

   66   S.A.T.B. Settings   13
   67   Keyboard Chorale Settings   21
   68   Longer Chorale Settings   23

INTERLUDE THREE: SURVEY OF PIECES BASED ON IMITATION   27

PART ELEVEN: DISSONANT CHORDS   37

   69   Dissonant Tones in an Expanded Context   37
   70   The Autonomy of Dissonant Chords   39
   71   Summary of $^6_4$ Usages   40
   72   More on Tonic Prolongations   42
   73   More on Dominant Prolongations   44
   74   More on Applied Dominants and Leading-Tone Chords   46

PART TWELVE: MUSICAL FORM AND FORMS 1   49

   75   The Classic-Romantic Phrase   49
   76   More on Musical Texture and Space   53
   77   Motive and Development   57
   78   The Single Phrase   62
   79   Groups of Phrases   63

PART THIRTEEN: CHROMATICISM 1   67

  80   Introduction to Chromaticism   67
  81   Mode Mixture 1   69
  82   Chromatic Chords; More Vocabulary   71

PART FOURTEEN: MUSICAL FORM AND FORMS 2   77

  83   What Makes the Form of a Piece?   77
  84   The Single-Idea Piece   79
  85   Comprehensive Analysis of Mozart's Variations on *Ah vous dirai-je, Maman,* 145   81
  86   Rounded Binary Form   86
  87   Comprehensive Analysis of the Minuet from Haydn's *London Symphony,* 133   90
  88   Ternary Form   94
  89   Comprehensive Analysis of Chopin's *E-Major Etude,* 148   95
  90   Forms Used in Song and Aria   97
  91   Introduction to Sonata-Allegro Form   100

PART FIFTEEN: CHROMATICISM 2   107

  92   Chromatic Motions 1: Prolonging Motions   107
  93   Chromatic Motions 2: From I to V   110
  94   Chromatic Motions 3: Other Connecting Motions   113
  95   Chromatic Motions 4: Modulations and Tonicizations 114
  96   Mode Mixture 2: Motions in 3rds   116
  97   Toward Continuous Dissonance   120
  98   The Decline of Tonality as a Unifying Force   121

PART SIXTEEN: THE EXTENSION OF TRADITIONAL TONALITY   123

  99   Background   123
 100   Tonal Structure 1   125
 101   Tonal Structure 2   126
 102   Vocabulary   128
 103   Chord as Line   130
 104   Tonal Structure 3   131
 105   Formal Aspects of 170 – 179   134
 106   Comprehensive Analysis of *Nature, the Gentlest Mother,* by Aaron Copland, 180   138

POSTLUDE: BEYOND TONALITY   141

CODA   157

MUSICIANSHIP AT THE KEYBOARD   159

GLOSSARY   162

LIST OF BOOKS REFERRED TO IN THE TEXT   168

WORKSHEETS   169

GRADUS

BOOK II

Title page of *A Plaine and Easie Introduction to Practicall Musicke,* by Thomas Morley, published in London in 1597.

PART NINE
ADVANCED CONTRAPUNTAL TECHNIQUES

62

Florid Counterpoint

The study of counterpoint involves not only pitch relationships, but also rhythmic ones. The systematic organization of the exercises previously undertaken has led from note against note, the simplest rhythmic relation possible between two lines, through two notes against one, to four notes against one. The last type of counterpoint exercise to be studied here uses all those possibilities in a free mix, approaching the rhythmic flux of a piece of music.

By *florid counterpoint* we simply mean that whole notes, half notes, quarter notes, and (occasionally) eighth notes are all available for use against the *cantus firmus*. How are they to be used? What we already have learned about the shaping of pitches into a coherent line will be applied to the counterpoint; however, there have been very few rhythmic alternatives available thus far. How can we make the most of different note values in a single melodic line?

The answer cannot be given in any formula, but principles may be discovered in musical works. We may take two fairly simple Renaissance pieces, 102 and 103, as models. Looking at the individual phrases, we see that each one begins with a half note or with a note of longer duration and ends with at least a half note. Within the phrase, shorter notes are heard. A first observation, then, is that a line begins and ends with longer notes and moves more actively in the middle. Thus, the longer notes provide rhythmic stability, desirable both at the starting point and at the final resting point.

Remembering that the half note represents one beat, we may also observe that quarter notes are used in groups with but few exceptions. They serve as connections and embellishments; they are PTs and NTs. Occasionally, as in 102, 6, a quarter note is an AN. In the Lasso piece, groups of quarter notes flow across the bar line, making the downbeat less obvious. In the Claudin (as Sermisy was known to his contemporaries), groups of quarter notes may begin on relatively accented beats.

Eighth notes, always in pairs, are used in two ways. In 102, 19, the first eighth note of the pair is dissonant, a PT. A PT is often used to prepare a SUS. In 103, 6, the first eighth note is consonant, the second a dissonant NT.

Returning to the domain of pitch, the interplay of consonance and dissonance that controls the relationship between the parts has more scope than in simpler exercises. All types of diatonic dissonant usages are available. As you might expect, PT and NT predominate, their effect being to make more options available rather than to raise the level of dissonance. The strongest dissonance is the SUS. The leading tone, a chromatic note in both 102 and 103, seems inevitable because it functions as the resolution of a SUS. Other SUSs add to the interest in various ways. A reduction of the last four measures of 102 shows the structural notes behind the embellished resolutions of the SUS. The alto's descent from F to E is embellished by one of the favorite melodic turns of the Renaissance, known as a *cambiata*. We would call the dissonant E an IN, but the four-note figure is used consistently enough to have acquired an identity of its own. The first and third notes are always consonant, the second dissonant, the fourth either.

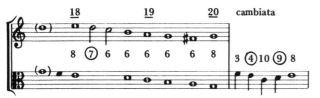

For study

Write figures to show all interval relationships between the parts in 102. Circle all that are dissonant. Identify each dissonance as PT, NT, or SUS.

Exercise

To focus on the problem of writing a florid counterpoint to a *cantus firmus*, examine the exercise below from Fux's *Gradus ad Parnassum*.

The counterpoint, in the lower voice, has a simple but effective curve. It descends from the initial D to the lowest note, G, which is heard twice—once in a rhythmically weak position and once on the strong beat. Then the line works its way back up, past the D to the high point, F, after which an embellished 3–2–1 brings the line to a natural close.

Rhythmically, both beginning and end are weighted with long notes. Quarter notes are much in evidence, and half notes fall on the weaker beat, where they may be tied to quarter notes or half notes in a variety of ways. Beyond these obvious characteristics and the play of consonance and dissonance regulating the interaction of the lines, is there anything more fundamental to be discovered?

Underlying every line there is a tonal structure, and that is as true of an exercise as of a symphony. This exercise, then, affords one more opportunity to study the relationship between the skeleton of the piece and its complete embodiment, between structure and prolongation. Reduction of Fux's melody shows a firm foundation of note-against-

Florid counterpoint by Fux

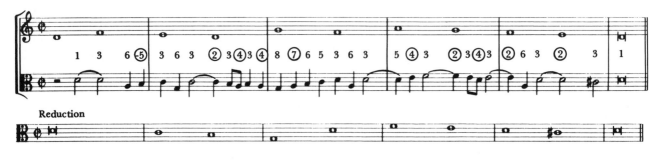

Reduction

Another counterpoint based on the reduction

note consonance under the florid counterpoint. And, having reduced the florid line to a basic one, it would be possible to elaborate the structural notes into an altogether different florid line.

Before writing a florid counterpoint to a *cantus firmus*, another look at melodic elaboration is useful. Have musicians of the past left us any clues to help develop this basic skill? We should not expect to find writers of the past using the same terminology as we do, but if the concept is valid it must have been in use since the beginning of the tonal period. Here is an excerpt from *A Plain and Easy Introduction to Practical Music* (1597), a valuable (and amusing) book by the Elizabethan composer Thomas Morley:

MA.* Here be three plainsong notes, [notation], which you may break thus: [notation]; thus: [notation]; or thus: [notation];

and infinite more ways which you may devise to fit your canon, for these I have only set down to show you what the keeping the substance of your note is.

PHI. I understand your meaning, and therefore I pray you set down that example which you promised.

MA. Here it is, set down in partition because you should the more easily perceive the conveyance of the parts.

Salvator mundi Domine

The plainsong of the hymn 'Salvator mundi' broken in division, and brought in a canon three parts in one by Osbert Parsley.

* MA. is the Master; PHI. is Philomathes, a student.

Like most instruction books of the time, and like Fux's book, Morley's treatise is written in the form of a dialogue between master and pupil. The teacher begins by explaining how to "break" three notes of a plainchant. Looking at the result, we see that this is nothing more or less than what we call elaboration or prolongation. Each of the three illustrations is informative.

First: the A is shifted down an octave, as is the second G. The first interval, a 2nd, is inverted and becomes a 7th, which is filled in with PTs.

Second: the A is prolonged. The interval of a 4th up from A is used, filled in rising and falling with PTs. Then, instead of moving directly to G, the line first steps up to B, then moves back to G, the B elaborating the G with a skip.

Third: the A is decorated with a skip to C, which, in turn, is elaborated with a NT. B, again, embellishes G with a skip—or, rather, two skips.

When Morley speaks of "keeping the substance of your note," he shows an awareness of the difference between those notes we call structural and those we call elaborative. His distinction corresponds to our division between structure and prolongation.

Morley then quotes a canon whose melody is an elaboration of the plainchant, using still another version of the first three notes. This time, G is embellished with a skip and A is left unadorned. The second G is anticipated by a quarter note in a typical SUS embellishment. The F of the plainsong has been altered to F♯, showing a tendency away from Mixolydian to G major. But the major does not win out completely, for F does play a role in the piece. By "partition" the author means score.

5

In Morley's canon, bracket all notes in the leading voice (tenor) that may be grouped together as elaborations of one note of the chant. Identify each group.

☞ Worksheet 24

63

Imitation

A MATTER OF TEXTURE The Renaissance choral pieces studied in *Gradus* I, Parts Two, Three, and Four, were written in a predominantly note-against-note style. Such a texture, homogeneous and almost unchanging, is sometimes called *homophonic*. But if that term means the opposite to polyphonic it does not describe the music accurately. All tonal music in more than one part or voice is, by definition, polyphonic. How, then, can we distinguish between the choral works in the note-against-note style and such pieces as 102 through 106? All come from the same period, but the musical fabric, the texture, is quite different.

CHORD AND LINE One of our ongoing preoccupations is the pull between the demands of the line and the chord. In all tonal polyphonic music, both are present all the time. But they are rarely in equal balance. The texture of the note-against-note pieces favors the chordal aspect; the texture of the other pieces brings the linear aspect to the fore. We may speak of the two kinds of texture as chordal and linear, respectively.

IMITATION In composing linear music, musicians long ago invented a way of letting the listener know, at the outset of the piece, what kind of texture should be listened for. The problem does not arise if, throughout the entire piece, the melody is in the top line. But if each of the voices is important, that basic fact of texture can be communicated quite readily. At the beginning, when the listener does not know what to expect, the composer starts with an idea in a single voice, perhaps only a note or two or perhaps a lengthy subject. This initial idea is called *dux* (Latin: "leader"). A second voice, *comes* (Latin: "follower"), answers with the same idea, and each of the voices that is to participate joins in, one at a time, with the same melody. In this way all levels of pitch are set forth and the musical idea is heard at each level. The procedure, whether in two voices or more, is called imitation. It was used in a great variety of pieces from the Middle Ages well into the twentieth century.

MODELS To proceed from writing one line in florid counterpoint to writing two such lines together is a logical step. But what is to provide the unity between the lines? In addition to the unifying factors of tonality, rhythm, and similarity of style, imitation can be useful here. Fortunately, at least a few composers have written exercises and short pieces that may be used as models for imitative writing. 100 consists of such models. A survey of these studies will guide you in writing your own.

The source of 100A is the counterpoint book of Gioseffe Zarlino, considered to be the best contemporary description of the Renaissance vocal language. Number 1, in Dorian, begins with imitation at the octave (two lines starting an octave apart). The distance is one measure (bar lines added). As in most Renaissance pieces, only a few notes of *dux* are heard before *comes* enters with the imitation.

Not until the late sixteenth century did the practice begin of setting out an entire melody before commencing with its imitation.

The melody starts neither on the tonic nor on the dominant, but on 3. The tonality-defining 5th makes its presence felt only in 2. Both voices proceed to a cadence on 5, in 5 – 6. The upper voice then sings the first three pitches of the opening idea, which is not imitated, and both voices flow on freely to the cadence on the Dorian tonic.

Number 2 is also in the Dorian mode. This time *dux* has two long measures before *comes* imitates. Then the first note of the melody is shortened to get the emphasis off the downbeat. More important, the intervals of the melody are inverted in *comes*—we have imitation by inversion. A cadence on 4 has little punctuating effect; there is no pause in the motion. No imitation follows the cadence, but there is internal imitation in 8.

These two pieces show but a few of the possibilities of imitation in Renaissance music. 102 through 106 will reveal many more.

100B consists of three examples written by Henry Purcell for a book printed in 1683 by John Playford, the leading English music publisher of his time. By the word "fuge" Purcell means imitation; "Per Arsin & Thesin" means inversion.

Three types of imitation are shown. Number 1 illustrates a type that was to become increasingly popular in the Baroque. Taking the first six notes as the idea to be imitated, we find that the imitation is a literal one at the 4th below until the last note. Then the skip of a 5th, from 1 to 5, is replaced by a skip of a 4th, from 5 to 1. The answer in which tonic and dominant notes replace each other in the melody is called a *tonal answer*. The other type of answer, in which *comes* responds with the same intervals that *dux* set out, is called a *real answer*.

Number 2 shows imitation by inversion, with both voices taking turns at the original and the inverted forms of the melody.

Number 3 is longer than its predecessors because the *augmentation* of the melody takes time to unfold. Purcell seems to have been interested in the possibilities of this treatment, and he pushes the exercise through a tonicization of VI in 7. Although the heading does not say so, 10 brings yet another kind of imitation, using the opposite of augmentation, namely, *diminution*. It appears only once, in 10. Imitation at different intervals also helps lengthen the illustration: we hear imitation at the octave, then at the 5th (5–6), the 4th (7–8), and those intervals again in the remaining measures.

Another early Baroque model is the set of exercises from Sweelinck's *Rules of Composition*. The most renowned organist and composer of his time, Sweelinck was also a much sought-after teacher, and this little book was written to fill the needs of his many students. Interestingly enough, the exercises in the first part of his book are taken literally from Zarlino. We realize that many of the principles and even style characteristics of Renaissance music were still considered useful in the first half of the seventeenth century. But where Zarlino leaves off, Sweelinck goes on, and the examples of 100C are all his.

Number 1 shows a tonal answer in which the initial skip from 1 to 5 is answered by a skip from 5 to 1. Number 2 is the inversion of number 1. In what sense? The melodies are the same; where is the inversion?

INVERTIBLE COUNTERPOINT While the lines of number 2 are identical to those of number 1, their spatial position is reversed. The higher line has become the lower and the lower line has become the higher. This technique comes under the general heading of *invertible counterpoint*. Specifically, if two voices are involved we speak of *double counterpoint;* three voices are in *triple counterpoint;* four, in *quadruple counterpoint.* How is the intervallic relationship between the lines affected by this treatment?

Inversion of a 3rd will yield a 6th, and the reverse is also true—in each case a consonance is replaced by another consonance. 2nds and 7ths are both dissonant, hence interchangeable in invertible counterpoint. 4ths are dissonant, and their replacement by consonant 5ths can hardly create any problem. But consonant 5ths become dissonant 4ths under inversion. Either the two-part counterpoint must be written in such a way as to avoid 5ths altogether, or the 5th must be treated as a dissonance. 3 demonstrates one way of using a 5th. In number 1, of course, it is a consonant PT. In number 2, the 5th is inverted into a 4th and is a dissonant PT. It might also be observed that the last sound in the measure is an augmented 4th in number 1 and a diminished 5th in number 2, a dissonant tritone as well as a PT in both cases.

For study

Write out the inversion of 100C, number 3 (which is number 4). Indicate all intervals in both. Is the answer real or tonal?

The next models, 100D, are by the Spanish organist-composer Cabezón. In four parts, they begin in what looks like S.A.T.B. texture. But each of the short imitations breaks up the large note values into smaller ones as it progresses, arriving at eighth notes that lead to the cadence. The melody is that of a chant, the Magnificat. All answers are real. Imitation is at the octave and the 5th, above and below. The Mixolydian mode of the chant is retained for the most part, and most of the F♯s are saved for the cadences. Since C has an important role to play in this mode, it receives quite a bit of attention and is the first note heard in two of the examples. A 5th below C is F, whose presence imparts much of what we call the Mixolydian flavor.

The examples by Salvatori, 100E, show the developing instrumental style of the early Baroque. The lines are much less vocal in character than the Cabezón. The first two examples retain the close imitation, while the third presents the entire one-measure melody before the imitating voice enters.

Number 1 is in C major. The first two voices enter in paired imitation. Answers are real. In contrast to the close imitation of the first measure, the third voice waits until 3 for its entry. The fourth entrance is delayed, by comparison with the second, so that the imitation is not predictable. Once a voice enters, it does not drop out. Each voice has the subject just once. The result is a very brief piece.

Number 2 is in the Dorian mode. Again the first two voices are close, the others more spread out. In order to get the emphasis off the downbeat, the composer shortens the duration of the initial note of the subject in the third entrance, and that foreshortening persists until the end. Entrances are all on the tonic and the dominant; answers are real. Each voice pauses after completing one thought, then enters with the subject for a second time. This means that imitation resumes with the upbeat to 7, and four entrances are heard. A prolonged dominant in 10–11 adds weight to the end of this example, which is twice as long as the previous one.

Number 3, in C major, has a subject with a markedly instrumental character. It runs to the first note in 2; only then does the answer begin. This is extended for half a measure. Such an extension prevents the entrances from being too regular, and became a feature of fugue writing. All answers are real. Each voice has the subject once and then continues to the end.

☞ Worksheet 25

64

Canon

A PROCEDURE, NOT A FORM When imitation is carried out rigorously through a piece, that piece is called a canon. Canon is actually a procedure, not a form. The imitation controls neither the tonal structure nor the development of the material. Perhaps it would be more accurate to say that the piece is written in canon. The minuet of Haydn's *String Quartet* Op. 76 No. 2, the trio of Beethoven's *Sonata for Violin and Piano* Op. 30 No. 2, the concluding section of Chopin's *Mazurka* Op. 63 No. 3, and both the opening and closing sections of Igor Stravinsky's *In Memoriam Dylan Thomas* are written in canon.

The canons of 101 are in a variety of styles. Some are in two parts, some in three, and some in four. It is interesting to see how canonic procedures were applied in Renaissance, Baroque, Classical, and Romantic styles.

The Purcell canon, 101A, is taken from the same book as the imitation models of 100B and uses the same musical idea. The difference between the imitation exercise and the canon is simply that in the canon the imitation is pursued to the end. To match the last two notes of *comes, dux* has an additional two notes, making the final cadence. In this way both voices can end at the same time. This example is a simple, clear model for canon at the octave in two parts.

To study the Byrd canon, 101B, score it first on Worksheet 26. It is a complex and varied piece, including SUSs that add to the richness of texture. This piece is usually printed in triple meter, but works as well in duple meter. Unlike the previous canon, the Byrd ends with each voice completing its part and dropping out. First we hear one part, then two, then three, then two again, and, finally, one.

The four-part canon by Haydn, 101C, written during the composer's first visit to England, has a rich chord vocabulary, including the dominants of IV and V. Most measures consist of the prolongation of one chord, but some have two. Despite the variety of chords, the demands of melody are met just as well, and each part is a singing line in itself. Furthermore, the first two parts sound quite good by themselves, as do the first three.

The Mozart canon, 101D, is based on chant. It is a tour de force of SUS in a canon, the level of dissonance increasing with the addition of each voice. The piece resembles a counterpoint exercise, but sounds heavenly, a marvelous combination of technique and expression.

101E, written in honor of the inventor of the metronome, uses only tonic and dominant chords. The rhythm mimics the ticking of that infernal machine in a good-humored way. The whole canon is contained within the interval of a 9th, but movement through the available space creates a constantly varying texture, with many voice crossings. Beethoven must have liked the tune; he used it again in the second movement of the *Eighth Symphony*.

Brahms's interest in Renaissance and Baroque music led him to write a number of canons, but a piece like 101F is utterly Romantic. The highly inflected line—A♯ pushes up to B, G pulls down to F♯—could be the melody of a song. A few well-placed dissonances add to the expressivity of the piece, and only three parts are needed to give this canon at the unison a full sonority.

The Dallapiccola canon, 185B, is atonal. However, it is certainly a canon and should be heard at this point to see how certain forms of tonal music persist into the posttonal era as well as to see another instance of the successful combination of skill and lyricism.

☞ Worksheet 26

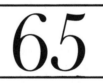

65

Short Pieces Based on Imitation

EXERCISE AND PIECE 102 through 106 are short pieces in two and three parts, based on imitation. They illustrate an aspect of Renaissance music not studied previously—where line rather than chord is emphasized. The techniques of imitation are used in all of these pieces. What is the difference between the exercises you did and these pieces?

The main difference is in form. Exercises consist largely of a single phrase or two phrases. Pieces are built of many phrases, which are strung together to make sections. These sections comprise the pieces. In vocal works, each line or phrase of the text has its own music, so that each new verbal

idea brings a new musical idea. This is true in both sacred and secular pieces. In sacred music a single word, such as "Amen," may have its own musical idea. Thus there are as many sections as there are groups of words. Sometimes, as in linear chansons, an opening section may return at the end to round out the piece, but more often the procedure is simply for one section to follow another until the text is used up.

TWO-PART PIECES Although the characters of 102 and 103 are quite different, the techniques are similar. The lovely Mass excerpt by Lasso and the gay chanson by Claudin both use imitation to start each section. In both pieces the initial idea begins with a long note and proceeds to shorter values. Later ideas convey a sense of continuation by beginning with upbeats. A cadence marks the end of each thought. But invariably while one voice holds the long note that concludes the phrase the other breathes, with or without a rest, and quickly moves on to the next idea. The leading tone, usually a chromatic note, is brought in as the resolution of a SUS, creating the tension that helps lead to the tonic. Both works use the same repertory of rhythms, but we have already seen how Lasso's music flows across the bar line, obscuring the downbeat, while Claudin gives his piece a decidedly metrical feeling. The opening of the Benedictus can be thought of in more than one meter; try 3 + 3 + 2 to start the soprano part.

Another interesting aspect of the Lasso is the way in which the second half grows by an intensified use of imitation. The first section is seven measures long, the second section, thirteen measures long. That tells us something—there is more development of the material in the second section. In the first part (1–7), the melody is stated once in each voice. The continuation idea is then set forth, imitation being closer than in the beginning of the piece. This idea, too, flows on to a cadence in 12 . But instead of ending at that point, Lasso resumes the activity immediately. At the point where the alto leads off in the upbeat to 8 , the soprano now begins. After starting the same idea for the second time, Lasso cuts it short. He drives home the first few notes, treating them as a motive. Close imitation between the voices, on different pitch levels, creates a climactic effect. As the soprano reaches the highest note in the section in 18 , a flow of quarter notes speeds the music toward its rhythmic and tonal goal, checked by the SUS dissonance (17–18) and the soprano's G (19). The subtle interplay of active and stable elements involves both rhythm and pitch. Imitation is concerned with both and plays an important role in the entire piece.

THREE-PART PIECES 104 , 105 , and 106 represent three different aspects of Renaissance music. The piece by the Flemish composer Ockeghem, 104 , whose great disciple was Josquin, shows an early stage of stylistic development which is just as mature, in its terms, as any other. The long, winding melodies proceed in independent fashion with little imitation. The motet by the Spaniard Morales embodies the systematic imitation characteristic of the High Renaissance. Quite different

in feeling is 106 , a *canzonet* (English for chanson) by John Wilbye, one of the many fine composers of the Elizabethan period.

The Sanctus, 104 , is the most remote from us, both in time and in the particular kind of religious mysticism that underlies it. The piece is in the Dorian mode, transposed to G. Leading tones of both 1 and 5 are heard, but only in a few places. In some measures we feel a pulse of three whole notes, but in others we feel two groups of three half notes. In either case, the music has little feeling of downbeat or upbeat. The one point of imitation starts in 23 at the unison. There is no other imitation, and we realize that nonimitative linear music can be just as convincing as imitative linear music. The complete triad is the norm for simultaneous sounds. One vestige of medieval music is the Landini cadence, still present in 15–16 and 17–18 . In other places the bass does make the skip that underpins the harmonic motion at the cadence, as, by implication in 12–13 and in 32–33 . When one voice stops at the end of a phrase, the others remain in motion so that there is no break in the overall flow of the music. Nor do differentiations of texture or sharp dissonances bring out any particular details. All the details, in fact, are subordinated to the continuity of the whole, as if in contemplation of the infinite. Perhaps this music needs more effort than most to identify with. The effort may be rewarded with the discovery of a work that has both beauty and spiritual depth.

Each section of Morales's motet, 105 , has its own text and its own music. The first idea appears successively in soprano, alto, and bass. The alto has a tonal answer, the bass a real answer. The careful listener will hear the time lag in the bass entry, which does not follow directly (one measure) after the alto, but waits two measures in the service of asymmetry.

The imitation that begins in 18 uses a melody with an offbeat start, again a typical procedure to ensure continuity. This time the alto is *dux*, the soprano *comes*, the real answer at the octave followed by a bass entry a 5th lower. From this point the imitation grows increasingly informal. "Et in terra" is imitated only approximately, as is "hominibus," with a suggestion of inversion. The use of imitation in the remainder of the piece is left for you to discover. Overall, we might say that while imitation is a powerful means of unifying the melodic material of a linear piece such as this, the composer had considerable leeway in determining just how much imitation was desirable.

While there are no technical features in this piece that have not been observed previously, the

10

skill with which Morales makes a full and satisfying sound with only three parts is worthy of attention. The lines, flowing in largely stepwise motion and in quarter notes for the most part, maintain their independence effectively. For example, consider 30–32. The soprano has three upbeats leading to the high point of the phrase, then a quick descent. The alto's independence derives from its rhythm, which may be heard as triple, with an upbeat. Despite the quarter notes the bass has its own identity, largely because of a mix of parallel, contrary, and oblique motion with the upper voices. Throughout the piece each line quietly but surely goes its own way rhythmically and in terms of contour; the lines come together for the cadential points, then break up either with or without imitation to launch the next phrase.

When we remember the extent to which English composers of the time were influenced by the Italians, we might be surprised to see just how English a piece like *So Light Is Love* sounds. But a long tradition of choral music enabled the English to assimilate all they wanted from the Italians and still retain their own identity. Without aiming for great emotional depth, Wilbye writes music that is so genial as to be irresistible.

In this piece, first and second soprano are equal, sharing not only the same range but also the same tunes. What the first sings in the beginning the second sings in 5, with the opening half note reduced to a quarter note, thus shifted from the strong beat. What the second sang in 2 is sung by the first in 6. Thus the music is repeated almost exactly since the alto part is unchanged.

The sections of the piece are clearly laid out, each ending with a V–I cadence. Sections are linked by the usual overlapping technique. At 51 the entire text has been set, and the piece could very well end. But in keeping with his practice of repeating the music with the two sopranos exchanging roles, Wilbye, at 55, repeats the material from 33 on, which explains why the piece is so long—all the music is heard twice.

This piece includes an example of word painting, a feature of many Italian and English madrigals. To understand it we must first be aware of a play on words in the text, typically Elizabethan. In the first phrase the word "light" refers to weight, but later when the poet speaks of "lightness to love" he means not taking love seriously, which he deplores. Up to 47 the composer has been satisfied to suggest the character of the text in the most general way. But at the words "so heavy on my heart he (it) sitteth" the texture becomes heavy, the register drops, and SUS plus a consonant 4th add more dissonance than we have heard hitherto—musically, an unexpected and welcome contrast, but brought into being by the composer's desire to express the words.

Seeing the similarities in the technical aspects of each work, including imitation, we have a basis for comparing them and finding the differences. Those differences are what make each piece unique. Each composer built upon the tradition he had inherited to create a work that embodied his own ideas.

Projects in tonal composition

In writing short imitative pieces, make each piece different by varying

1. the number of voices—two or three, equal or unequal;
2. the type of voices—female, male, mixed;
3. the modes—major, minor, others;
4. the character—sacred or secular.

Make a decision about each of these points before starting to write each piece.

☞ Worksheet 27

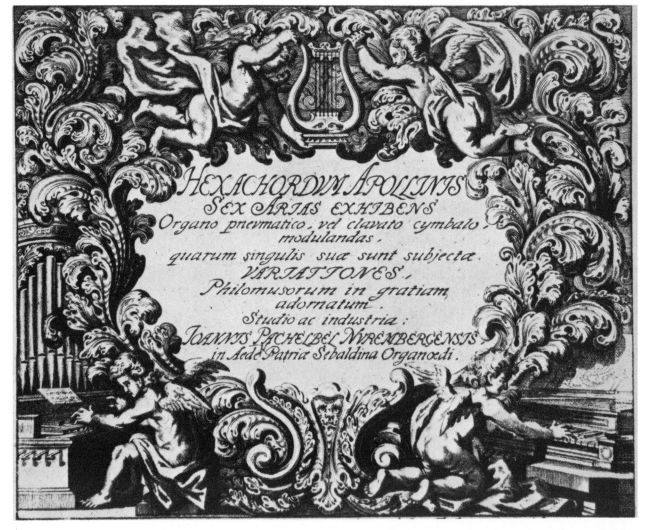

Title page of Johann Pachelbel's *Hexachordum Apollinis*, a collection of six sets of variations for organ and harpsichord, printed in Nuremberg in 1699.

PART TEN
THE CHORALE

66

S.A.T.B. Settings

PURPOSE OF THIS STUDY The fact that generations of music students have "harmonized" chorale melodies is not in itself sufficient reason to spend time doing such exercises. Are there specific gains to be made by setting chorale melodies and analyzing various settings? We set the following goals in Part Ten:

1. to learn the place of the chorale in the history of music;
2. to study further the relationship between line and chord;
3. to review and summarize the techniques of diatonic four-part writing;
4. to study elements of chromaticism in a relatively simple context;
5. to review and summarize tonicization and modulation;
6. to learn how chorale melodies were used as the basis of larger works;
7. to develop skill in writing such works, including the application of imitative techniques.

BACKGROUND Keenly aware of the unifying effect that group singing invariably has on a com-

munity, Martin Luther established congregational singing as a basic procedure in the Protestant service. He and his colleagues wrote religious poems, called hymns, and music was both adapted and composed to fit them. The musical works were also called hymns. The particular kind of congregational hymn used in what is now known as the Lutheran service is called a chorale. Other Protestant denominations, of course, use hymns in much the same way.

The melodies come from many sources. Some are plainchants on which metrical regularity was imposed to fit the new poetry. Some were popular songs of the day, since Luther believed that the Devil should not have all the good tunes. Some were actually composed as hymns in the early days of the Reformation, during the wave of enthusiasm for music that was part of the new religious movement. The chorale melodies were old before Bach was born, so that when we speak of "Bach chorales" we mean Bach's settings of traditional melodies.

SOURCE While chorale melodies were set by hundreds of Baroque composers, we concentrate on those by J. S. Bach, who summed up this aspect of composition as he did so many others. Observant students will soon realize that Bach's settings are quite sophisticated and may well wonder how the congregation could sing them. The answer is that the congregation did not usually sing them. These arrangements were taken from cantatas in which they were sung by a choir accompanied by a small orchestra. Very likely, the congregation joined in singing the more familiar tunes, but not the lower parts. We should bear in mind that Bach's chorus had instrumental support most of the time, not primarily for reasons of tone color, but because the chorus consisted of only a handful of boys who were studying at the St. Thomas School in Leipzig. Instrumental doubling for class performance is always acceptable. *A cappella* performance may bring out the lines more clearly for study purposes.

RHYTHM AND METER The music follows the meter of the poetry in a literal way, the settings being almost entirely syllabic. The poems are usually in iambic meter, following the following scheme:

∪ — ∪ — ∪ — ∪ —
∪ — ∪ — ∪ — ∪ —

This may be most simply translated into rhythmic values as

$$\begin{array}{c}4 \\ 4\end{array}$$ ♩ | ♩ ♩ ♩ ♩ | ♩ ♩ ♩̂ | ♩ ♩ | ♩ ♩ ♩ ♩ | ♩ ♩ ♩̂

or

$$\begin{array}{c}3 \\ 4\end{array}$$ ♩ | ♩ ♩ | ♩ ♩ | ♩ ♩ | ♩ ♩̂ | ♩ ♩ | ♩ ♩ | ♩ ♩ | ♩ ♩̂

FORM Many of the chorales consist simply of one phrase after another until the piece has run its course. But some are in *bar form*. This consists of an opening, usually a couplet, which is repeated, followed by a continuation leading to the end. The outline may be represented by AAB. Bar form, first found in medieval secular music, was also adopted by Wagner in his opera *The Mastersingers*, in which the German musicians of the Middle Ages were idealized.

Examine 107 through 114 and indicate which chorales are in bar form.

PHRASE Are phrase endings shown by the *fermatas*? Not necessarily. It is by no means certain that the *fermatas* were observed in performances of the cantatas. *Fermatas* were originally intended for congregational singing as a way of bringing untrained voices together at frequent intervals. Cer-

tainly there are pieces using chorale melodies in which the *fermatas* appear in the score but cannot possibly be performed. An obvious case is in 113, where 7 is hardly a complete phrase, nor is 8. If we are to find the phrase we must listen to the music, not look at the *fermatas*. As always, the cadence defines the phrase ending, whether it be an open cadence or one with more sense of closure.

CADENCE Reviewing the relative degree of closure that cadences may have, we find a continuum from the closed harmonic cadence, complete with melodic descent 3–2–1 and a 7th (described in detail on page 48 of *Gradus* I), to an open-ended cadence on V;. An overview of the cadences in 108 shows different effects of punctuation. The first cadence is harmonic, with 7–8 in the melody. The main thing that keeps the music going is the upward motion, which asks for a downward gesture to balance it. The second phrase ends with a motion to V. There is very little sense of stopping the tonal flow, because the stepwise motion in the bass moves right on to the next phrase; one may ask if this is a cadence at all. The third phrase ends with a cadence that is as conclusive as it can be, with 3–2–1 over the harmonic progression and a passing 7th. The melodic arch is complete and the piece could well end at that point, were it not so short.

The cadence in 14 is V⁷–I, which is to say a
$$\underbrace{\qquad}$$
of II
cadence in II. This implies a modulation, for modulation leads to a cadence *in*, not a cadence *on*. The final cadence, as expected, is harmonic and conclusive.

We should observe that the cadence on V; is not always based on the dominant of the piece. It may also be based on V of a temporary tonal center. In 112A, 6, a modulation from I to III leads to a cadence in III, and there is another in 8. III remains the tonal center for the next phrase, but the cadence is on its V;. This opens the way for the return to the dominant of F♯, and thence to the end.

We should remember that not every V–I or even every V⁷–I is a cadence, for the harmonic progression may be used in many ways. One way is to slow down the action near the end of a phrase or a piece, to prepare for the V–I that is, indeed, the cadence. The last phrase of 112A uses V⁷–I for that purpose in 11. Rhythmic placement of the tonic (third beat, not first), the fact that the top line is on 3 and not 1, and the motion of the bass away from F♯ keep the music moving through this harmonic progression.

14

MODULATION AND TONICIZATION In chorales as well as in longer pieces, modulation guides the tonal structure of a phrase to a scale degree other than the one on which the phrase started. Many of the chorales modulate somewhere near the middle, creating the need for a return to the tonic at the end. As an example, ⟨108⟩ turns toward II after the first couplet is repeated and confirms the shift with a cadence in II in 14. The tonal movement of the phrase has been shaped by modulation—or, rather, we call that process which shifts the key center temporarily to a different key center modulation.

In most modulations there is a pivot chord, which has one function in the key from which the music is coming and another in the new key. In ⟨108⟩, the phrase that modulates to II starts with I–V⁶, going into 13. V⁶ is interpreted as IV⁶ of II, abbreviated V⁶/IV⁶. From that point on the phrase is in II: IV⁶–II⁴₃–III⁶♯–VII⁷ of V–V–I. The last chord

of II

in the phrase is the pivot to the upcoming F major, so that I/II (I becomes II) in the return modulation.

CONSONANCE AND DISSONANCE One of the most obvious ways in which Bach's chorale settings stand out from those of his contemporaries is in his treatment of dissonance. Using the familiar procedures of NT, PT, and SUS, Bach enriches the settings with colorful and dramatic clashes between the voices; the resolutions, sometimes immediate and sometimes deferred, are all the more satisfying because of the strength of the disagreements. A study of dissonance and consonance in the chorales is a review of what has been learned up to this point as well as an object lesson in how much can be made of relatively few sounds.

DISSONANT NOTES PTs and NTs are used primarily for their melodic interest and secondarily for their dissonant qualities. But when they occur on the stronger half of the beat as P̆T and N̆T, their activity, tension, and need to resolve are greater. Such dissonant notes usually resolve to consonant sounds immediately. But successive dissonances are heard in a few places, such as ⟨111⟩, 3. The G in the bass is a PT. When it reaches F, the upper voices have moved, and that F, instead of being consonant, is dissonant with both alto and tenor and is thus a P̆T. The next bass note, E, is dissonant with the A in the so-

prano, and not until the D in the next measure does the bass reach a consonance. Three dissonances in succession are not found in every chorale, but they do occur.

A procedure that emphasizes the dissonant element is the SUS. Placement of the dissonance on the strong beat throws the disagreement into relief and makes the sound quite active. This quality is exploited in the II⁶₅, which often precedes the dominant in the cadence; resolution of the SUS in the II⁶₅ is to the leading tone, part of the V chord. Two examples are in ⟨112B⟩, 6 and 8. In these examples of II⁶₅–V the soprano and bass are the same, while the inner voices exchange notes. In neither example are any notes tied. The pitch is repeated across the bar line, the procedure is that of a SUS, and the absence of a tie does not affect what happens. Another strong SUS is heard at the final cadence, where the alto's G is continued (not tied) from the previous measure.

DISSONANT CHORDS A large vocabulary of dissonant chords is put to use in these settings. In addition to major and minor triads in all inversions, diminished triads in first inversion, and an occasional augmented triad, we hear both dominant 7th and diminished 7th chords in root position and inversion. A striking dissonance is the first sound in ⟨107⟩, an unprepared V² of IV in the Phrygian E. But interesting dissonant chords are heard in many places.

If one dissonant tone can follow another, one dissonant chord can follow another. An unusual example is heard in ⟨108⟩, 13–14. The move from F major to its II becomes quite chromatic as the bass finds its way to D, the dominant of II. The first chord in 13 is the consonant pivot chord V⁶/IV⁶. The first chord in G minor is II⁴₃, a half-diminished 7th in second inversion. What might have been a passing I⁶ on the third beat is inflected by a NT in the alto, producing an augmented triad. This linear chord is part of the motion to V (of II) and has no independent life of its own; to put a Roman numeral under it is an exercise in futility. The fourth chord in the measure is a diminished 7th whose function is VII⁷ of V. It is followed by V in a dissonant form because of the SUS. As that SUS resolves, the tenor moves up to the 7th; dissonance persists up to the last chord. Finally, G is reached as an intermediate goal of motion in the overall context of F major. On the way from I to II we heard five dissonant chords in succession, of which no two are alike in type.

Dissonances in 108 , **13–14**

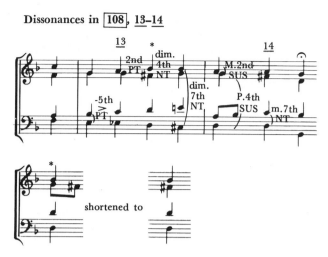

👉 Worksheet 28

TONE PROLONGATION, CHORD PROLONGATION

To learn more about the relation between line and chord we cannot look at music a note (or a chord) at a time. We must group the notes or chords into units. We have found such units through use of the concept of prolongation, in which one note (or chord) controls a group of notes (or chords). The application of this concept to chorales 107 through 114 can reveal much about the organization of lines and chords and their relation to each other.

110 begins with two measures that elaborate what is probably the favorite melody note in the major mode, 3. Within those measures we find two groups of notes. First, a SP in the soprano is matched with the same device in the bass, using contrary motion. Since the bass has skipped a 4th to the soprano's 3rd, it needs two eighth notes to return to the tonic in time. The third beat serves as the end of the first group and also as the beginning of the second. Having descended and come back a 3rd, the melody now rises a 3rd and returns while the bass does the opposite—contrary motion again. The prolongation of C as melody note has been set with a prolongation of the chord whose 3rd C is —namely, A♭, the tonic. Since the motion to A♭ has been stepwise, this is a contrapuntal prolongation.

The melodic control of C and the chord control of I continue for another five beats. The last C in 3 is met with C in the bass; but instead of I a substitute chord, III, is heard. This varies the color of the melody's C, making it the root of a minor triad. But the use of III also opens the end of the tonic prolongation so that it leads smoothly into VII⁶ of V;. When the same melody returns, starting with the upbeat to 7 , I is hardly to be heard, VI

is very much in the picture, and the prolonged C functions as the 5th of F minor.

A prolongation may include both contrapuntal and harmonic elements. The melody of 108 begins with a forceful rise of an octave, bounded by F, prolonging F. In the polyphony, five beats prolong F contrapuntally, the bass elaborating F with a PS. Then the IV–V–I brings a harmonic motion that completes the prolongation of I.

MOTION WITHIN A TRIAD AND CHORD PROLONGATION

Of course, melodic motion does not always center around one note. Another possibility is motion within a triad. Here, too, the unifying effect of the melody being stabilized around one sound (chord) is complemented by the group of chords set to the melodic unit. In 113 , the first seven notes of the melody circulate through the tonic triad, including PTs which are Bach's own addition to the tune. The corresponding bass motion is built on the motion from 1 to 3; but rather than rising, it descends, thus opening up the space of a 6th and making contrary motion possible. Bass and soprano start together on F, but when the soprano touches F again the bass has started its downward journey and is on D, so that we hear VI rather than another I. After I⁶, the NT of the melody generates a neighboring IV. This is a situation we saw in simpler choral pieces many times, and usually the bass simply skipped from 4 to 1. Here the interval of a 5th is filled with PTs, which imitate the opening of the soprano in inversion.

An interesting feature of the chorale's last phrase is the way in which Bach sets the descending scale of the melody. Is it all one move? The last two notes are set to the harmonic cadence, which is a unit itself. What about the first six notes? They may be read as motion within a I chord. Just as some prolongations end with substitute chords, this one begins with such a chord. By using VI, Bach avoids repeating I, which has just been heard and which will inevitably be the goal of the next phrase. And by stretching the bass to its lowest range he makes possible the contrary motion between the outer voices that shapes the prolongation and makes the musical gesture so grand.

Not all tonal structures are as clear as those discussed above, and often there is room for more than one interpretation. Sometimes a difficult problem may become simpler if the field of view is extended just a bit. The second phrase of 111 seems to fit into no category. There is an F-major triad in the melody, but it does not control the polyphony. An octave skip in the bass is filled with motion in the opposite direction, so that B♭ must be an important note in the bass. But what is its connection with the soprano? If our thinking is bounded by the *fermata* we are not likely to find any answers to these questions. But if we take the last chord of the first phrase as also being the first sound in the next group, we can hear a bass motion from 1 to 5 with one of the steps in that motion, 6, being elaborated through a SP that encompasses an entire octave. The two occurrences of B♭ are set under the two Gs in the tune, so that G is the main melodic note and IV⁶ the prolonged chord. This still is not as simple a group as, for example, the first six chords of the chorale, but we can see the tonal unity of the group.

DIFFERENT INTERPRETATIONS OF MELODY NOTES Is there only one possible interpretation for each note of the melody? Not at all. In fact, there are often several different possibilities, all musically valid. One way to see the different possibilities is to examine two settings of the same melody. Another is to find a melody with internal repetition and see how Bach set the repeated phrases.

TWO SETTINGS OF THE SAME MELODY 112A and 112B are settings of essentially the same tune. Comparison of the melodies shows that 112A includes a few PTs that 112B does not. These do not affect our comparison of the settings.

Write appropriate numerals, both Roman and Arabic, beneath each chord under a *fermata* in both settings, and compare them. Five out of the six are, identical. The difference is in the pause at the end of the third phrase; 112A is off to III while 112B still lingers at V.

This difference is one of timing, not of tonal direction. The overall motion I–III–V–I shapes both settings. Both versions have V; as goal in the first two phrases, both cadence in III under the fourth *fermata,* both cadence on III's V; under the fifth, and, of course, both return to I for the final cadence.

These initial observations were based on the chords under the *fermatas*. But we have seen how unreliable the *fermatas* can be as boundaries for tonal movement. In both versions the chord under the first *fermata* is V, which seems to imply that we heard a complete motion from I to V. But perhaps we have not looked far enough. In 112A, the bass continues after the *fermata* with a SP, a melodic prolonging motion. It continues on stepwise to regain the tonic, and only then is a large motion

completed, one which prolongs F♯ with motion through the triad. At the same time the soprano has been busy moving up, then down, through the tonic triad. The tonic prolongation runs through the *fermata* to the third beat of 3. The thought is only completed with IV–V;.

The prolongation that opens 112B is more obvious, but lasts exactly as long as the one that starts 112A. The bass moves through the octave from G to G. Perhaps the desire to set the first two Gs of the melody in different ways (as root, as fifth) gave Bach the idea of beginning the bass with an upward skip, the return from which starts the downward motion that continues to fill the octave. This time the opening prolongation of I is followed by II⁶₅–V;. IV and II⁶₅ have the same bass, and both function as connecting links between the tonic and the dominant.

Comparison of details throws further light on the technique of prolongation in relation to both melody and chord. Within the first large move, the first four notes of the tune move from the tonic to the 3rd of the chord. In both settings, I starts and completes this subunit. The difference is that in 112A, the bass moves through a PT to 3, generating a I⁶ as the second chord. The first inversion is connected with the root position by a VII⁶ and a
>
PT. The bass move sets up a voice exchange with the soprano between the second and fourth chords —another unifying device. In 112B, the bass skip gives the opening a different shape than 112A. The skip has an energy that launches the piece more vigorously than the steps. The contrapuntal chord supported by the skip is IV, which is then linked to VII⁶ with a PT. This comparison shows two ways of setting the top line 1–2–3 with a group of chords having the same purpose but differing in some of the specifics.

Comparison of 1–2–3 ascents

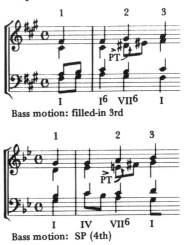

Bass motion: filled-in 3rd

Bass motion: SP (4th)

17

Comparison of the closing phrases shows, again, similarity of overall direction but interesting differences in detail. In both settings the penultimate phrase ends with V of III, and the last phrase returns to the tonic and the harmonic cadence. The melody includes the familiar descent from 5 to 1. But the individual notes are not set in quite the same way.

The last phrase of 112A starts with the E-major sound that ended the previous phrase, but in first inversion. V of III/VII, and the bass leads smoothly through V–I in 11 . This small harmonic motion prepares the way for the larger harmonic motion which is to come. The bass then moves stepwise to 4, where the SUS between soprano and alto helps generate a II⁶₅. The 7th of V⁷ is simply a PT. The rate of chord change was four to a measure throughout the piece, so we expect to hear two chords under the G♯ of the melody. The two, of course, change the function of G♯ from root of II⁶₅ to fifth of V.

The last phrase of 112B does not return to the tonic quite so quickly. The first two notes of the melody are interpreted as 2–3 in III; the prolongation of B♭ continues with V–I. Then III takes its place within G minor, and the melodic descent begins. I does not appear until the final moment. Its substitute, VI, appears instead, under the B♭. II⁶, delayed by a strong P̌T, leads to the dominant. The same SUS between soprano and alto that we heard in the previous setting is used, this time incorporated within the dominant chord. It is interesting to see how the SUS and its resolution plus the move to the 7th of V⁷ create the sense of chord change we expect here, even through there is but one chord in the two beats under the melody's A.

ROOT, THIRD, FIFTH (AND SEVENTH) One factor that makes it possible to hear a given note or group of notes in different ways is that they may be heard in relation to different tonal centers. Another is that, again, a melody note may be heard as the root, third, fifth, or even the seventh of a chord. Beyond that, even if two settings of the same melody note use the same chord, the inversion (bass) may be changed, as in the opening of 112A. All these variables must be taken into consideration when analyzing a setting or when making your own setting of a chorale melody.

COMMENT ON 107 Among the group of chorales we are studying, one has a tonal structure quite different from the others. The melody of 107 begins with a tonality-defining 5th; and after the B

is prolonged, the second phrase fills the 5th with a descent to what is clearly the tonic. Thus we know that E is the center of tonality. But what is the mode? Where we expect F♯ in the descent we hear F♮. There are F♯s in the setting, but they are used mostly as leading tones to G. The tonic triads, on E, are not preceded by their dominants. The mode, then, is Phrygian, defined originally by the melody and confirmed by Bach's setting.

Bach was well aware of the differences between those tunes that have modal traits and those that are straightforward major or minor. A survey of his chorales will show that in many cases he made an effort to preserve Dorian, Mixolydian, and Phrygian characteristics in his settings. Both Dorian and Mixolydian pose no problems at the cadence, where the leading tone is customarily introduced. But in Phrygian there is no leading tone, and the V–I cadence is not used. A look at 107 shows some of the ways in which Bach closes his phrases without using V–I. We focus on the cadences on E, the tonic. The cadence in A, the all-important subdominant in the Phrygian, is harmonic, as is the cadence in III.

In each case, the approach to the E triad, which is always major, is linear—indeed, stepwise for the most part. In 2 , 3rds in soprano and alto are counterpointed against 10ths in tenor and bass, arriving at a chord that has A in the outside voices and leads directly to the I. The cadence in 5 again uses contrary motion, the bass moving against the three other voices. Root movement and chord progression tell us nothing about this cadence; voice leading is everything. The final cadence on E is a bold stroke. Bach takes every sound from the second note in 11 to the second beat of the last measure as a huge prolongation of the A-minor triad, mixing G and G♯ and, more surprising, B and B♭. Both contrary and parallel motion are put to use until the melody arrives at E. Then the lower voices move obliquely to the E. When Bach has wrung everything possible out of the A-minor prolongation, that chord takes its place as IV of E. To a listener with any sensitivity to the Phrygian mode, this cadence is as convincing as any V⁷–I could be.

Phrygian cadences in 107

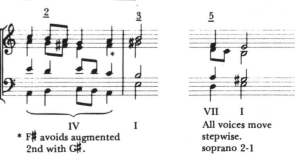

* F♯ avoids augmented
2nd with G♯.

All voices move
stepwise.
soprano 2-1

18

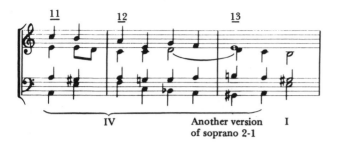

IV   Another version   I
of soprano 2-1

HEMIOLA Most chorales are in $\frac{4}{4}$, but a few, including $\boxed{114}$, are in $\frac{3}{4}$. On page 14 we saw that the rhythm of the poetry lent itself to either. One interesting device that is used in triple meter is the hemiola. Singing the first line of $\boxed{114}$, the natural accent of words and music is:

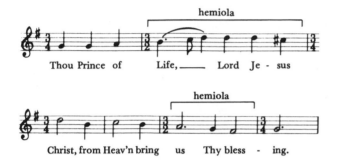

The natural accent shifts from $\frac{3}{4}$ to $\frac{3}{2}$, and the bar line in the middle of the "large measure" is disregarded. The effect is to slow down the rhythmic drive before the goal chord. The hemiola is found in triple-meter music from the sixteenth century through the nineteenth, but is most frequently heard in Baroque music. Not all the cadences in $\boxed{114}$ involve hemiolas. Study the setting to determine which cadences use hemiola and which do not.

For further study

The collection of 371 chorales by Bach (see list of books on p. 168) should be studied in as great detail as possible, following the lines of this introductory investigation. Earlier chorale settings are of considerable interest, as the two versions of *Out of the Deep* included in Davison and Apel's *Historical Anthology of Music,* I (no. 111), suggest.

☞ Worksheet 29

☞ Worksheet 30

☞ Worksheet 31

Projects

Set chorale melodies for S.A.T.B., approximating the style of the Bach settings. Suggestions for procedure:

1. analyze the melody for cadences in and on;
2. determine the tonal function (scale degree) of each note;
3. sketch a bass note (or two) for each cadence;
4. analyze the melody for tone prolongations and motion within a triad;
5. sketch bass notes to accompany these;
6. complete the bass;
7. write the inner voices.

Additional chorale melodies for setting

If God were not _ with Is - ra - el, To fight the _ cun - ning e - vil foe, Then we'd be _ lost for - ev - er.

3.
Je - sus will I nev - er leave! He did give Him - self _ for _ my life. Close - ly to Him do I

cling, He's the light of all _ my _ foot - steps. Hap - pi - ness and joy are mine, Je - sus will I nev - er leave.

4.
1. O God from Heav - en look _ be - low, Let Thy com - pas - sion fall on us.
2. Thy mer - cy comes from Heav'n a - bove, And with its bles - sings heals ____ us.

Thy ho - ly ones are _ but a few, And faith _ is but a flick - 'ring flame, In all the sons of man - kind.

5.
1. Lord Christ, _ the on - ly God's Son, Our Fa - ther ev - er - more,
2. Who brings _ us all His good - ness, Our Sav - iour ev - er - more,

He _ is the star of morn - ing, A - far and wide his light goes, More bright - ly than the sun.

6.
O God, en - dur - ing God, The source of all our good - ness, With -

out whom we are naught, From whom we have our life and _ joy, O grant me life and

health, And peace with - in my soul, And keep me free from sin, My God, en - dur - ing God.

7.
Ah, how fleet - ing, emp - ty noth - ing, Is our life and be - ing. As a mist it

soon is gath-er'd, As a mist is soon dis-pers-ed, Dust un-to the __ dust re-turn-eth.

8. Now is the great and glo-ri-ous day, Let us sing praise to our Lord God, He comes now in tri-umph o-ver all foes, So praise the Lord with full __ hearts, Al-le-lu-jah.

9. Dear my Lord re-buke me not, In Thy fear-ful an-ger. Sin is ours, Sin and pain, We go down __ to the a-byss, But for Thy com-pas-sion.

67

Keyboard Chorale Settings

Deeply involved in music and worship, the church organist finds it most natural to give the congregation a few measures of the hymn they are about to sing or to remind them of what they have just sung. Since no one has ever found out how to keep organists from improvising, their "preluding" before the singing of a chorale must have become part of the normal course of events long ago. The simplest way to accomplish this is to use the chorale melody as a *cantus firmus,* while the lower voices do any number of things in counterpoint. The melody stands out from the lower voices, perhaps because it moves more slowly, perhaps because of the choice of registration by the organist.

Two early Baroque examples show two different approaches. 116 is hardly more than an S.A.T.B. setting, although it was meant to be played and not sung. The melody is predominantly in half notes.

The lower parts also move in half notes, but smaller values are used for a bit of a flourish in prolonging the triads at cadential points. The Dorian mode is maintained for the most part, lending a particular color and charm to this piece. But in 115 the melody soon dissolves into figuration, and the whole notes become sixteenths. The melody is elaborated with every embellishment Sweelinck knew. Moreover, the rhythm is infectious, the sixteenth notes moving from one register to another. Imitation appears from the very beginning, making the texture more complex, more interesting. A sudden switch from sixteenth notes to triplets, a delightful change of pace, is one of Sweelinck's specialties. Although written perhaps half a century before the Scheidt piece, Sweelinck's is more "modern" both in tonality and in the use of musical space and the keyboard. This does not make one piece better than the other, but it does make them different.

For study

In comparing the chorale on which 115 is based with Sweelinck's figurated version, you find all the techniques of florid counterpoint combined with polyphonic melody (see below). Be sure that you understand how each note of the elaborated version is related to the original tune. Examine the first four phrases, in which the relation between the original tune and the elaborated version is described. Then do the same for the remaining phrases.

The type of elaborated setting of a chorale called a *figurated chorale* (chorale melody plus figuration) reached its highest stage of development in a collection by Bach called the *Orgelbüchlein* (*Little Organ Book*), possibly written while the composer was in prison in Weimar. In 117, the melody moves serenely in quarter notes, the three lower voices in sixteenths; thus we may speak of a *cantus firmus* approach. The *fermatas* are not to be taken

Elaboration of chorale melody in 115

as anything but the composer's unwillingness to change even the appearance of the traditional melody. One rhythmic figure suffices for the three lower voices, and the inner parts move in 3rds and 6ths almost all the time. The music begins with the first part of the figure in the inner voices and the second part in the bass—or, if you like, the reverse. Those who are familiar with organ music know that octave coupling or playing on a shorter (or longer) stop can change the register that we hear, so that, for example, the melody may be doubled an octave higher in this piece, or the bass an octave lower.

Another piece from the same organ book is 118, in which the chorale melody is in canon with itself at the octave. Not content with that, Bach accompanies that canon with another, also at the octave, in smaller note values. Hence the "double canon" of the title. The notation was probably quite clear to Bach's contemporaries, but we might point out that the triplets should be quarter notes, not eighths, in modern notation. More important, no one would have played three against two in 3 and similar measures. The quarter notes are not equal. They are triplets that fit with those in the lower voice, which could be notated in the manner of 25 .

The last of Johannes Brahms's published works was a set of organ preludes. Some are modeled after those of Bach, but some use quite original procedures. Reaffirming his identification with German musical tradition, Brahms revived a genre that has included many great works of the past. The result, to be sure, is pure Brahms. The familiar melody in 119 is in the top voice. Each cadence is echoed twice, which does not happen in Bach's pieces. As the indications for the three manuals show, each echo has a different tone color. The melody is elaborated to some extent, but is easily recognizable. In the second measure, a lovely chromatic figure emerges to play an important role in the piece. The rich five-part texture is enhanced by lush SUSs at every opportunity. Brahms is known to have felt that the great age of musical composition was drawing to an end, and this music is something of a farewell to the art he loved.

☞ Worksheet 32

Projects in tonal composition

Write a figurated chorale for organ, piano three hands, or an available instrumental combination. The melody may be heard in augmentation, the lower parts moving in smaller note values. One polyphonic melody may replace two inner voices. You may take an existing S.A.T.B. setting as your point of departure. Contrapuntal chords in an S.A.T.B. setting may be replaced by others if the more animated lines move in different tonal directions, but the structural chords should be kept.

68

Longer Chorale Settings

The short figurated chorale follows the form of the melody, usually without so much as a prefix or suffix. Longer settings are constructed in a variety of ways, sometimes following the form of the melody, sometimes expanding it with an introduction or with material added between the phrases of the melody. These settings may take the form of cho-

rale preludes or movements of a cantata or a larger work. The main types are:

1. a piece in which the chorale melody is used as a *cantus firmus*, set against lower parts which are independent—examples: number 1 of the *Schübler Chorales* by Bach; the first chorus of Bach's *St. Matthew Passion;*

2. an imitative piece based on material not directly related to the chorale melody, with the melody super-imposed—examples: number 14 of the *Seventeen Chorale Preludes* that are included in part 3 of Bach's *Clavierübung;* number 4 of the *Schübler Chorales; Chorale of the Two Armed Men* in act 2 of Mozart's *The Magic Flute;*

3. a piece in which the chorale melody is imitated in all voices in the manner of a motet—example: number 17 of the *Seventeen Chorale Preludes* by Bach;

4. a piece in which the chorale melody first appears in all voices but one, in imitation; then the remaining voice brings in the melody in augmentation—examples: number 3 of the *Schübler Chorales* (over a nonimitative bass); number 2 of the *Eighteen Chorale Preludes* by Bach (page 254 in the edition cited on page 168); the opening chorus of *Cantata No. 80* by Bach.

These compositional procedures can be applied not only to chorale preludes, but also to cantata movements and movements from oratorios. At this point, we concentrate on the imitative chorale prelude, in which all the musical material grows out of the chorale melody.

A simple example is 120 . It is based on the same tune as 111 and 115 . There are only three parts, and the organ pedal is not needed. Overall, the form of the piece takes its shape from the chorale melody. But before the melody is heard there is a preparation; between the phrases there are interludes; and the last melody note is extended into a postlude, all very short. In each phrase, the melody is anticipated in imitation, in smaller note values than the tune. Such anticipatory imitation is called *fore-imitation.*

The lowest voice starts the piece, quickly followed by a tonal answer in the middle voice. The first note of *dux* is 5, the last, in 3 , is 1. In the tonal answer, *comes* begins with 1 and moves to 5. To make the answer fit, the initial interval of a 3rd is reduced to a 2nd, but the contour of the line is easily recognizable.

As *comes* reaches its last note, the top line brings in the first phrase of the chorale, in half notes, and the lower parts become subordinate until that phrase has run its course. Then the lowest voice brings in the second phrase of the chorale melody, again imitated closely by the middle voice. The answer is real this time. Neither part includes all the notes of the upcoming phrase. Once the melody appears in the soprano the lower voices are more or less accompaniment. The same procedure is followed for each phrase.

Comparing this piece to Sweelinck's prelude 115 , aside from the textural differences, we see that where the earlier composer stopped the activity at the end of each phrase with whole-note chords, Telemann prolongs the chords with contrapuntal motion. This keeps the rhythm flowing, and each of these points is a small study in techniques of chord prolongation. Returning to texture, Sweelinck varies the densities by moving about the keyboard and shifting registers, while Telemann relies on imitation to accomplish the same purpose.

If J. S. Bach traveled two hundred miles to hear Dietrich Buxtehude play his (Buxtehude's) music on the organ, there must have been good reason. 121 is an example of the imaginative way in which the Danish master built a prelude upon a traditional chorale. Compare it with 111 , 115 , and 120 . The Buxtehude piece starts with an elaborated version of the melody in the top voice, accompanied by rich chords and dissonances in the three lower voices. But no sooner is the first phrase completed than the texture changes. On the upbeat to 6 , fore-imitation begins in the inner voices, followed by the bass. The soprano continues its elaborated version of the melody. In effect, the soprano is moving twice as slow as the lower voices, but the figuration, full of fantasy, moves more rapidly. To clear the way for the top line, the texture of the lower parts thins out, but all four join in the cadence on V; in 11 .

This is followed by imitation based on a chromaticized version of the phrase to come. Only two of the three lower parts introduce the thought before the top line enters. Again, the basic notes of the chorale are given two beats each, but the elaborative notes have shorter values. The bass then seizes the opening notes of the phrase and gives them a motivic significance by repeating them a 5th higher. In 17 and 18 , another element is added by introducing not only the upcoming phrase in the middle voice, but also a new idea which starts after an eighth rest. The middle voices are occupied with this figure for the phrase that unfolds, as bass and soprano play the unadorned melody in canon at the octave—yet another texture. The inner voices continue to function as a pair in the next phrase, starting in 23 , with imitation suggested but with no clear reference to the chorale. Bass and soprano move through a series of SUSs which lead to the cadence in III. In 29 , the inner voices anticipate the final phrase of the melody, and the bass replies with the beginning of a tonal answer. But then the soprano takes over, embellishing the melody ornately. It swoops down to the area of the inner voices in 33 , as it prolongs G through the octave. The fanciful elaboration of the D-major triad that fills the last three measures imparts weight, duration, and unwinding of the musical energy, bringing the piece to a strong conclusion; the last chord can be quite long.

Following no fixed pattern, marvelously unsystematic, this music shows the chorale melody in ever-changing guises. Buxtehude has the ability to vary textures, densities, contrapuntal treatments, and dissonant usages, making a fascinating piece of music.

Fore-imitation is carried to what seems to be its limit in 122, the last piece Bach wrote. Imitation by inversion occurs at the outset, and remains a feature of the work throughout. No sooner has the bass brought in the third statement of the idea than the alto starts again, now directed toward the dominant. The fore-imitation occupies seven measures. When the chorale melody enters in 8, the lower voices do not abandon their imitation, which was the case in the Telemann, 120. They stress the first four notes of the idea, giving it a motivic significance.

As we might expect, the end of the first phrase is followed by fore-imitation of the second phrase, starting in 11. But when the top voice takes up the second phrase, the lower voices revert to the first idea, which continues under the chorale melody. Bach uses the same procedure in the rest of the piece: fore-imitation leading to the soprano's statement of each phrase, the latter then accompanied by an imitative texture based on the opening notes of the chorale. The insistent return to the first idea adds a unifying motivic factor that is unusual in Baroque music.

In each of the four cadences, bass and soprano arrive at their goals at different times. This helps to keep the phrase endings moving and adds to the overall sense of continuity. Again, we might compare the procedure with that of the Telemann. In 120, the prolongations heard at each cadence maintain the rhythmic flow in a simple way; Bach's cadences are more elaborate.

The first cadence is in 10. The melody's G is first met with the bass's E, and VI; then, through I⁶ and IV, the motion arrives at I. The G has been

heard as the fifth, third, fifth, and finally root of a triad. The second cadence, in 22, is in V. It plays with the melody's A as root and fifth of the temporary tonic. In the third cadence, the melody's D of 31–32 presides over a scale in the bass that projects a tonic prolongation (still in V). The final cadence is much like the first, with VI–I⁶–IV (now tinged with mode mixture) plus other contrapuntal chords to strengthen the ending.

For study

Each movement of Bach's *Cantata No. 4* is based on the chorale melody *Christ Lay in Death's Dark Prison*. Describe the different ways in which the melody is used. First listen without a score, jotting down your impressions of how the tune is treated in each movement. Check against the score, and listen again.

For further study

Four chorale preludes based on the same melody comprise *Historical Anthology of Music*, II, no. 190, affording an excellent opportunity for comparison. Read through Bach's *Little Organ Book* at the piano, with one, two, or three players. With the score, listen to a recording of Bach's *Schübler Chorales,* which contain some of the composer's most imaginative larger organ settings.

Projects in tonal composition

Write a chorale prelude in three or four voices using fore-imitation. 120 is a good model. Be sure to keep the musical flow unbroken at the phrase endings. The same techniques that are used to build an instrumental chorale prelude may be applied to the chorus. Bach's *Cantata No. 4* has two examples.

Kyrie of the Mass *Ave maris stella* **by Josquin des Pres (1512).**

INTERLUDE THREE
SURVEY OF PIECES BASED ON IMITATION

From the early Renaissance through the late Baroque and even well into the Classic period, many musical works were based on the imitative techniques we have studied. The following is a simplified outline of the main genres:

What do these have in common?

1. All voices enter in imitation at the beginning of the piece.
2. Imitation is usually at the 4th or 5th and the tonic-dominant polarity is emphasized.
3. Density of texture builds to a cadence at the end of each section.
4. One section follows another, most beginning with imitation.
5. Repetition of a section is rare.
6. Sections are in keys closely related to the tonic—i.e., dominant, relative major or minor, mediant.
7. Sections may be linked with episodic material, varying the texture and modulating to the key of the upcoming section.
8. The last section emphasizes the tonic.
9. Musical interest shifts from one register to another as the main ideas move from one voice to another.

10. All voices have an approximately equal share of the interest, and all are independent.

In this survey we include:

1. *Mass movements.* The same imitative techniques and general layout are to be found in Renaissance Mass movements, motets, and madrigals. For purposes of comparison, we will study four Kyries.
2. *Ricercare, canzona, fantasy.* In the transition from vocal to instrumental style and texture, early instrumental pieces were modeled after the French chanson (linear), the result being called (by the Italians) a *canzona.* Each section is a short piece in itself, or, we might almost say, a small fugue. The *ricercare* (literally "research," "study piece") is a more general term; one of its meanings is "a contrapuntal study, sometimes based on a single idea, sometimes on more than one idea, like a *canzona.*" Not too different are the *fantasies* of the English composers. These are also in several sections, of which at least the first is imitative.
3. *Fugue.* The division between discernible sections in Renaissance pieces gives way to a larger continuity in the Baroque fugue. All sections are based on the same subject. If two subjects are used, we speak of a *double fugue,* and the two are often heard together. Originating at the keyboard, the fugue was adapted to the chorus

and even to the orchestra. Later, Haydn and Mozart used fugal techniques, sometimes complete fugues, as movements of orchestral and chamber works; Beethoven changed the nature of the fugue in his later piano sonatas and string quartets, building in the elements of contrast and development so characteristic of Classical forms. Certain twentieth-century composers have been intrigued with the textural possibilities of fugue, even without the tonic-dominant basis on which earlier fugues were constructed.

FOUR KYRIES The four settings of the first section of the Ordinary of the Mass, ⌷123⌷, show differences among four highly original composers—this despite the fact that three of the pieces are in the Phrygian mode. They also demonstrate how much all four composers relied on a common musical language. Not only do the voices enter in imitation, but they are often grouped in twos, as in ⌷123A⌷ and ⌷123B⌷, so that one pair is imitated by the other. This is the paired imitation that the Netherlandish composers brought down to Italy at the beginning of what we call the Renaissance. Imitation is based on tonic and dominant, except for Phrygian music, where the subdominant is at the other end of the axis from the tonic. The texture is carefully controlled, voices entering and leaving in a way that makes for a constantly changing musical fabric. The rests are worth noticing. They show phrase endings; they clear the way for the next entrance; they lighten the texture. But phrase endings are obvious only at the end of sections, if at all. Otherwise they are hidden by overlapping voices. Together, these techniques create a remarkable sense of continuity and little contrast.

⌷123A⌷ The High Renaissance style is seen in the compact but eloquent piece by Victoria, one of the Spanish composers who worked in Rome. Paired imitation opens the first Kyrie. Soprano (later tenor) leads off; alto (bass) responds with the tonal answer. But since the mode is Phrygian, the 5th is between A and E, and the dominant function simply does not exist. While the two lower voices complete their statement of the material, the two upper voices proceed with a continuation not motivically related to the opening, but similar in nature. This carries the soprano and alto through the first section while tenor and bass repeat their opening lines, the first note shortened to shift the emphasis off the downbeat. From 10 , all voices are engaged. The increased flow of quarter notes and the parallel 10ths between the outside voices in 14 move the music toward the Phrygian cadence. This

is embellished by a lovely SUS whose resolution leads through unexpected parallel 4ths to the E-major triad.

The Christe is marked "Three voices," suggesting that it was sung by soloists. The opening 5th is E–B, but the tonal movement is toward A, which emerges as the center of gravity. G♯ and C♯ function as leading tones, and B♭ is heard as NT between two As. A is affirmed in 24 and prolonged through its IV, D minor, and that chord's V⁶.

The motivic aspect is particularly clear in the second Kyrie. The melodic kernel is worked out thoroughly, usually in close imitation. All entrances are imitative. Tonally, C♯ keeps pushing toward D, but the bass keeps firmly grounded on E and A. The A has its own leading tone, but takes its place as IV as E gains control. Modal tonality does not stress the tonal center, but plays on subtle shifts within the main notes of the mode. Its ambiguity is part of its attraction.

⌷123B⌷ The *Pange Lingua Mass* of Josquin takes its title from the plainchant that provides the melodic material for the entire Mass. Each of the three sections of the Kyrie begins with paired imitation. The pairs are alternated: the first Kyrie pairs tenor 2 with bass; the Christe groups tenor 1 and bass; and the second Kyrie groups the (low) soprano with tenor 1. The pairings persist much farther into the piece than is the case in the other works studied here, and there is more two-part music in this Kyrie than in any of the others. The duet texture makes a fine contrast with the three- and four-part textures and is a notable feature of Josquin's style.

The mode of the chant is Phrygian, which means that A, G, and C are important centers. The melody's E is heard often as a 5th and a 3rd, but not until the end of the Kyrie as a root. The tonal movements comprise one of the most imaginative aspects of the music, and even a quick survey shows some of the ways in which Josquin moves from one tonal area to another to create tension and interest.

Hardly have the opening E and its NT, F, been heard than the bass enters with A, the all-important "opposite pole" in the Phrygian. A retains control until 12–13 , where it moves down through G, F, and D to C. But C is not the goal. C is interpreted as the IV of the Mixolydian, and the tonal direction turns to G for the cadence. It is a closed ending, including the harmonic motion V–I, yet it promises more to come because it is so sudden.

The texture of the Christe is lighter; two-part writing predominates; and for twenty-seven measures no four-part sound is heard. When all voices

28

join in, we know that the end is near. The 5th most prominent in this section is C–G, so that C is the center of gravity to 48. Then the melodic 5th A–D and the bass motion centering around A as dominant lead into D for the IV–I cadence. One reason that this sudden move to D is convincing is the tripled D at the beginning of 49, which prepares the ear to accept D as tonic.

The second Kyrie begins with the C–G 5th, in a different register than at the outset of the Christe. The second pair brings the tonal movement to G in 59, but C retains its overall control to 65. Josquin solves the age-old problem of how to end a piece with a gradual thickening of texture, guided by the parallel 10ths between the outside voices and an increasing stabilization of the C-major triad. But E plays an important role in soprano, tenor 1, and bass. The outer voices finally converge on the tonic in 66. The last tonic prolongation is especially beautiful. Soprano and tenor 2 hold the E, while the other two voices spin out lines that elaborate the same note with skips and PTs, reaching the final 5th with no 3rd. Josquin has moved from one tonal area to another, contrasting C, G, and A with each other and leading from them to the tonic, which, not often emphasized, nevertheless seems the inevitable goal. It is difficult to know which to admire more, the subtle variety of textures, the elegance of the tonal movement, or the calm expressivity of the lines.

123C One of the few English Catholic composers of the Elizabethan age was William Byrd, whose Kyrie shows the five-part chorus much favored in late Renaissance music. The two sopranos are equal voices. As in all Renaissance music, the one flat is not a key signature, but rather the sign of a transposed mode. Examining the music, we find that A is the center of gravity, with the subdominant and the subtonic as secondary centers. The mode is Phrygian, transposed up a 4th (which is what the flat tells us); A is tonic.

Each section of the Kyrie is quite short, and in no section do all five voices participate in the imitation. Yet imitation is still the way in which texture is controlled. The independence of the lines and the beauty of the chord successions are quite impressive; chord and line are in a rare balance. The SUSs are woven into the fabric to add just a few dissonances at well-chosen moments. The composer takes advantage of the rich sound that a five-part chorus can produce, and most of the voices are singing most of the time.

As in most Phrygian pieces, the tendency toward IV is very strong, and much of the first Kyrie sounds as if it is in D minor. At the cadence, the last chord contains a major 3rd, rather than the minor 3rd one might expect. The major 3rd, supplying the final sound in a piece in minor, is called a *Picardy 3rd*. Perhaps the reason it came into existence is to eliminate the clash between a minor 3rd and the major 3rd that is the fourth overtone of the bass note. Whatever the reason, the Picardy 3rd may be found in choral music as far back as medieval times, and has become a standard feature of sacred vocal music.

The Christe starts with two voices at once, the tenor supporting the first soprano. The opening B♭-major triad is a deliberate contrast to the D-major sound that ended the previous section. The Christe first moves toward D, but then turns toward a cadence in G, again major.

Imitation is used more methodically in the second Kyrie, four out of the five voices entering in close succession and the outer voices repeating the main idea. D is again stressed and is gradually located as IV of the Phrygian A.

Brief though this movement is, it shows us in a masterful way both imitation and tonal movement in the service of musical expression. Although relatively few notes are used in this closely knit piece, the listener is left with an impression of infinite resource.

123D The calm, rather abstract Kyrie by Palestrina embodies one expression of religious feeling as surely as the more personal music of Josquin and Byrd expresses another. For any number of reasons Palestrina's music was long considered to be the very model of what Catholic church music should be, and many generations of composers strove to emulate him. While we do not believe that the study of counterpoint should be based on the language of any one composer or of any one style, Palestrina's music stands as a noble monument in the literature and is well worth studying for its own sake.

Despite the use of six voices, each line has room in which to move. A glance at the page shows that in most measures at least one voice is at rest; a four- and five-part sound predominates. The sound is a particular kind of euphony based on triads and a few carefully placed SUSs, clear and luminous, the hallmark of the Palestrina style.

We also observe that although there are six parts, there are only four different voices. Tenors 1 and 2 are equal voices, as are basses 1 and 2. The equal voices share the same register and thus cross frequently. Other crossings are less frequent.

If each voice were to go on at length before it

was answered, the first Kyrie might be inordinately long. But Palestrina almost always starts with close imitation, whether the voices are many or few. All voices participate in the imitation, some more than others. But not all entrances are based on the main idea of each section. Indeed, each of those ideas disappears gradually during the course of a section to be replaced by others. The continuation ideas are not imitated systematically. The voices simply weave their lines together as they move toward the goal.

The rate of chord change is slow, which helps create the sense of serenity that informs the piece. C major is never threatened, and the cadences that conclude the two Kyries are both in C. The Christe ends on G. The spacious prolongation that concludes the first Kyrie is characteristic: the soprano reaches C, the bass avoids it with A. VI substitutes for I on the strong beat, and I only arrives on the last half of 21. Since the soprano is stationary, the motion in the alto becomes decisive for the embellishment, and the NT A (in G–A–G) generates the neighbor chord that the bass matches with its arpeggiation of IV.

The same procedures are found in the Christe, except that three voices enter at the beginning of the section. Tenor 2 and bass 1, as a pair, imitate the soprano and bass 2 a 4th lower. This turns the tonal direction toward V, but only for a moment. The cadence may be heard as I–V in C major or IV–I in the Mixolydian G.

The second Kyrie begins with compact paired imitation. Again, a second, continuing idea appears, and, again, it is imitated. As often happens, a climax is built by insisting on a short motivic idea; but here it is a gentle climax even though it serves to bring the section to a sonorous close.

Each line flows with complete smoothness, stepwise motion prevailing, the skips balanced by motion in the opposite direction. The result is that to the ear the lines are somewhat subordinated to the chords despite the fact that the lines generate those chords. It is difficult to follow the individual lines precisely because of their smoothness, and it is easy to hear a succession of simultaneities which are lovely in themselves and which follow each other in the most natural way.

RICERCARE [124] is an instrumental piece to be played by any combination of equally balanced instruments. There are four sections. The third section ends with a transition that leads back to a reprise of the opening, so that the fourth section has the same music as the first. In outline:

section	measures	cadence	texture
first	1–14	on I	imitative
second	14–26	on V;	14–20, imitative; 21–26 chordal; continuation
third	26–47 (second ending)	on I	imitative
fourth	47 (second ending)–14	on I	imitative

Not only does each section have its own melody, it also has its own meter and texture. There is but one tonal area. The piece fits the traditional definition of a *canzona*, and if Gabrieli called it a *ricercare* we can only conclude that the terms were not mutually exclusive.

Although specific instruments are not mentioned in the score, the style is not vocal but instrumental. This is clear from the very opening, whose repeated-note motive lends itself to string or wind instruments. The opening five notes of the motive are the most decisive, judging from the fact that when the motive is shortened in the course of the section, those notes retain their identity as a group. To bring things together after the fragmentation that has occurred, the top voice plays the entire motive once through, starting in the middle of 11.

The next part is based on a triadic two-voiced idea, which permeates the entire section. After the imitations have run their course, a short concluding pattern in quarter notes starts in 21 and rounds off the section. The prevailing texture here is chordal, but there is a bit of imitation, too.

The third section changes to triple meter and opens with paired imitation. A short transition brings back quadruple meter, and leads first to a repeat of the third section, then to the restatement of the first section that concludes the piece.

This music was published during Palestrina's lifetime, and there are many similarities between it and Palestrina's Kyrie just studied. Both are in C major and are quite diatonic. Both center around tonic and dominant. Both use paired imitation. Yet the spirit of the two seems quite different. In the Gabrieli, the motivic aspect is very strong. In each section, a clear, decisive idea dominates, being driven home again and again with an insistence that is far from the contemplative music of the Roman master. Strong emphasis on the downbeat suggests dance rhythms. In every way, Palestrina's is sacred music, Gabrieli's secular.

FANTASY By *fantasy* the English composers meant a genre much like the Italian *canzona,* written for keyboard or strings. The stringed instruments in use at the time were members of the viol family, which had not yet been superseded by the more brilliant violins. Purcell's fantasy, 125, is in two long imitative sections in fast tempo, connected with a short, slower part that has little imitation.

The long, flowing lines contain short motives that are used in a variety of ways. At the beginning, imitation is by inversion, and both the original and the inverted forms are used throughout the section. Hardly a rest is found on the page, yet the lines are subtly punctuated in their rise and fall. For example, the opening line (tenor) goes without a stop into the ninth measure. We may feel the end of a thought, however, in 3, after the D; in 6, after the G; in 8, after the A; in 10, where the first G both ends one thought and begins another; in 13, after the F; and in 15, after the first F♯. One gesture melts into the next, all based on the leading motive, creating an extraordinary kind of continuity.

The whole piece is a study in just how expressive diatonic dissonance can be. The first beat in the measure often includes a SUS, and the frequent use of PTs helps keep the dissonant level higher than in any of the pieces studied in this section. An example of Purcell's use of dissonance is heard in the first measure, where a PT followed by a P̆T gets the music out of the measure and into the SUS that starts the next. The consonant 4th is still used, as we see from the cadence in 14–15. Indeed, every type of diatonic dissonant usage is put to work here.

A page covered with quarter notes may not promise much in the way of rhythmic interest, but the opening section of the piece has a fascinating way of moving through time. The grouping of the quarter notes does not follow the bar line in the way the Gabrieli piece did. The natural accent of the lines is anything but regular. For example, the opening of the top part may be heard as

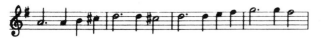

This also means that where one part has a strong beat another may have a weak beat, a Renaissance style trait that carries over well into the seventeenth century. By contrast, all the voices move together in the slow interlude, and the dance rhythm of the final section adheres closely to the beat.

Chromatic notes appear as early as the second measure and are rarely absent from then on. Many involve mode mixture; some are applied leading

tones. The slow section is the most chromatic. The color of the chromatic notes combines with the pungent dissonances to create a kind of emotional intensity that is unique to the music of Purcell.

FUGUE In the middle of the seventeenth century, the imitative types coalesced into one genre, the *fugue*. Most of the concerns that underlie the earlier forms are in evidence in the fugue; we note imitative procedures, variety of linear textures, overlapping of phrases, and the pursuit of the main melodic idea from one register to another, together with shifts of tonal area to help delineate the form of the piece.

How can we distinguish the fugue from other genres? The fugue is continuous; most fugues contain no changes of tempo or meter. One idea is followed throughout; in a double fugue, there are two ideas, which appear simultaneously for the most part. The close imitation that sometimes obscured the melody in earlier music is replaced by imitation that permits the entire subject to be heard before the second voice answers.

A fugue grows out of a salient musical idea, a clearly recognizable melody known as the *subject*. This subject may be long or short, fast or slow, but it is always clear-cut and easy to identify. It is presented in all the registers and voices of the fugue in the opening section, in imitation. This first part of the fugue is known as the *exposition*. Subsequent sections in which the subject is prominent may alternate with those in which the subject is not heard, or in which only part of the subject is heard. These latter sections, usually quite short, serve as continuing links and are known as *episodes*. An episode frequently uses fewer voices than the total available in the fugue, for textural contrast. The voice that is silent is usually the one in which the forthcoming entrance of the subject will appear.

The sectionalization of a fugue is subordinate to the overall continuity. As a result, the level of tension is fairly constant throughout the piece, sometimes building to a climactic statement in the lowest voice at the end. Intensification is also achieved in some fugues by shortening the distance between entrances, thus introducing close imitation again. This device is known as a *stretto* (Italian: "close," "pressed," "narrow").

Some of these characteristics are illustrated in a short organ fugue, 126, by Guillaume Gabriel Nivers, a little-known composer of the French Baroque. The six notes that comprise the subject have a distinctive character, partly because of the

31

off-the-beat start, partly because of the two eighth notes that push the line into the upcoming measure.

The subject enters in the bass (the S.A.T.B. format is not far in the distance), and a real answer appears in the tenor, written in the treble clef until 6 . Before the answer is quite completed, the alto makes the third entrance. The three voices extend the material before the soprano enters on the upbeat to 7 . At the end of 7 the exposition is complete, but there is no pause in the flow of the music. An episode follows in 9 and 10 , featuring a new motive with an upbeat of three eighth notes. The alto is silent for just one beat, at the start of 11 , then enters with the subject again, answered by the bass at the end of 12 . When that statement of the subject has run its course, another brief episode ensues (14–15), made up of bits of the subject. Again, the sense of sectional division is minimized, so that the piece seems to have but one long gesture. The final bass statement starts on the upbeat to 16 , and the alto answers, its first note being held from the previous measure.

The tonality of the piece is a **D** minor that still evokes memories of the Dorian mode. B♮ occurs more often than B♭, creating the modal coloration that accounts for much of the charm of the fugue. It is interesting to note that elements of modal tonality lingered on well into the seventeenth century, particularly in sacred music. At the beginning of the piece, we might well think that it is in **A** minor. Not until the second voice brings in **D** do we suspect that A is not the tonic. The third voice presents A as the fifth of a **D**-minor triad, and that is as conclusive as the piece will be. The center of tonality shifts back and forth between **A** and **D**, and only at the end are we quite certain that **D** is the tonic.

The organ, like the chorus, is particularly suited to bringing out the dissonant element in the SUS. The subject has the resolution of a SUS built in, so that every entrance can introduce a dissonance. If the resolution is to a leading tone, so much the better.

In the pieces studied up to this point, the musical material heard together with the subject did not take on any particular character. In close imitation, the same material was heard in all voices at the start, and later entrances of the main idea were accompanied by subordinate material of a "continuation" nature. This is no criticism of the music; the composers simply focused their attention on the main idea. But as musicians developed greater mastery of fugal techniques, the melody that ran counter to the subject, called the *countersubject,* began to take on a motivic significance of

its own. It was still not as important as the subject, but in many cases it came to have some degree of independence. Since this is true of both 127 and 128 , we study those two fugues together.

Both fugues are built on subjects that stress 1 and 5; tonal answer is heard in both. Handel has to squeeze the descending 5th into a 4th to preserve the tonic-dominant exchange; for the same reason, Bach has to expand the descending 4th into a 5th in his tonal answer. Both retain the characteristic intervals that give the subject its shape, the initial half steps in Bach and the diminished 7th in Handel.

In both, the answer is accompanied by a countersubject, and for the rest of the piece the subject is never heard without its partner. Since the subject appears in all voices at one time or another, the countersubject is heard sometimes above and sometimes below the subject. This means that the subject and countersubject must be written in double counterpoint.

Handel's fugue starts with the sopranos, and works its way down. When the sopranos have finished with the subject and the altos start the answer, the sopranos proceed with the countersubject. When the tenors enter with the subject, the altos sing the countersubject and, as an added touch, the sopranos imitate the countersubject in 16 . The bass entry with the tonal answer is met with the countersubject in the tenor, which is imitated in the alto. Through the end of the exposition, the subject has always been heard below the countersubject.

But in 25 the sopranos begin with the subject—or, more accurately, the tonal answer. It is the basses' turn to sing the countersubject, reversing the position of the two melodies. The double counterpoint is at the octave. Where the countersubject had begun a 3rd above the subject it now begins a 6th below. Consonances and dissonances retain their identity in the inversion.

Double counterpoint in 127

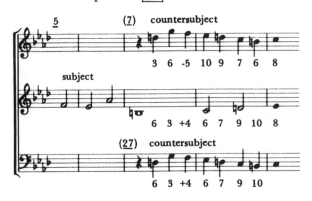

32

From here on, either version of the double counterpoint may be used, and Handel takes advantage of both to make the most of his material. He also gives the countersubject special attention, using the first notes as a vigorous motive that helps propel the piece toward its goal.

Bach's countersubject, too, makes its appearance under the tonal answer. Subject and countersubject are then inseparable until the ending, where the subject is set with chords. At the third entry of the subject, in 7 , the countersubject moves above the subject in double counterpoint at the octave. The 6ths of 3 become 3rds (10ths, in fact) and the dissonances are carefully controlled. The only 5ths in 3 and 4 were diminished, and their inversion into augmented 4ths leaves them as dissonant as they were.

When the subject appears in E♭ major in 11 , the countersubject is below it; when the subject is heard in G minor in 15 , the countersubject is above it. 20 is a rearrangement of 7 , with three voices participating in the exchange; this is triple counterpoint. Since the intervals involved are mostly 3rds and 6ths, the spatial inversion poses no special problems. We see how essential the technique of invertible counterpoint is when the composer is presenting a small amount of material in the largest number of ways (see below).

Both fugues are continuous rather than sectional, but they accomplish their purposes in somewhat different ways. Handel's piece simply drives on from beginning to end without pause, the rhythmic impulse pushing through cadences (or what would be cadences if there were time to let them make their effect). Overlapping helps maintain the continuity, too; the bass ends the exposition in 26 , but the soprano has already started the next statement of the subject in 25 . Close imitation of the countersubject rather than the subject builds up tension toward the end, helped by a progression in 5ths starting in 73 . The subject and/or countersubject are present virtually all the time.

Bach alternates short sections in which the subject is heard in its entirety with short episodes based on either the characteristic opening motive of the subject or similar material. The episodes modulate. The episode in 9–10 moves from I to III; the one in 13–14 returns to I, or seems to, since the tonal answer pushes on to V at once; that in 17–19 takes us back to I. The episode starting in 22 seems about to modulate, but does not; it is, tonally, a motion from I to V. When it reaches the dominant, in 25 , it continues until the middle of 26 , emphasizing V to prepare for the bass statement of the subject. After that the bass holds a tonic pedal over which the subject is proclaimed in the soprano, the texture growing more chordal and emphatic.

The episodes, far from weakening the continuity of this fugue, add to it. How is this done? One answer is that the episodes use the same figures as the subject so that the same melodic material pervades every measure. But another unifying factor is the connection between the episodes themselves. Consider 17 . Haven't we heard this music before? Yes, in 5 . Of course, the position of the voices is reversed (double counterpoint again), the lines are transposed, and a third voice is added. What happens in the middle of 18 ? Isn't this 17 all over again a 5th lower (or 4th higher), with the bass and middle voice inverted? Look at 22 . It bears a suspicious resemblance to 9 .

This fugue is a lesson in how to make the most of minimal material. Every aspect of music that

Triple counterpoint in 128

Bach can bend to his purpose is put to work, the emphasis being on lines and their combinational possibilities. Any idea may appear in any register together with any other idea, and invertible counterpoint is the technique that makes it possible.

What role does tonal movement play in a fugue? It provides a foundation on which the contrapuntal orderings and reorderings can be built. Every tonal shift brings out a change of texture, another combination of the lines. This is as true in the Handel as it is in the Bach. 127 stays in F minor, with the customary swings to the dominant and subdominant through 41 . Then, a move to the dominant of III takes effect, leading to the relative major in 56 . The major mode is a strong contrast; the subject is the same, of course, but is now seen in a new light. III is confirmed with a cadence in 62–63 , but the rush of quarter notes prevents any sense of stabilization and the tonic reappears at once. The progression in 5ths that starts in 73 brings the end near, and the piece concludes on the dominant. The next chorus, in F major, follows directly.

The tonal structure of 128 is not too different. The alternation of tonic and dominant characterizes the exposition. The episode in 9–10 modulates to III, while 13–14 returns to I—but not to stay. The tonal answer brings us to V so that the episode of 17–19 has somewhere to go, regaining the tonic after dwelling on G minor for a moment beyond the cadence in V. From 20 , all entrances are on the tonic, and the motion to V culminates in the final two statements, both heavily emphasizing I.

The spirit and much of the technique of the fugue lives in the second movement of Stravinsky's *Symphony of Psalms*, 176 . While tonality has been extended to include many chromatic melodic and chordal types and the V–I relationship has almost disappeared, there is no doubt that key centers are heard as a vital part of the piece. The textural aspects of the fugue, including imitation, are in the forefront of the piece. A discussion of the tonality of the piece is on page 127 .

Listening for an overall impression, we find not one fugue, but two—or, perhaps more accurately, a double fugue. The orchestra has its own subject, set forth in four parts. It is in C minor, in the middle and high registers, with middle C the lowest note. The chorus has its subject, in four parts. It is in Eb minor, exposed to the accompaniment of the orchestra playing its own subject and material drawn from it. A short episode, starting at 47 in the male voices and orchestra, leads to a *stretto* (52–

60), sung very quietly *a cappella*. The orchestra's answering episode stresses the first four notes of its subject, which take on increasing importance. Over a G pedal (66–69), a version of the instrumental subject is introduced in dotted rhythm. Without warning, the climax of the piece bursts out, the chorus singing in rhythmic unison, the orchestra building on the dotted figure. Just as suddenly the serene epilogue starts, the voices reiterating the Eb that is the goal of motion for this movement. The orchestra calmly insists on a motive made of the first four notes of the subject. Such a literal reiteration of a short idea is called an *ostinato*.

The tonal centers are quite clear in most of the piece. The techniques of elaboration and the norms for simultaneity will be the subject of Part Sixteen, but we can see now that the triad is much in evidence both as line and chord. Embellishing tones added to the triads impart the strong dissonant element that propels the music from one point to another. Mode mixture is abundant, provoking many clashes between lines and giving the sound its astringent quality.

While the first (orchestral) exposition is built on C and G, the only chord resembling a dominant is the leading-tone chord that is heard for a brief moment before the chorus enters. Once C minor is left, it never returns, and Eb becomes the overall tonic. The first subject (orchestral) evokes the spirit of Bach's polyphonic melodies. Built on minor 3rds and their inversion, the tune prolongs C for four measures; then, in 5 , both strands of the polyphonic melody are directed toward G. On that note the answer begins. It is a real answer, as are all the answers in this fugue. Two statements of the five-measure subject are followed by a two-measure extension, then the third entrance in 13 . The fourth entrance follows directly (18). Then we hear six measures which continue working out the figuration that has accompanied the subject. The top line of the polyphonic melody reaches Eb, and that becomes the center of gravity for the next section.

In the second (choral) exposition, the sopranos start with a 4th that defines Eb as tonic, the orchestra providing the minor quality at once. The two subjects flow side by side, and that procedure could easily have been followed for all four entrances of the chorus. But Stravinsky chose instead to continue with the short figures that were heard at the end of the first exposition. While the texture of the first exposition began at the center of that section's range and spread out, the chorus begins with its highest voice and works down to the lowest. The episode that follows has the nature of an extension, leading to something resembling E♭'s dominant.

The *stretto* is used not so much as a climactic device as it is a résumé of the preceding exposition. When all voices are involved, we have a *master stretto (stretto maestrale)*. This marvelous piece of close imitation begins a choral section that gradually diminishes in dynamics and leads tonally to the dominant of the dominant. The orchestra comes in with the expected B♭ in 61 , featuring the four-note motive derived from its subject. The bass moves slowly down from B♭ to G. A four-note idea starts in the high register and is imitated in counterpoint to the dotted rhythm that is transforming the motive.

The passionate music that follows is torn between G minor and B♭ minor, then between B minor and C minor. Despite all the activity and the full texture, there are no more than three real parts because the rhythmic unison of the chorus sounds like one gigantic voice against which the orchestra presents its two with octave doublings. The chorus, bearer of the message, has the leading part. The orchestra serves to inflect the sung line, starting with its (the orchestra's) opening motive and gradually diverging from it. The top line moves from G through F♯, F, and F♭ to E♭, the goal. The last chord is E♭ major, with an added 6th and an added 2nd, a chord type that could also be represented as a series of perfect 4ths. The tonicity of E♭ is firmly established by the chorus.

The sharp contrasts between sections seem to grow from the meaning of the text, or perhaps Stravinsky chose to illuminate the text with those contrasts. The opening expression of faith is calm and deliberate and continues long enough to set the mood and character of the piece. But when the Psalmist sings of a new song to his Lord, Stravinsky bursts forth with music that is quite appropriate in its harsh way. There is no transition to or from this section; it is just there. The calm of the last line embodies the sureness of hope shared by the Psalmist and the composer. But in spite of the sharp contrasts, the piece has continuity. While one section confronts another, the tempo remains constant, the material presented in the two expositions is heard throughout the piece, and the overall tonic, E♭, exerts its unifying influence.

This piece is but one example of twentieth-century fugue; there are many others. The links to the past are obvious, yet these sounds could only come from the period between the two world wars. Just how Stravinsky manages to make so many aspects of Baroque music serve his own purposes is, of course, one of his miraculous secrets.

For further study

Read the articles "Canzona," "Ricercar," "Fantasy," "Fugue," and "Imitation" in *Grove's Dictionary*. A most useful book is Alfred Mann's *The Study of Fugue*. The first part gives an account of the history of fugal theory; the second contains "how to do it" information selected from the writings of Baroque theorists, and is illustrated with numerous examples.

Bach wrote three collections of fugues: *The Well-Tempered Clavier, The Musical Offering,* and *The Art of Fugue.* The latter contains imitative pieces other than fugues. For simpler examples, Pachelbel's fugues on the Magnificat and Telemann's *Easy Fugues* are suggested. The fugues in Handel's harpsichord suites are more easygoing than those of Bach and are enjoyable to play.

Classical composers were trained in fugal writing and put their skill to use in various ways. Haydn used fugue for the last movements of string quartets, but gradually gave up the practice as his music moved away from its Baroque antecedents. But when he turned to writing oratorios in his later years, fugue proved to be a powerful means of expressing his ideas, Handel being his model more than Bach. The fugal numbers of *The Creation* and *The Seasons* should be compared with the choruses from Handel's oratorios. Mozart was involved with fugue all his life, but he was more interested in integrating fugal elements into larger forms than in writing fugues as such. The finale to the *Jupiter Symphony* is a case in point. But the Kyrie from Mozart's *Requiem* is a fugue, and should be compared with 127 . Beethoven, too, had a strong background in fugal technique, but not until his last years did he successfully incorporate the fugue into his overall formal concept. The fugues in *Piano Sonatas* Opp. 101, 106, and 110 and the *Great Fugue for String Quartet* Op. 133 stand comparison with the works of Bach, and tackle formal problems of a magnitude that simply did not exist in the Baroque.

Nineteenth-century fugues are rarely convincing, perhaps because the tonic-dominant axis was losing its significance. The texture of a fugal exposition still intrigued composers, however. A short section in which a subject was introduced in imitation, called a *fugato,* was used in the course of longer pieces by Schumann and Brahms as a developmental technique.

The "back to Bach" movement of the 1920s and the revival of interest in many aspects of Baroque music led to the creation of many fugues and pieces with fugal sections. The most conspicuous fugue composer of the period was Paul Hinde-mith, whose works include a set of piano fugues and interludes called *Ludus Tonalis.* Atonality does not often lend itself to fugal writing. One example of a nontonal fugue is in the opening of Roger Sessions's *Second String Quartet,* which has the design of a double fugue. Anton von Webern's arrangement of the ricercar from Bach's *Musical Offering* is a remarkable illustration of the effect of twentieth-century thought on the way we might hear an eighteenth-century piece.

PART ELEVEN
DISSONANT CHORDS

69

Dissonant Tones in an Expanded Context

Before going more deeply into the study of dissonant chords, we pause to observe that dissonant tones continued to be used as embellishments and connections even after dissonant chords had evolved. In fact, dissonant chords, originally resulting from the adherence of dissonant tones to triads, are themselves elaborated with additional dissonant tones. In the nineteenth century, there is an ever-increasing level of dissonance in music, leading to a chromatic language in which consonance has less and less place.

PT The PT on the weak beat is an essential device. It makes possible the stepwise motion that is so often sought after. In the Classic-Romantic style, the P͞T is more appreciated for its ability to highlight the dissonance. Both types are used in 161, together with other melodic elaborations. In the voice part, a long chromatic PT and its elaboration occupy 17, the A connecting the A♭ of 16 and the B♭ of 18. The C of 18, itself anticipated, is a P͞T that clashes with the D♭ in the accompaniment and resolves, 7th to 6th. The same event takes place in

each of the next two measures. Looking back at the orchestral part, in 7 an inner voice moves through E, a chromatic PT that colors the V⁷ with an augmented 5th from the bass.

NT Both diatonic and chromatic NTs are at the fingertips of every late eighteenth- and nineteenth-century composer. In the voice part, the first measure of 161, a chromatic NT (E♮) is used to round off the lower part of the expressive melodic arch. The unexpected A of 9 is given a moment to settle in by the use of two NTs, and an IN in 10 bends the line down to play against the prevailing upward motion. Not all neighbor notes are of short duration. A long IN is used to slow the line in 33.

The expressive power of the N͞T is shown in another aria, 159. In 12, the tenor's high B♭ is dissonant with the V⁷ of the orchestra. Here, to be sure, is the origin of the V⁹ chord. A dissonant chord with an independent existence, V⁷, is elaborated by yet another dissonant note. This additional dissonance, in turn, soon cleaves to the chord to which it is a NT and generates a more dissonant

Poster for the first run of Carmen at the _Opéra comique_, Paris, 1875 (Bettman Archive).

chord. When the 9th has made its point it resolves stepwise down to A♭.

SP, PS The skip followed or preceded by a stepwise motion to or from the main note constitutes a basic device of melodic embellishment. SP is used in ⟨161⟩, 6–7, to spin out the end of the first phrase. 14 consists entirely of a SP with octave displacement, A♭ being the main note. The same note is immediately embellished with a rising SP, in which the dissonant PT, B♭, is a bit longer than we might expect, forming a 9th with the bass. These two elaborations are the means by which A♭ maintains its control of 14–17. Through the study of melodic elaboration, we begin to see beyond one note at a time. Starting from the second beat of 18 through 20, B♭ is the structural note. First it is the base of a SP, then of two skips that make an embellishing triad and PT that return.

SUS As in earlier styles, the SUS is valued for its dissonant quality and as a way of getting across the bar line. ⟨161⟩ owes much to the dissonances that fall on strong beats. These color the melody and enrich the orchestral fabric. The bass line and an inner voice move through a chain of SUSs in the first phrase, 7ths resolving to 6ths. The melody, consisting mostly of top-line notes, shares some of the SUSs. When the bass skips down to E♭ to vary its stepwise motion, another inner voice sets up another SUS relationship. As one dissonance is resolved another appears, and dissonance is continuous until the tonic goal of the phrase is reached.

Not all SUSs resolve so quickly. In ⟨161⟩, 12, an inner-voice G♯ is held over the A in the bass for the entire measure; and by the time it resolves to G♮, the bass has moved to B♭. SUSs also play a role in the gradual resolution of the I$^6_4$ in 14. The two upper voices move into their notes of the V⁷ in 15, as expected. But the suspended D♭ persists, resolving only in the second half of the measure.

☞ Worksheet 33

70

The Autonomy of Dissonant Chords

EVOLUTION OF DISSONANT CHORDS Until the late sixteenth century the only simultaneity to have an independent existence was the consonant triad. Dissonant notes were used to connect and embellish those triads, but the dissonant notes were completely dependent on the consonances to explain their function. With the shift of musical emphasis from the chorus to the keyboard, Baroque composers grew more interested in the chords themselves, an interest that has persisted to this day. The sound of a PT, NT, or SUS together with the triad it was embellishing was recognized and not only tolerated, but cultivated for its own sake. Seventh chords became part of the vocabulary; and dissonant chords began to have a life of their own, even though their relation to consonant chords remained direct and clear.

In studying dissonant chords, then, we begin by looking for their function in relation to the consonant chords about them. In earlier pieces this relation is quite obvious; later the consonances are needed less, and the dissonances begin to predominate. The interplay between consonance and dissonance changes from one piece to another, and is a valuable guideline in defining styles. In the Haydn quartet movement ⟨147A⟩ almost every dissonant chord is surrounded by consonant ones. Indeed, consonant and dissonant chords alternate in the first phrase except for the two dissonant chords in 8–9. By comparison, the Chopin *Prelude in E Minor*, ⟨144B⟩, contains exactly five consonant chords in the entire piece, of which only one is in root position. In the Haydn, the energy of each dissonance is immediately absorbed by a consonance, while in the Chopin, very few consonances are used and the activity and color of dissonance is exploited. Here is a clue to the sense of repose that we hear in many parts of the Haydn, and to the tense striving that the Chopin has despite its slow tempo.

Once a dissonant chord exists as a recognizable entity, it, too, may be elaborated with dissonant tones. These, in time, adhere to the chord they were originally embellishing and form an even more dissonant chord. We saw this process taking place in the incipient V⁹ of [159]. In this way, composers developed ever greater degrees of dissonance in tonal music. The search for dissonance and its expressive power brought late nineteenth-century music to the point where dissonances outnumbered consonances in many passages. Chopin's *E-Minor Prelude* is an unusual piece, but after Chopin led the way, others followed with ever-increasing levels of activity. Finally, Arnold Schoenberg was to speak of "the emancipation of the dissonance." By this he meant that dissonant sounds were accepted into the musical vocabulary on their own, without explanation from consonance.

☞ Worksheet 34

71

Summary of $\frac{6}{4}$ Usages

The $\frac{6}{4}$ position of the triad is dissonant, by definition, as long as the 4th is considered dissonant. Since the 4th is used either to embellish a consonance or to connect two consonances, $\frac{6}{4}$ chords may be used to embellish a triad or to connect two triads. The 4th may be a PT, NT, or SUS, and its resolution determines the behavior of the chord.

I$^6_4$ IN THE CADENCE Rarely in Baroque music, and increasingly in eighteenth-century music, does the dominant in the cadence begin with I$^6_4$. The Roman numeral is misleading because the chord is part of the prolongation of V, not the tonic. The $\frac{6}{4}$ position creates expectation, for we want the 4th over the bass to resolve to a 3rd. When it does, we hear V or V⁷, and the tension releases toward the upcoming tonic. I$^6_4$–V⁷–I is a typical formula for the harmonic cadence in Classic and Romantic music.

Both phrases in [129A] use I$^6_4$ as dominant prolongation in the cadence. In both, the 4th is a P͞T. The illustration below shows the progression in reduced form.

To compare harmonic cadences with and without the use of I$^6_4$, listen to both [129A] and [129C].

The cadence on V; can also be entered through I$^6_4$. The first half of [129B] ends with I$^6_4$–V; with the 4th as a SUS.

I$^6_4$ IN THE PHRASE The usages studied above are all in cadences. But I$^6_4$ is useful in other parts of the phrase as well. [131] opens with a tonic prolongation, and the first part ends with a cadence in I. Gluck begins the second section by modulating to the dominant, but holds off the arrival at C, the new tonic, by prolonging its dominant from 12 to 16 . Pedal points in the outer voices frame the prolongation. Within that framework the strings elaborate V with a neighbor I$^6_4$. Study the dominant prolongation in detail, paying particular attention to the way in which the 4th functions.

II   I$^6_4$ V⁷   I

IV$^6_4$ While any triad may appear in $^6_4$ position, IV$^6_4$ is the most frequent, after I$^6_4$. IV$^6_4$ is a neighbor chord that occurs fairly often in Classical works, less often in early Romantic music. One example is in the first section of [140]. The first four measures are taken up with a tonic prolongation. The sketch shows how the two upper lines prolong the main notes with NTs. The linear chord generated is IV$^6_4$. It is a dependent chord, elaborating the tonic, and has no "subdominant" quality. The second four-measure group continues the musical idea, the NT growing into a DN. Again, IV$^6_4$ is heard as a linear chord, as is the II^2 which follows it. An interesting detail is the inner-voice move through the chromatic PT, C$\sharp$, which intensifies the motion to IV$^6_4$.

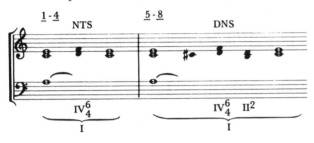

ELABORATION OF THE $^6_4$-POSITION TRIAD

Itself an elaborative chord, the $^6_4$ may in turn be embellished by higher degrees of dissonance. A simple example is in the cadence of [139B]. $\underline{6}$ is indeed the I$^6_4$, but elaborated with a strong SUS that clashes with the bass before resolving. [140A] has a neighboring $^6_4$ in $\underline{2}$, embellished by a SUS in the melody, then a NT. In 142A, we hear a neighbor to I$^6_4$. In $\underline{6}$, the dominant is reached, but the music pushes on to IV, which acts as a neighbor to the I^6, then returns to the V that is implied by the Gs. Another interpretation: the I$^6_4$ is a passing chord on the way to IV, which is followed by the cadence.

In [144B], a delayed resolution of I$^6_4$ gives Chopin time to unwind the tension built up by the high level of chromaticism. The dominant, the goal of the chromatic motion, is reached in $\underline{17}$ and prolonged until the last measure. $\underline{22}$ brings the I$^6_4$ followed not by V, but by a neighbor chord. As in [140A], the neighbor chord delays the move from I$^6_4$ to the dominant. The move to V is taken one voice at a time—first the G steps down to F$\sharp$, generating the stark SUS chord that follows the pause; then the E resolves to D$\sharp$, and the dominant triad is complete.

An elegantly embellished resolution of I$^6_4$ graces the first cadence in [147A], $\underline{9}$-$\underline{10}$. A master of timing, Haydn knows that the listener needs a moment to recover from the surprising chromatic chord in $\underline{8}$. So he spins out the I$^6_4$–V^7 over an entire measure of slow music. The 4th first sounds between the viola and the cello. But instead of resolving directly, the viola line moves up chromatically at the same time that the first-violin line is on its way from 5 to 1, elaborated by skips. The A$\sharp$ for which the ear is waiting is first mentioned by the first violin, an octave higher than we had expected. By the time the viola confirms it, the cello has reached the tonic. The SUS chord on the downbeat of $\underline{10}$ absorbs the remaining energy of the dominant and eases the motion to the stable tonic.

Embellished resolution of I$^6_4$ in [147A]

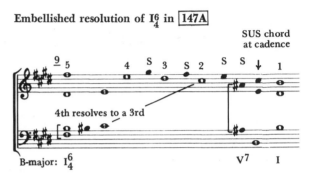

Still another, far-flung prolongation of I$^6_4$ occupies the excerpt from Verdi's *Otello*, [160]. The bass motion starts on 5 to which it returns in $\underline{8}$. During that time it travels through quite a chromatic PS motion. But that move itself is elaborated. The lowest note of the figure, G$\sharp$, has a still lower note, its leading tone F$\times$. We hear that once in $\underline{5}$, with its function clearly that of a chromatic NT. Then the bass skips through E, not to F$\times$, but to G, which is 3 in E minor. Over that note sounds a VI$^6_4$ minor, its effect almost consonant in this dissonant context, after which the V^7 finally appears, heightened by an expressive $\overset{>}{\text{NT}}$. The sketches below show the bass and soprano in an imaginary evolution from their main notes.

[160] **Prolongation of B in bass**

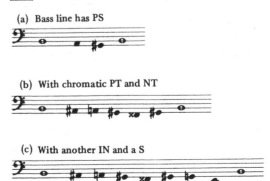

Prolongation of B in top line and descent to E

(a) Melodic descent   (b) With NT; skip 4

5 (4) 3 2 1   NT   NT   NT to NT   *   IN

(c) Octave shift and arpeggiation at * (d) Elaboration of (e) With inner voice

NT   IN by SP

5

to inner
voice

(5) B prolonged

3 2 1

☞ Worksheet 35

72

More on Tonic Prolongations

The large majority of Baroque and Classical pieces start with tonic prolongations, as do many Romantic works. The musical reason is not hard to find. The tonic represents stability and the reference point for the entire composition. If this is impressed upon the ear of the listener at the outset of a piece, the composer is free to move to contrasting tonal areas, creating variety and interest, always with the tonic as home base. The tonic may be prolonged in any number of ways, but prolonging motions are basically of two types—contrapuntal and harmonic.

V⁷ INVERSIONS A simple and effective way to start a piece is to elaborate the tonic with contrapuntal chords such as V⁷ inversions and leading-tone chords. Beethoven used this technique in many of his works, and ⌷132⌷ is a lesson—or rather several lessons—in this type of tonic prolongation.

To identify each move we ask two questions:

1. How many chords make up the group?
2. How are the chords related to the tonic and to each other?

At the start of ⌷132⌷, we may say that five chords are in the orbit of I. The first, third, and fifth chords are, of course, the tonic itself. The second chord grows by way of NT motion in the outer voices; it is V₃⁴. Then, the melodic ascent 1–2–3 introduces the PT, D, which is set with a NT in the bass, the chord being V₅⁶. It is quite clear that root movements have nothing to do with this chord progression, and directed motion of the lines has everything to do with it.

Consonant and dissonant chords alternate in ⌷147A⌷, too, probably one of the works from which Beethoven learned how to begin a piece with a tonic prolongation. The prolonging motion ex-

42

tends into the beginning of $\underline{5}$. Identify all the chords in the tonic prolongation.

PEDAL POINT A simple and effective way to fix the tonic in the listener's ear is by means of a pedal point over which the upper voices may generate chord changes without shaking the control of the tonic. $\boxed{131}$ opens with an F in the bass, over which the two upper lines move through contrapuntal chords that elaborate the tonic. A short pedal point opens $\boxed{135}$, the three upper instruments moving through tonic and leading-tone chords while the cello holds D. I–V⁷–I over a pedal is quite common; it is heard in $\boxed{136}$, $\underline{9}$–$\underline{12}$, where it is $\underbrace{\text{I–V–I}}_{\text{of III major}}$, and in $\boxed{150}$, $\underline{23}$–$\underline{24}$. In $\boxed{153}$, $\underline{14}$–$\underline{16}$, the progression is enlarged by preceding the dominant with its dominant, and then replacing the V⁷ with VII⁷ minor. The pedal note is strengthened by doubling in the upper octave. The voice leading may be seen most clearly in the left-hand part.

$\boxed{154}$ is a song in three stanzas. The first two are built over a tonic pedal point, which persists into the beginning of the third verse for a total of twenty-eight measures. The pedal C moves up and down an octave for textural variety. Contrapuntal activity in the middle and upper voices moves the music along, with no dominant or leading-tone chord. The entire song is colored by mode mixture, almost resulting in a hybrid major-minor mode. However, although the mode is variable, the key is not. The song is as firmly rooted in its tonic as any by Schubert or Brahms, but the approach to tonality in French music depends much less on the dominant-to-tonic drive than it does in music by German and Austrian composers.

Another long tonic pedal point ends the aria $\boxed{161}$. The final tonic is reached in $\underline{34}$ and prolonged to the end of the piece. Over the pedal there is a complete tonal movement:

I–VII⁷–I–VII⁷ minor–I–VI minor–I–V⁷–I–I–V–I,

$\underbrace{}_{\text{of II}}$ $\underbrace{}_{\text{of V}}$

the last tonic being elaborated itself.

DN A linear motion of a DN prolongs a note; such a motion in the bass supports a prolongation of the chord built on that note. $\boxed{129B}$ opens with the harmonic prolongation I–V–V–I (discussed below). A NT in the bass follows, over which a neighboring V⁶ acts to prolong I further. Starting in $\underline{6}$, the last note of that three-note group is also the first note of a five-note group. The five notes consist of the main note, E♭; a chromatic PT, E, on the way to the upper of the NTs, F; the lower neighbor D; and E♭ to complete the group. E is the leading tone of F, and the chord over E is V⁶ of II. V⁶–I is then followed by $\underbrace{\text{V⁶–I}}_{\text{of II}}$, creating the third unit in a large tonic prolongation.

Diatonic DN	plus	chromatic PT

I–V–V–I The harmonic prolongation is often expressed as four chords to create an opening gesture. Simple examples may be seen in the first measures of $\boxed{129B}$ and $\boxed{129C}$. In both, each chord completely fills a short measure. In $\boxed{129B}$, the bass line simply skips; in $\boxed{129C}$, the bass line fills in the space from 1 to 5 with PTs in a rhythm that answers the melody. The tune includes a dissonant chromatic $\overset{>}{\text{P}}$T which collides with the F♯ in the bass. The common tone in I and V, D, is the center of a tiny figure in the winds which adds yet another touch.

For study

In each of the following, determine how long the opening tonic prolongations are and bracket them: $\boxed{129A}$, $\boxed{130F}$, $\boxed{136}$, $\boxed{141}$, $\boxed{144A}$, $\boxed{145}$, $\boxed{147A}$. Identify all linear chords used in these prolongations.

73

More on Dominant Prolongations

V and V⁷ often appear as single chords. But, like any chords, they may also be stretched out over longer spans of time by means of prolongation. Such prolongation was known to Baroque composers. However, Classic and Romantic composers took greater advantage of prolongation, exploiting its dramatic potential and using chromatic resources to increase tension and the drive to the cadence.

DIATONIC LINEAR CHORDS The dominant note in the bass may be prolonged by a simple NT, which will then support a linear chord that may be heard as being under the dominant's control. A clear example is in the chorale [114], 6–7. The D in the bass is prolonged with a NT, E. The soprano moves within the dominant triad, its passing G meeting the bass's E to frame a VI chord.

A DN serves the purpose of prolonging V in [121], 32–34. The sketch below shows the tonic, the approach to the dominant by way of IV, the prolonged dominant, and the concluding tonic, reduced to outer-voice main notes. The linear chords that embellish V are VI and IV.

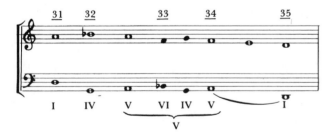

LONGER PROLONGATIONS It is no coincidence that many of the pieces that can be outlined ABA utilize the prolonged dominant to prepare the return from B to A. By prolonging the dominant the music accumulates tension and expectation. The resolution then leads into the restatement of the opening material and of the opening tonic as well. This is precisely what happens in [133], [134], [137], and [140].

The entire middle section of [134] from the double bar through 16 is a dominant prolongation. We may better understand it if we take it as two motions, each four measures long.

In the first four measures the bass prolongs the dominant in the simplest way, with the pedal note A. The upper voice moves within the V⁷ chord from A up to G. The chords are I₄⁶, V, and V⁷, all dominant in function, plus a linear I underpinning the passing F♯ in the top line, 11.

The second half of the prolongation begins on the upbeat to 13, its upbeat character helped by the rest in the lower part. The bass, now an octave higher than it just was, has a chromatic NT, G♯ (15), adding to the prolongation. Still within the dominant chord, the top line now descends from the high point, A, to C♯. The inner voice, which had moved together with the top line in parallel motion, now is counterpointed in contrary motion. Two SUSs enrich the texture as a result. The chords are the dominant in the form of I₄⁶, a single V in 12, and the leading-tone chord of the dominant. The space between the top two lines is used up by the contrary motion a measure before the phrase ends, and Mozart simply inverts the position of those lines to make 16, resolving the 4th to a 3rd as he does so.

Surveying the entire eight-measure phrase, we see that chords and lines have the same function —to prolong the dominant—and they combine for that purpose without wasting a note.

Another short piece whose middle section is built on a dominant prolongation is [140]. The first section ends with a cadence on V;, and the expectation is that the dominant will be followed by the tonic. But for the eight-measure phrase that comprises the next part of the piece, the return to I is deferred, creating anticipation and interest. If we look at the bass line for a clear, controlling direction, it is difficult to find one. This suggests that

Sketch: Reduction of 140 , **9–23**

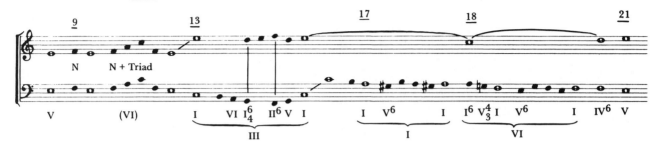

Further reduction

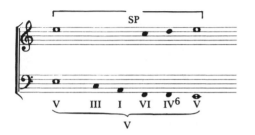

the bass does not always direct the motion; the soprano may do that job. The sketch above shows how a SP in the top line is projected over eight measures to prolong 5; and under that, V is prolonged.

The first move is purely melodic as all voices move in unison, a marked contrast to the previous phrase. Then the neighboring F is itself elaborated by means of a triad (11), another melodic embellishment. The E skips up an octave as the bass begins to move. The prolonging chords III, I, and VI are each tonicized. At the VI, the top line skips to C and works its way back through the D to E. Schumann has used not only three prolonging triads, but their own dominants as well, making a richly colored dominant prolongation.

Of course, not all dominant prolongations precede the return of the tonic. The dominant of the cadence itself may be prolonged, as in 138 , making a six-measure phrase out of what could easily have been a four-measure unit. Had the V on the last beat of 24 resolved to I, the piece would have been over. But the musical impulse pushes on, and the E moves not to A, but to a chromatic NT, D♯. This supports a chord whose function is VII⁷ of V. Part of the extension lies in the way that the top line refuses to resolve the leading tone, returning to C and repeating its descent to the final tonic. The four upper lines elaborate notes of the dominant or move within that chord, generating

dissonant sounds of considerable tension. That tension might not be satisfied by a direct resolution to I, and the linear motion moves through the point at which the bass does arrive at A, until bass and soprano agree and the energy is expended.

Dominant prolongation built on a NT in bass

☞ Worksheet 36

74

More on Applied Dominants
and Leading-Tone Chords

The good-natured theme on which Beethoven based the variations that comprise $\boxed{132}$, the second movement of his *Piano Sonata* Op. 14 No. 2, contains many tonal motions that are typical of the composer's vocabulary. We are now particularly interested in ways of using applied-7th chords, both in root position and in inversion.

3–4 include a bass motion from 1 down to 4, the interval of a 5th being divided into two 3rds. VI functions as a way station between I and IV, as it often does. The first 3rd, from C to A, is filled with a PT, B. In contrary motion, the top line gets from G to A by way of a chromatic PT, G♯. The PTs in the outer voices conspire to create a passing chord, V$_3^4$ of VI.

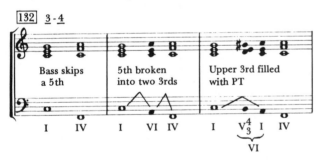

A modulation to V in 6 establishes G as temporary tonic, with an accented I^6 helping the new key to gain a foothold. On the way from that I^6 to I$_4^6$ there are two passing chords. The first is II$_5^6$, a diatonic dissonant chord. The second is built on the leading tone of the dominant; it is VII♭ of V. The B♭ is, in effect, A♯, moving up from A to B.

Having stressed tonic and dominant, Beethoven moves toward the subdominant, tonicizing IV and II. First, F♯ is canceled out. The tonal movement swings through I, and B♭ is heard as a PT in V^2 of IV, 9 . IV is stabilized with its dominant in 10 , II in 11 . Inevitably the section heads toward V. VII$^{7♭}$ of V in 12 leads to V, preparing the return of the tonic.

12–15 are by no means a carbon copy of the first four measures of the piece. The first two measures have the same tonal structure in both cases, but the restatement is varied registrally: first it is contracted; then expanded. The melody's G enters a beat early, at the end of 14 , beginning the melodic descent to C. On the way, the composer takes advantage of several ways to make that descent more interesting. G enters on a weak beat and is reiterated even more strongly. The *sf* chord is another applied dominant, VII$_5^6$ of II. Its resolution is delayed by two SUSs: one is in the soprano, forcing the G to move on; the other is in the tenor, where the leading tone of 2 is delayed for a beat. The sound on the third beat of 15 is an example of the interesting chords that can be grown by linear means and that cannot be described as a collection of 3rds.

As if to sum up the applied-dominant usages found in the piece, Beethoven brings several together for the last phrase. V^7–I is followed by V^7–I and V^7–I . The succession of applied-domi-

of II of III

nant and offbeat accents both stop with the strong V$_3^4$ of 18 , and the unaccented tonic that follows prepares the way for the final I.

It might be thought that applied-dominant chords would weaken the tonic's control. On the contrary, they may extend that control into new regions. Such chords are related to the tonic not directly, but through the triads they emphasize. A marvelous example is the recapitulation of the first movement of Beethoven's *First Symphony*, $\boxed{162}$, 182–198 . The top line moves through a chromatic scale, an octave and more. Except for 3, each degree of the scale is tonicized, preceded with its own V^7. Consonance and dissonance alternate. But if every scale degree is to be tonicized, what about 7? A triad on that degree is a diminished one, not a usable goal for an applied dominant. Beethoven solves the problem by using the 7 of C minor, which is B♭. How readily the modes can be interchanged may be suggested by the convincing way in which the borrowed VII fits into the progression.

Much less clear-cut is the opening of the symphony. What key is it in? Just from hearing the first two chords, no listener would conclude that the piece is in C major. But is it in F? The next two sounds make that unlikely and point toward A. Then a strong emphasis on the dominant of G is followed by G as dominant, and C is the center without a single I chord having been heard. The way in which all the chords so far are related to C is: V^7–I, V^7–I, V^7–I .

of IV   of VI   of V

VII⁷ The 7th chord built on the leading tone of the dominant offers a smooth motion to V or I^6_4. In the minor mode, it is a diminished-7th chord, and that sound was so well liked that it often was "kidnaped" into the major. We saw VII⁷ᵇ of V at the end of the dominant prolongation in 134 , at a point where the mode had become quite variable. Another instance occurs in the introductory phrase of 150 . We hear I, a space-filling VI, then not IV or II⁶, but VII⁷ᵇ of V, which leads into the dominant. The E♯ in the bass is the leading tone of the dominant. The D is both a chromatic PT and part of the leading-tone chord; it also suggests mode mixture.

Applied-leading-tone chords may add their tension to any part of the phrase, not only to the cadence. 138 starts with I–VII$^6_5$–I⁶. Transposition of the first motive a 4th higher results in I–VII$^6_5$–I⁶ .

of IV

The 7th chord, built on the leading tone, in first inversion, acts as a passing chord to connect I and I⁶, then IV and IV$^6_5$. In 150 , 28 , VII$^6_5$ of II is heard again, inflecting a melodic descent much as it did in 132 .

☞ Worksheet 37

Quartet evening at the home of Alexis Fedorowitsch Lwow, lithograph by R. Rohrbach (1845).

PART TWELVE
MUSICAL FORM AND FORMS 1

75

The Classic-Romantic Phrase

THE PHRASE The phrase will serve as the unit of study in our investigation of the way pieces are put together. Individual chords are grouped into units that build phrases; phrase groups build sections. If we understand the phrase, we will have a way of seeing how the details of a piece add up to something larger; we will also see how the whole is built up.

It is useful to remember the vocal origins of the phrase even when we are studying instrumental music, for instruments often follow the vocal type of gesture ("make the piano sing!"). A phrase has two essential attributes: it embodies a complete thought, and it draws breath at the end.

THE CADENCE Taking the second point first, we draw breath when we have reached a goal of one kind or another. The fall of the voice at the end of a thought is what we call a cadence, whether it be the purely melodic cadence of unaccompanied folk song or the harmonic cadence of a Bach cho-

rale. Does the voice always fall at the end of a phrase? No, because composers learned to use rising inflections for open-ended cadences. But even those cadences are eventually answered by closed cadences with a falling line, manifesting what we might call "music's law of gravity."

HARMONIC CADENCE The cadence that gives the most complete sense of closure consists of the harmonic motion V–I or V^7–I. Here the connection of the roots of the chords, a 5th apart, is decisive. But all such cadences do not have the same degree of finality. The forces that are in play include:

1. the melodic descent 3–2–1;
2. the bass skip 5–1;
3. an inner-voice motion 7–8;
4. an inner-voice motion 4–3, resolving the 7th;
5. rhythmic placement—weak-strong or strong-weak.

If the first four factors are present, the sense of closure is maximum. Finality is greatest if V^7–I coincides with weak-strong rhythm—the so-called *masculine ending*. If V⁷–I is set to strong-weak, the end is rounded off a bit—the *feminine ending*. Even if all pitch factors make for closure, the rhythmic activity may push on to open the phrase ending. The first phrase of the aria from *Carmen*, 161, ends with a clear V⁷–I. How final is it? The melody ends not on 1 but on 5; the rhythm of the accompaniment figure pushes on. The two factors work together to move the music through the harmonic cadence, thus producing the effect of a light punctuation mark but by no means a full stop.

Cadences in early Beethoven piano sonatas

The cadence is preceded by a SUS chord. The top line moves 7–8 rather than 3–2–1. After the complete V⁷ there is an incomplete I. Octave doubling emphasizes the top line. There is enough stability to end the piece, but rhythmic activity continues at once.

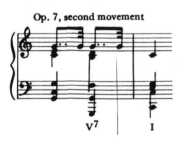

The same cadence as in Op. 7 above, but in the parallel minor.

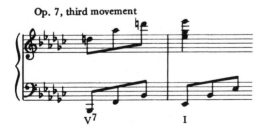

The cadence is complete, and stability is maximum. 3 appears as an IN to 2. The dominant is prolonged by I⁶₄.

The cadence is quite strong, and the tonic prolongation, sweeping through the registers, adds stability. The melody is polyphonic; there are at least three voices. 3 appears as the soprano in I⁶₄.

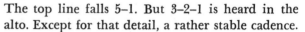

The top line falls 5–1. But 3–2–1 is heard in the alto. Except for that detail, a rather stable cadence.

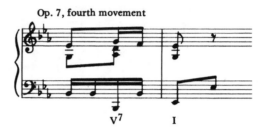

A harmonic cadence with a **maximum** sense of closure. The II⁶ that connects I and V⁷ varies the descent of the top line, but does not weaken it.

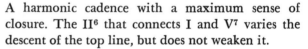

The SUS chord softens the masculine ending in the cadence. Note the voice exchange between soprano and tenor.

Not in two parts. The play of registers is the striking feature of this harmonic cadence.

50

The customary roles of bass and soprano are exchanged here. The bass descends stepwise to the tonic, and the soprano leaps 5–1.

Op. 2 No. 1, third movement

All of these cadences show the masculine ending, weak-strong. While some of the cadences in Schumann's *Carnaval* Op. 9 are similar to those in the early Beethoven sonatas, others have different features, including various rhythmic placements of V–I and V⁷–I.

Strong-weak cadence—the feminine ending.

Strong-weak—the feminine ending. The rest in the right-hand part suggests syncopation.

The melodic descent is hidden in an inner voice, and is shortened to 3–1. The D is an unresolved NT. If it were resolved, we would hear 2.

The weak-strong feeling is blurred by the delay in the bass, which reaches the tonic only on the second beat of the measure.

Weak-strong ending. The inner-voice E♭ shifts up an octave, covering the top line's 3–2–1 descent. The bass delay puts off the final arrival at the tonic until the last moment.

139A

Weak-strong or strong-weak? Placement within the measure means nothing here, since there is only one chord to a measure. But in a fast tempo, the first measure sounds like a downbeat and the second like an upbeat. This is another strong-weak ending.

Even though the tempo is slow, one measure is the unit of pulse, probably because of the septuplet. The effect is strong-weak. The descent takes place entirely over the tonic chord.

CADENCE ON V; The particular value of a cadence on V; is that it presents a complete musical thought yet tells the listener that more is to come. We see this clearly in 140. The initial eight-measure phrase, firmly grounded in the tonic, ends with a cadence on V;. This leads to a repetition of the first part. The second time, the V; prepares the way for the middle section of this short piece. The I⁶₄ prolongs the dominant and gives it added weight. The same type of cadence in 139B, 6–8, has little weight, constituting the lightest of punctuation marks. Why? Partly because the flow of the rhythm is not halted at all, and partly because the

51

dominant is suspended, as it were, into the next phrase.

PHRASE LENGTH Identifying the cadential point may help answer the question: How long is the phrase? Locating a complete tonal motion from I to V is also useful in defining the phrase. Thus we may be tempted to think of ⌈134⌉ as being in four-measure phrases. The first four measures make up a tonic prolongation, ending with V⁶–I. But the rhythm moves right through the fourth measure, the prolongation continues, and the tonal center shifts. Only after the cadence in V do we breathe, and we realize that the phrase is eight measures long. Indeed, there is a small division at the end of four measures, but it does not have the strength of a cadence.

It is customary to think of phrases as being four or eight measures in duration, and these lengths may be taken as norms. But such norms are only a rough approximation. Phrases may be quite long or quite short. An unusual example is in ⌈135⌉, which begins with a three-measure unit prolonging I, incorporating a quick melodic ascent. The long descent that follows is grouped into two measures, then two more, and a concluding three. The continuity is unbroken, and the piece has begun with a ten-measure phrase. What has happened to the symmetry and balance of the Classical style? Are those features to be found only in music-appreciation books? Not entirely. Balance in music is much more than adding together phrases of equal lengths. Mozart's ten-measure phrase is balanced, setting up tensions that are worked out in the course of the phrase in a manner that is quite satisfying, if not quite symmetrical.

The first phrase of ⌈135⌉

MODULATION AND TONICIZATION The motion that changes the tonal course of a phrase, leading it to a cadence in a center other than the one in which it began, is defined as *modulation*. Such a tonal shift has a bearing upon the large dimension of musical form. Any piece with more than one section probably uses modulation to achieve the tension of departure from the basic tonal center and the satisfaction of return. The force of tonal shift is at work in a fugue, a minuet, a song, a piano piece, a movement of a symphony. It is one of the most powerful ways of arousing and maintaining interest that is available in tonal music.

In a small context, any scale degree that can support a consonant triad may become a temporary tonic. The dominant principle may be applied to that scale degree, and the resulting chord is an applied dominant. Or we may have applied-leading-tone chords, or applied subdominants, or any other function. What we might call secondary tonics may involve any of the functions of the main tonic. But this brief motion, *tonicization*, remains a detail. It is often an expressive detail, but one that does not shape the tonal flow of the phrase or the section. Many tonicizations are quite short, consisting of only two chords; but some are extended, and there is a gray area between a long tonicization and a modulation that cannot always be clearly differentiated.

TONAL STRUCTURE OF THE MELODY The rise and fall of the melody is built over a framework of structural notes which we have seen in all melodies from folk song and chant to Bach. The Classic-Romantic melodic language is rich and varied, but its methods represent a continuation of past practice. A reduction of the melody of ⌈150⌉, first section, shows the basic notes behind the line.

52

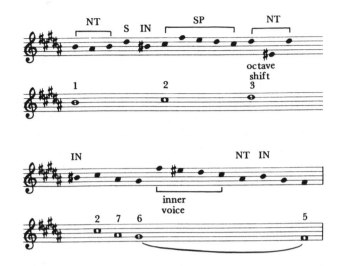

and admired the music of Bach. Octave transfer adds to the interest of a polyphonic melody, as this reduction of the melody of [139A], 1–4 , shows.

In the first phrase of [141], two lines, a 3rd apart, are enmeshed in one melody. The skip keeps them separated. The 3rd spreads to a tritone, then a perfect 5th. At the end of the phrase, PTs link the two strands, but the 3rd emerges again at the end.

POLYPHONIC MELODY While some of the melodies we study are as one-dimensional as most folk songs, others are filled with implications of more than one line. Perhaps this trait is most obvious in the works of composers who have studied

76

More on Musical Texture and Space

Few of the pieces in this part of the study have the note-against-note texture of earlier music, nor are many completely linear. What we find is a great variety of textures, often several within a single piece. To be sure, change of texture is not only interesting in itself, it is also one of the composer's ways of signaling that a new thought is under way. Thus it can be a crucial element in building musical form.

MELODY AND ACCOMPANIMENT One frequently used format is simply a melody with accompaniment, often based on a repeated figure. One would expect to find this texture in songs, and Schubert's [150] is just one example. The introductory phrase in the piano has the melody in the right hand, supported by left-hand chords. The

alternation of hands that follows is familiar to anyone acquainted with the song literature. The change to a fuller texture at 11 underlines the punctuation of the cadence in V; the same is true of the second cadence, in 19–20 . The new section begins with a new accompaniment, built on a four–sixteenth-note figure. The texture is as full as the first section's was thin. As the emotional temperature rises, from 35 , the rate of chord change increases and the texture swells to six parts, with much doubling, now moving in eighth notes. The very first texture never comes back, but the sixteenth-note figure returns at 41 and stays with the melody to the end. The epilogue owes at least some of its effect to the descent of the accompaniment figure through the middle to the low register, which frees the upper register of the piano for the concluding remarks.

A simple chordal accompaniment may be combined with a vocal or instrumental part with satisfying results. The first half of 153 has an accompaniment figure of eight note–quarter note, while the melody makes much of the figure quarter note–eighth note. Together they fill every eighth. At the same time, the bass motion is slower, joining the upper part when it moves in groups of three eighths, later moving into octaves for clearer definition of the contrary motion with the top line. Again, both hands move together at the cadence. Thus far the accompaniment has been low, its dark coloring in keeping with the meaning of the words. As the mood shifts to start the second verse (14), the upper notes of the piano come into play for the first time. At the same time, the accompaniment grows more active, introducing a figure of four sixteenths and an eighth in the left hand; the right goes on with the first figure in its highest note, but also includes inner-voice chords. Three levels are engaged at once, helping to create the feeling of emotional intensity that makes this brief song so substantial. The way in which the range of the song grows and diminishes also reflects the progress of the poem. Starting from a rather small range, it expands to three full octaves in 16–18 , then gradually contracts to the end. The eighth note–quarter note accompaniment figure, transferred from the highest register to the lowest by the last line, ties the song together motivically.

Another song, 154 , by Fauré, also uses an accompaniment figure as a unifying device. The unit of two eighth notes and a half note, the second eighth sometimes tied to the half, is heard in every measure up to the final chord. The right-hand part stays in a limited range until the moment when the voice descends at the end of a verse; then it moves faster and rises to its high point, and falls back to the chord that starts the next phrase. The last descent, starting in 42 , leads to the final tonic, and it is extended just a bit to round off the conclusion of the piece.

Other songs show a few more of the many ways in which a vocal line can be accompanied. We might contrast 155 , which moves in quarter notes from beginning to end (but what quarter notes!), with 157 , which shifts textures frequently to dramatize the utterances of the characters. The relentless eighth notes of the latter, punctuated by chords, accompanying the opening narration, provide the texture that is interrupted by Death's footsteps in unison with the singer. Tremolos, triplet figures, chordal movement of various kinds, all are pressed into service to meet the demands of the poem.

The eighteen measures that make up 169 offer several different textures. The first three measures are entirely chordal, in four parts. Then the left-hand part begins to move, and two measures later that movement infects the right-hand part. The continuous eighth-note motion is stabilized by longer notes in the low register, and the two hands gradually equalize until 15 . At that point, both move together in a telescoped version of the first three measures. The eighth notes move against quarter notes to the final chord, slowing down the momentum to the end. No accompaniment figure is used, but a motive based on a minor 3rd prevails throughout the song.

The accompaniment to 170 is close to being a piano piece in itself. Melody and accompaniment are both in the instrumental part. The very first measure covers four and one-half octaves. What the piano first plays has the character of a refrain; it returns at the middle of the piece, in 18 , and is remembered in the concluding measures. The active texture of the piano part fits perfectly with the *parlando* (Italian: "in the manner of speech") nature of the voice part.

The vocal line of 173 also resembles speech as much as song, and, again, the piano seems self-sufficient. A chordal texture prevails without any motive predominating. The texture is quite thick; many chords have seven or even eight notes, and in the first chord all eight are different.

Many of the accompaniment textures that originated on the keyboard were readily translated into orchestral terms. Alternating bass and chord starts 159 , and a variant of that accompanies the melody of 165A . Repeated chords with a simple syncopated figure are behind the melody of 161 up to the orchestral coda, where an arpeggiated figure, also derived from piano usage, accompanies the melody taken by the violins. The simple chordal accompaniment of the first section of 158 is the perfect background for Don Octavio's opening lines; when the words become more expressive, Mozart seizes the opportunity to introduce new, more active textures, which change with each shade of the text's meaning.

PIANO TEXTURES A straightforward melody and accompaniment serve well for piano music, especially in pieces of a relatively simple nature. The group of Schubert waltzes, 130 , includes examples in which the left hand plays a regular accompaniment while the right plays the melody. The same is true of the Schumann piece 139B . In all those pieces, the piano sounds quite full because the left hand covers more than an octave. But in

139A , the left hand, with the entire accompaniment, uses a restricted range, thus contributing to the intimate character of the music.

But piano textures may take almost any shape. In the Schubert waltz 130B , the phrase begins with a doubling of the right-hand chords in the left hand, switching to support of the chords with octaves, and finishing with a rhythmic unison. The second phrase follows the same course. 130F has virtually an S.A.T.B. format with octave doubling. The Mozart minuet, 134 , possibly written with harpsichord in mind, is in two parts for the first phrase, then thickens the texture for the middle section, which is one of its significant contrasts. The Clementi sonata excerpt, 138 , starts with chords in five real parts—that is, without octave doubling. Later phrases introduce linear textures and imitation. When the initial melody returns, the fact that it is to be varied is communicated at once by the changed texture. Chordal textures are heard in 140 , where the left hand plays the chords and the right plays a melody based on arpeggiation of those chords.

The preludes of 144 should be studied in detail to identify the many ways in which the keyboard's possibilities can be exploited, keeping in mind the use of the pedal. The two halves of 149 are differentiated by texture as much as anything else. In both halves the melody is in the right hand, in octaves, a procedure that continues up to the concluding section in 33 . But in the first half of the piece the left hand blends with the right. The lower part supports the melody first with single chords, then with a rhythmic figure derived from the melody. Eighth notes link the end of the first section with the beginning of the second; they also forecast the texture of the second section and the location of the left-hand part in the piano's lowest register. When this ends, the piece concludes.

171 has some fascinating textural aspects: the opening up of the total musical space in the first five measures; the way in which melodies are set over, under, and around the repeated C♯; the complete change of texture at the new idea in 38 and again at 67 ; and the sudden intrusion of a chordal texture, suggesting the guitar or mandolin, in 109 . The shifting textures and densities are an integral part of the piece and do much to impart its kaleidoscopic nature.

ENSEMBLE TEXTURES An ensemble in which all instruments are (more or less) equal affords each the opportunity to participate in the conversation. This is the ideal of chamber music. Such a guideline cannot be taken too literally, for in tonal music the outer voices will always have more to say than the inner ones. But we may observe that in chamber music, simple accompaniment figures are less favored than in piano music, and the linear aspect plays a more important role.

More than anyone else, Joseph Haydn defined the string quartet as an ensemble. A look at the second movement of his *G-Minor Quartet,* 147A (the second movement is in E major!), will give us some insight into the medium.

The first measures employ the S.A.T.B. format. When the phrase explodes with a chromatic chord in 8 , the space is expanded by an octave. The parallel 10ths between violin 1 and cello open out, the upper instrument moving up a 3rd, the lower down a 6th. From that point on, while the S.A.T.B. concept is still in the background, Haydn takes advantage of the flexible use of musical space first developed in the Baroque. Observe how the solidity of texture is broken up in 9 , 14 , 21 , 39–41 , 51 , 53–55 , 57–58 . From 60 on, the thinning out of the texture and the cello's descent into its lower region are means to signal the approach of the end.

136 demonstrates a particularly resourceful use of texture and space; the texture changes to characterize each idea. The two violins present the four-note motive (often shortened to three) together, with simple chordal accompaniment from the lower instruments. Moving toward the cadence that ends the four-measure phrase, violin 1 takes over and violin 2 joins the accompaniment. After this open texture, the closely packed chords of the middle section offer a strong contrast. After that, new textures follow in quick succession. Particularly interesting and amusing is the relation between the two phrases that begin in 30 and 34 respectively, where the instruments exchange roles with a bit of double counterpoint. Imitative entrances build the climax in the last phrase, and the ascent is answered by a quick descent in the first violin, covering three full octaves. Textures in the trio section are simpler and change less. At the end, violin 1 swiftly rises three octaves in a gesture that balances the end of the scherzo, and is itself balanced when the scherzo is repeated.

A simple example of a five-part piece is 137 . But it is covered with rests, and the five instruments play together for relatively few measures. The composer uses the quintet by calling upon smaller groups, usually, three at a time, thus changing the tone color in many ways. The horn has little to do, and the inner voices are supportive rather than independent. The accompaniment, as in much Classic and early Romantic music, involves a good many repeated notes.

A more complex five-part weave is to be found in 141. The richness of sonority grows out of the activity of all five instruments and the fact that they are not all doing the same thing at the same time. Texture thins only at the cadence, 7–8, where Brahms lets in just a little air. The melody of the first eight-measure phrase is carried by the clarinet. In the lower parts, a triplet starts on every beat in a different instrument. The rhythm of three against two accounts for much of the density, especially since the two is syncopated, its notes dovetailing with those of the melody. The strings are quite low; and when the first violin starts to repeat the melody in 9, the sound is fresh. At that point the clarinet repeats what the first violin had played originally, and a mosaic arrangement distributes the triplet among the three lower strings. The third phrase, starting in 17, brings a third texture; violins play the continuation melody in octaves, while the clarinet plays a countermelody. The viola has a syncopated triplet figure that it had introduced during the end of the previous phrase, and the cello plays a simple polyphonic part made up of an inner voice and a pedal note, both above and below the viola. Observe, too, the crossing between the clarinet and the upper strings, and the clarinet's descent at the end of the phrase.

A short contrasting phrase is ushered in by the clarinet arpeggio, starting in 25, covering two octaves as it brings the instrument into the high register. Equally important is the silence of the strings, a breathing space after the dense texture we have just heard. The clarinet melody, starting in 32, is accompanied with bits of the triplet idea and the syncopated eighths. When the clarinet sings the main melody again it is doubled an octave higher by the first violin, bringing in a new register. The second-violin part covers a large space and suggests two lines, as do the viola and cello parts. Small wonder the texture is so rich.

ORCHESTRA While the study of the orchestra and what it has meant in the history of Western music is a large undertaking, the ideas introduced here can provide a basis for a preliminary survey. Even with a few examples we can see some typical ways in which the larger ensembles have been used to convey musical ideas; in particular, we can see how composers controlled texture and the use of space.

The different functions of the main choirs in the Classical orchestra are seen in microcosm in 129. The strings predominate; first violins play the melody, second violins play the inner voices, cello and bass play the bass line in octaves. There are no violas. Winds double the violins, highlight them, or add comments. The horns sustain the chords or repeat them, in which they may be assisted by the winds. The center of interest is in the first violins, while the bass line is counterpointed against it in such a way as to make a simple dialogue without distracting the ear from the melody.

The orchestra of 131 includes violas, but not horns. The sustained notes, which create much of the orchestral dimension, are played by violas and winds. The bassoon part simply duplicates the low strings. The first violins still monopolize the melody, the second violins moving with them in parallel 3rds. The two flutes double the two violin parts in the first measure, but in 3 the inner voices literally come to the top as the first flute doubles the second violin an octave higher, now moving in 6ths with the second flute. For the rest of the phrase, the flutes play an important role and actually take over the top line in 6, where the first flute's B♭ is heard as a continuation of the violin's C, while the violin's E and F are inner-voice notes. Such interaction among instruments is another characteristic of orchestral writing. The format is not simply S.A.T.B. paralleled by the winds; voices are reflected in different registers, and the scope of activity is expanded in space.

Several different textures may be observed in 164. At first, the oboe's melody (207–224) is accompanied by syncopated chords in the strings, all in the middle register. Then, starting with 225, clarinet and cellos have a duet above and below the continuing chordal accompaniment. This dies out as the oboe answers the clarinet (235). A sudden ff in 237 brings a complete change of texture. In this orchestral unison, the violins play the top line in octaves, doubled by the first flute. In counterpoint, a bass line is played by violas, cellos, and basses, doubled further by bassoons and the third trombone. The remaining wind and brass instruments fill in the inner voices, and the timpani adds punctuation. After only seven measures, the tutti changes texture. The second violins drop out of the melody to join violas and cellos in a rapidly moving countermelody. To reinforce the top line, all the flutes, oboes, and clarinets are pressed into service. Horns, trumpets, and the first two trombones fill in. At 250, the thirty-second notes move to the low register, bassoons joining the low strings. A striking contrast is made by the solitary notes of the oboe in 253, answered by another ff tutti. In the transitional passage that follows, the melody is shared by strings and winds, as is the chordal accompaniment.

The coda begins in 268. The division of labor is

now particularly clear. The winds, then the horns, play a chord progression whose top line forms a scale, counterpointed by a pizzicato line in the lower strings. Note how the combination of two horns and two bassoons sounds much like four horns. Starting in 280, the first violins lead into another phrase. Again, winds do one thing and strings another, answering each other until the last measures.

In the first five measures of 166 the melody is in the lowest part, for a change. It is played by violas and cellos in unison, doubled an octave lower by the basses. Wind chords that suggest organ sonorities accompany the melody. Starting in 6, a different thought is presented with a different texture. The strings are set up virtually in S.A.T.B. format, except that the motion toward the intermediate goal, the dominant, is reinforced by the timpani. Double stops in the strings add to the thickness of sound at the cadence on V;.

The allocation of separate roles to strings, winds, and brass began to disappear during the nineteenth century. In the music of Wagner, for example, almost any instrument can have almost any role. Doubling is to be found in one passage after another, and the sound is a blended one. The orchestral instruments sound together like one huge instrument. Stravinsky's comment about Wagner—"He plays the organ"—is to the point, although it need not be taken with the negative implication that was intended. 167C shows a small sample of Wagner's procedure. The initial chord blends clarinets, bassoons, trombones, and low strings in one dark sonority. A four-part progression in the horns

presents a single tone color. It is answered by the mixed sounds that start in 9, in which oboe, clarinet, and bassoon are heard with cellos and basses. So far the sounds have been in the low and middle registers. A rushing scale passage in the violins (12) leads to the high point of the excerpt, the loudest sound, filling all registers (13). As the massive chords descend, a rising line emerges against them, played by trumpet, violas, and cellos, a special color indeed. Observe how the instruments are withdrawn as the phrase subsides. The last melodic fragment in flute and oboe is projected against a chord held by oboes, clarinets, horns, bassoons, trombones and tuba, timpani, violas and cellos. The timpani roll carries through the two final B-minor chords, and dies away to end the phrase. In this excerpt we find a good deal of doubling. This makes for a dense coverage, even in the far-flung tutti chord. The way in which that large space gradually diminishes to the final note in the timpani is a study in itself; that spatial diminution is one of the factors in the overall sense of closure.

Even from this brief survey we can see how important texture and movement through musical space can be in defining the form of a piece. These elements have interested composers since the Renaissance. But since Beethoven, their significance has increased. They are factors whose importance was not diminished by the dissolution of tonality. On the contrary, as pitch relationships ceased to be all-important, nonpitch aspects of music came to the fore.

☞ Worksheet 38

77

Motive and Development

What makes a melody coherent? Two factors are in play, whether in a folk song or symphony. Tonal unity is the means by which all the notes are related to a tonic. Motivic unity grows out of both the pitch and the rhythmic aspects of music; we focus on that now.

Music moves through time very quickly, and the listener cannot go back to pick up a detail that was missed. In order to make it possible for the listener to remember a tune, composers have used repetition of recognizable features of the melody. A motive is such a recognizable feature. A *motive* is a short group of notes with a well-defined pitch and rhythmic contour; whether the pitch or the rhythm is the more decisive element varies from piece to piece. A motive does not exist by itself. A pattern becomes a motive only when it is repeated, either literally or in varied form. Mere repetition can lead to monotony. Varied repetition and development are necessary if music is to have both unity and variety.

THEME A term that is often used to designate the main melodic idea of a piece is *theme*. A theme may be one phrase long, but is often two or three. A theme has to be capable of being developed, which means that every melody is not a theme. Most themes are made of motives, repeated and varied. Our approach to the topic of melodic organization is through motive as the basic unit, and theme is included only informally. A special use of *theme* is in the form known as *theme and variations,* in which the theme is a complete statement with a tonal structure that is, in part, the basis of each variation.

FIGURE In many pieces, we have found tiny groups of two or three notes that were used and repeated, and we called those *figures*. Baroque melodies are usually built up of several such figures; Classic and Romantic melodies use more emphatic motives. Accompaniments often rely heavily on figures, which do not have the importance of motives but still give definition to a subordinate part. The distinction between figure and motive lies as much in what happens to them in the course of the piece as in the nature of the configurations themselves. A continuous melody spun out of a few notes whose characteristics are repeated would suggest figuration; development of a short idea, perhaps on many levels, in an insistent way suggests the use of motive. Obviously, there is some ambiguity between the two. The prelude of 128 is certainly based on figuration, and 136 lives on the development of a motive. But can we be sure about 139B?

MOTIVE Very often, it is not the motive itself that is so important as what happens to it. Many a Classical piece starts with a rather simple and almost neutral motivic idea, from which a complex and interesting work develops. Motivic development is one of the most important processes in music, and we will encounter it again and again. Motives may have extramusical associations. For example, Wagner associates musical motives with the characters and ideas in his music dramas, developing the mo-

tives symphonically in the manner he learned from Beethoven.

Just how all-pervading a motive can be is shown in 136. The first four notes in the violin 1 part are treated as a motive; immediately, in violin 2, the first note is omitted, but the kernel of the idea remains. So heavily do the first eight measures rely on the germinal idea that a strong sense of contrast is created by its absence in the subsequent phrase. The piece has some sections that do not mention the motive and other sections, quite different, that use it. In the latter, the motive permeates all registers and is played by all the instruments.

REPETITION OF THE MOTIVE Once stated, a motive, with or without accompaniment, may be repeated, usually transposed to a different scale degree. This is the case in the beginning of both 138 and 166. The same is true in the statement of the first theme of 162. Such immediate repetition has the effect of impressing the motive on the listener's ear.

RHYTHMIC MOTIVE Where is the motivic unity in 132? We have the impression that everything hangs together. But why? The succession of pitches heard in the first two measures returns only twice in the piece, each time varied. But the rhythmic pattern of the first two measures is everywhere. This rhythm, the time aspect of the music, has greater power than the pitch aspect to organize the melody and, through it, the piece. 3–4 repeat the rhythm of 1–2. An upbeat leads into another use of the rhythmic aspect of the motive (or the rhythmic motive) in 5–6. Then the second measure of the motive is broken off and played twice in the two measures that conclude the phrase, creating a rhythmic drive toward the cadence that works together with the tonal movement toward V. In the next section of the piece, the rhythmic contour of the motive prevails even though the staccato articulation is replaced by legato. Returning to the original idea in 13 means returning to the original articulation of the rhythm. But the half note at the end of the motive is too static for this late stage of the piece. In 14, after the last note of the motive on the third beat, the upcoming strong beat is anticipated with a *f* chord, and the next version of the motive bends across the bar line. At 17, the pitch shape changes into a rising line, but the rhythmic motive is very much alive, given a new dimension by the offbeat accents. In the last two measures, the first note of the motive is tied over from the previous accented note, but the basic idea is still there. Every measure has utilized the rhythmic motive.

58

Treatment of the rhythmic motive in 132

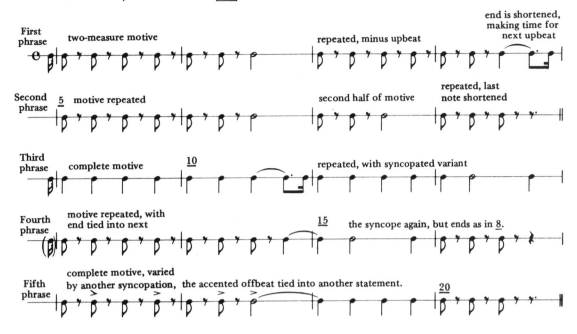

Each two-measure unit represents the motive in some form.

EXTENSION OF THE MOTIVE In the first section of 132, we saw part of a motive used as a short group. Can motives be extended, too? They often are. When a two-measure motive has been heard twice we might expect that two more occurrences would fill out an eight-measure phrase. But the composer may also choose to complete the phrase by expanding the motive to four measures. This is precisely what happens in 129A, 129B, and 130F. A sixteen-measure phrase made up of two four-measure phrases and an eight-measure extension comprises the first section of 137.

The soaring lyric phrase from the end of the first act of Verdi's *Otello*, 160, begins with a two-measure motive that reaches its high point with a skip of a 3rd. The motive is repeated with the leap extended to a 5th. The third time, the climax of the entire phrase gets its impetus from a leap of a 9th, and there is so much energy that the motive is now drawn out to four measures, giving the melody time to regain its original register. Extension in time works together with expansion in space.

CONTRACTION OF THE MOTIVE Of the many examples in which the composer has seized upon part of the motive and used it developmentally, we do well to study 129A. Following the initial eight-measure phrase, based on a two-measure motive, the second section begins with the first five notes of the motive, presented four times in an in-

sistent unison. This intensifies the expression by bringing the units closer together, the one-measure unit being emphasized by the *sf*.

OTHER WAYS OF DEVELOPING A MOTIVE The only limit to the ways in which motives may be developed is that of the composer's imagination. One particularly intriguing example is in the oboe melody which begins 164. Schubert follows Beethoven's example of making a long melody out of a short idea. In this case the idea is just two notes, rising a 3rd. This nucleus is repeated at once a step higher. Then it is contracted in time—two measures are reduced to one. When this, too, is repeated a step higher, the top note, F, is reached, the high point of the melodic arch. That note is the longest in the melody. While it is sustained, the chords underneath change, altering the role of F as they do. Then the melody begins to descend. The motivic interval of a 3rd is woven into the descent, too. Near the end of the line the two notes that began the phrase, A and C, return. Their rhythmic placement is now shifted off the downbeat. The E that concludes the phrase makes for an open ending, and the next phrase follows at once. Behind this very natural-sounding melody lies great artifice of melodic construction.

A characteristic rhythmic motive may be strong enough on which to build an entire piece. Two short Romantic piano pieces that use one such motive throughout are 139B and 144F. In each, the rhythmic motive is unvaried, appearing once in every measure but the last. The pitch contour of

59

the motive changes considerably in both pieces, and that, combined with the expressive chord changes, provides the musical interest that each piece has.

A brief example of the way in which Wagner manipulated motives, varying their pitch and altering their coloration with chord changes, may be seen in 167B. The short motive, half a measure in length, descends two and a half octaves in short order. When it returns to the first level, the chord under it has shifted, and the motive does not sound quite the same as it just did. A variant of the motive has a bit more rhythmic activity. In 3, the motive leaves its base on I and the intervals begin to shift. Observe how different each setting of the motive sounds in 4–7, due largely to chord changes in the background.

Large-scale development of motives is the great melodic device of Classic-Romantic instrumental music. The drama of Beethoven's *First Symphony*, first movement (which is discussed on pages 101–104), depends in good measure on the development of a small group of incisive motives. These are drawn from the first theme. Taken out of that theme, they are then built up into sections within the development, working out the possibilities of the material systematically and relentlessly. The same is true of a very different piece—168. In this glowing music, a two-measure motive is expanded, contracted, and elaborated with utmost resource. In the course of the piece other motives materialize and are woven into the rich fabric of Wagner's polyphony. Beethoven's technique of using short motivic ideas to build long phrases and large-scale pieces is altered to suit Wagner's purposes.

THEME TRANSFORMATION In the course of a large-scale work, a theme may appear in a number of different forms while retaining its identity. This is most likely to happen in a work with a *program*, with a theme that has a literary association. As the dramatic idea progresses, the theme changes to express the literary events. Such modification of a theme is called *theme transformation*. Below are some of the appearances of the main theme from Berlioz's *Fantastic Symphony*. The excerpts from the first movement show motivic development, as in a Classical work. The other excerpts show how the theme is transformed in the course of the subsequent movements.

Main theme or *idée fixe* from *Fantastic Symphony*, by Berlioz

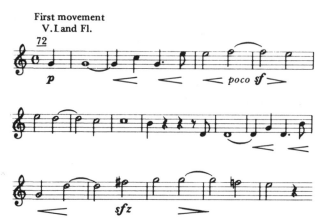

First movement
V. I and Fl.

Beginning of the development section. The first motive is built into a climax, through a sequence on rising half steps.

low strings

An imitative section, based on the first motive of the theme. A quiet moment in the coda to the first movement.

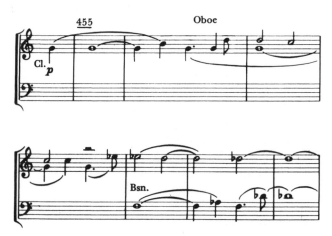

The first four notes of the theme are made into a figure which is contracted from the space of a 6th to a 2nd as part of a long diminuendo. This leads into a quiet restatement of the theme, near the end of the coda.

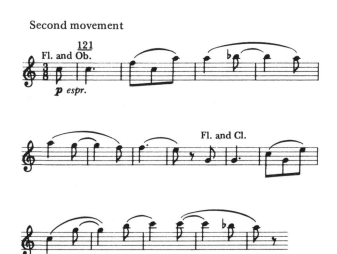

The theme is transformed into a waltz tune. The many dynamic changes that characterized the original are gone, and the melody is much more even in quality.

Second movement

In a slow tempo, the melody changes character again. Compare the rhythms of this version with the one above.

Third movement

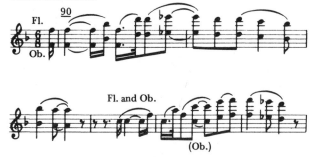

Only the opening motive of the theme is heard in this brief reminder, interrupted by a loud minor triad.

Fourth movement

The legato melody has been transformed into a caricature, disjointed and bizarre. The strained quality of the small clarinet adds to the color of this final version of the theme.

Fifth movement

For study

Listen to 162 and identify the motives in the exposition. Where are those motives used in the development? Do any appear in the coda?

☞ Worksheet 39

78

The Single Phrase

When we say that a phrase is that length of music that expresses a complete idea, we must remember that not every phrase ends with a sense of complete closure. We know that most phrases, in fact, do no such thing; if they did, pieces would have to be very short. But we look for a complete tonal movement, such as a motion from I to V or a prolongation of I followed by V, and a motivic structure that adds up to a unit of one kind or another. The cadence and a resting point in the rhythmic activity mark the end of a phrase.

THE EIGHT-MEASURE PHRASE Since dance pieces are likely to have a fairly predictable phrase layout, we look at the Schubert waltzes, 130, which raise some of the issues of phrase definition. In the first waltz, 130A, we hear two-measure units, four-measure units, and an eight-measure unit. Which is the phrase? Which do we want to define as a phrase? We call the two-measure unit the motive. The four-measure unit marks the repetition of the motive a step higher, but does not complete the tonal move. The dominant is prolonged in 4–7, and the cadence arrives at its goal in 8. At that point we breathe, and then the phrase has run its course. The eight-measure phrase is lightly punctuated in the middle, as are many eight-measure phrases. But there is not enough feeling of closure at the end of the fourth measure to end the thought.

A similar situation occurs in 130F. The two-measure motive is repeated without a sense of close, then extended for four measures to make an eight-measure phrase. But in the second half of the piece the accent on the chord in 11 and the length of that chord suggest a four-measure unit, and only the fact that the tonal movement continues through that chord gives support to the idea of an eight-measure phrase.

SHORTER PHRASES There are phrases shorter than eight measures that embody complete statements and close with a cadence on I or V. 130C begins with a four-measure phrase whose tonal

structure is I–V⁷, and is followed by a second four-measure phrase whose tonal direction is I–V⁷–I. The second half of the piece also consists of two four-measure phrases. 130D begins with the dominant, and also falls into four-measure groupings. 130E is longer than the other waltzes, but every fourth measure has a dotted half note and a goal chord that ends a phrase.

Four- and eight-measure phrases are not the only possibilities. One of the interesting features of the early Romantic piece 138 is its unusual phrase structure. A two-measure motive opens the piece, then is repeated a 4th higher. A connecting link of sixteenth notes leads into a third statement of the motive, altered to fit the cadence in V that marks the end of the phrase. Three statements of the two-measure motive add up to a six-measure phrase. When the same idea returns in 21, the motive is extended to three measures. Then the first measure is used twice over a dominant prolongation, and the phrase is drawn out to six measures. The internal rhythm of these six measures is quite unlike that of the opening six-measure phrase.

LONGER PHRASES If we take the eight-measure phrase as the norm, we find that many phrases are shorter. But some are longer, too. One way to extend a phrase is to repeat one of its units. 130B is an example of this. If 3–4 were omitted, the phrase would be eight measures long. Repetition of the first two-measure motive stretches the phrase out to ten measures.

A more complex example is the first phrase of 135. Here, the upbeat moves the music across every bar line; each rhythmic unit crosses the bar. A three-measure motive is built on a tonic prolongation. Two-measure groups grow from the initial idea, with the characteristic dotted eighth-note–sixteenth note playing a crucial role. The next three measures lead to the cadence, still in I. The phrase is ten measures long, the grouping $3 + 4$ (i.e., $2 + 2$) $+ 3$.

If the rate of chord change is slow and the tempo

fast, we may see even more than ten measures in a phrase. The scherzo from Reicha's wind quintet, 137, takes four measures to state the tonic and the same number to set forth IV. The next eight measures modulate to a cadence in III, completing one tonal movement and giving us a sixteen-measure phrase.

TONAL STRUCTURE OF THE PHRASE While there is no general formula for the tonal structure of the phrase, we often find a prolongation of I followed by a cadence or by a motion to the dominant or (if in minor) to the relative major. Within this general description, no two phrases are alike. Each work must be studied as something individual. The tonal structure of 129A is fairly typical of Classical phrases, although the elaborative chords are not necessarily typical of anything.

By contrast, the tonal structure of the first phrase of 139B is quite unusual. The tonic is not stabilized at the beginning. A Romantic restlessness propels the music from one dissonance to another.

Reduction shows Schumann's characteristic preoccupation with lines, here in contrary motion.

THE INDEPENDENT PHRASE Most phrases are part of phrase groups. But there are some that are self-sufficient, often standing at the head of a piece or a section. Beethoven wrote a number of such phrases. Two of them are 142A and 142C. The first is the theme for the *Variations in C Minor*. The second is the opening of a short interlude, hardly a movement, between the two fast movements of the *Waldstein Sonata*.

165A , 183 , is the second theme of Tchaikovsky's overture *Romeo and Juliet*. It is one long eight-measure phrase, with a motion in 5ths that ends V^7–I, and is barely punctuated in the middle. It is self-contained, and what follows is, in fact, something of a contrast.

The second movement of Schubert's *Unfinished Symphony*, 164A, has as its second theme a remarkable phrase, played by the oboe. We have already seen how the melody builds on the melodic interval of a 3rd. Using that as a unifying element, Schubert spins out the long phrase without a pause, following a two-measure introduction. The quickening in 211–212 allows no time for breath, and the long descent is unbroken. The tonal movement goes far afield of the tonal center, A, and returns as the melodic arch reaches its resting point. Excluding the introduction, the phrase is eighteen measures long. It is a complete statement of a theme, and is followed by a new phrase, continuing the same material.

☞ Worksheet 40

79

Groups of Phrases

The independent phrase is the exception; phrase groups are the norm. We may hear two, three, four, and even more phrases as a unit. What binds them together? A single tonal movement, most often.

PHRASE PAIR Each of the two eight-measure phrases that comprise 130A has its own complete tonal movement, starting from the tonic and ending with the harmonic cadence. The cadences are identical. Each phrase is self-sufficient. Their similarity lies in their common motivic material, key, tempo, registral movement, and general character. Because of all these factors, the phrases are defined as a pair. This type of two-phrase group has the least binding connection tonally.

ANTECEDENT AND CONSEQUENT A more binding connection between two phrases is seen in 130B. The first phrase, ten measures long, ends with a cadence in V. This demands continuation. The second phrase begins by adding an F to the V, returning the tonal movement to the orbit of C. The cadence on I completes the tonal movement. The entire piece has a single tonal direction, from I to V and back to I. The two phrases are related tonally, and each needs the other. The first phrase, which sets up the expectation of things to come, is called the antecedent phrase; the second phrase, which flows from the tonal implications of the first and satisfies them, is called the consequent phrase.

PERIOD The particular group of two or more phrases that is built on a single tonal movement is known as a *period*. Most music of the Classic-Romantic era is organized in periods. Identify the two-phrase periods that begin 131, the trio of 135, and 136. In what way does the consequent phrase fulfill something that is left incomplete in the antecedent phrase?

☞ Worksheet 41

LONGER PERIODS The four-phrase group is as old as folk song. It can be used to project a long melodic arch, kept in motion by three open cadences and closed off by the single harmonic cadence. Such is the format for the opening section of many Romantic pieces.

The following is a summary of phrase groups in 130:

1. pair of phrases, each phrase ending with a harmonic cadence: 130A 130C 130D;
2. two-phrase period, antecedent and consequent: 130B;
3. four-phrase period: 130E.

INTRODUCTIONS, EXTENSIONS 155 begins with four three-measure phrases, comprising a period. Only the fourth phrase has a harmonic cadence, which is not quite stable because of the C♮ that is in the inner voice. The large sense of punctuation is felt, but there is also a need to continue. At the beginning of the song, the piano plays a one-measure introduction, which may be con-

sidered part of the first phrase because it contains the chord that opens the phrase.

In another song, 150, the end of a period is extended. The first four-measure phrase, in the piano, is complete in itself and not a part of the period. Two phrases, each eight measures long, follow. But the goal Schubert has in mind is I, not V. A sixteenth-note flow goes right on from the F♯-major triad and leads back to B. This extension is part of the phrase, which is nine measures long.

In later Romantic music, periods grew to ever-greater lengths. In the quest for long, continuous utterances, the punctuation that marks phrase endings was weakened, sometimes lost altogether. The desire to keep the music moving over long spans of time, avoiding closed cadences, is manifest in the music of Wagner. 168 is one example. The phrase grouping is outlined below. The degree of closure at the end of the period is only relative since there is only one full close in the piece, at the very end. It should be noted that two measures can be a phrase in this music because the tempo is so slow. But there are very long phrases, too.

Phrase Grouping in the *Liebestod*, 168

measure numbers	phrase groups
1–11	2 + 2 + 4 + 3
12–28	6 + 8 + 3
29–43	9½ + 5½
44–60	17 (16½)
61–79	9 + 10

Composers who came after Wagner could hardly avoid being influenced by his force and emotional intensity. The closed forms of the past must have seemed quite obsolete by the end of the nineteenth century. Continuity was the goal; clear-cut phrases were avoided. Berg's song, 169, is the work of a youthful genius still under the shadow of Wagner, but already seeking his own way. The piece is a tightly knit succession of phrases, each phrase ending blended into the beginning of the upcoming phrase. The concept of antecedent and consequent phrases does not apply here. The division between phrases is minimal; we hear the song as a single, unbroken gesture. The phrase groupings in 169 are 4 + 4 + 6 + 4.

Those musicians who pursued chromaticism into atonality began by writing music in fairly clear phrases. In time, the phrase structure disintegrated to a large extent. An overview of the short orchestral piece by Webern, 182, raises some important questions. With tonality and the cadence no longer available to serve as guideposts, how are we to tell if there are phrases? And yet the piece, brief though it is, does not seem to be continuous from beginning to end. We fall back on the basic definition of a phrase: Where does the music draw breath? We may hear the first four beats as introductory. In the very slow tempo of this piece, the four-note melody of the solo violin is a unit, a phrase. The background sounds that served as introduction continue to create a tiny interlude. Three notes in the horn are an answering thought. Perhaps here we find a remnant of antecedent and consequent phrases; the context is not tonal, but the second idea complements the first.

A contrasting melody that is handed from clarinet to viola constitutes, again, a short phrase, complete in itself and punctuated by silence at the end. A varied version of the opening introduces, accompanies, and follows the final phrase in the muted trombone. We hear, then, that the entire piece is organized in phrases, without the aid of tonality. Between each pair of phrases there is either silence or a continuation of the background sound. Thus the definition of each phrase is made clear to the listener.

Twentieth-century composers who extended the concept of tonality also continued the phrase format associated with tonal music of the past. The phrases of [170], [171], [172], and [177], to name the most obvious, resemble the phrases of the past in their regularity and in their motion from and back to tonic chords. But the types of polyphonic motion and the decreased reliance on dominant and leading-tone functions set them apart from earlier music.

☞ Worksheet 42

VORABEND:
DAS RHEINGOLD

ERSTER TAG:
DIE WALKÜRE

ZWEITER TAG:
SIEGFRIED

DRITTER TAG:
GÖTTERDÄMMERUNG

From an 1899 edition of *The Ring of the Nibelungs* by Richard Wagner.

PART THIRTEEN
CHROMATICISM 1

80

Introduction to Chromaticism

DIATONIC AND CHROMATIC We have defined as diatonic those seven notes that spell out the major or minor scale on which a piece is based. The remaining five notes of our tempered scale are defined as chromatic. Strictly speaking, the inclusion of any of those five notes in a piece is considered chromaticism.

In that literal sense, almost every piece of tonal music has some element of chromaticism. Few, indeed, are the composers who could make an interesting piece out of diatonic notes alone. If we try to think of music that is completely diatonic, we think of most plainchant, some folk songs, and some medieval music. But more than a few folk songs use chromatic notes, and the leading tone as a chromatic note in the minor mode goes back to the Middle Ages.

That a piece is diatonic means that it is *prevailingly* diatonic and that chromatic notes are relatively few. If we say that a piece is chromatic, we mean that chromatic notes are relatively numerous. This is not intended as a hard and fast distinction, but we can compare two pieces, sections, or phrases and say that one is more chromatic than another.

TECHNIQUES OF CHROMATICISM In this section we survey various means by which chromatic notes are brought into use. They are mode mixture, chromatic embellishing tones, tonicization and modulation, and voice leading by half steps.

MODE MIXTURE Mixing major and minor (and other) modes over a common tonic is one of the oldest means of gaining the use of the "other five" notes. Music in the minor mode uses the leading tone, derived from the major, as part of the dominant function. Since late medieval times, pieces in the minor have often ended with the major triad, using the Picardy 3rd. By the seventeenth century, chords in the major mode were often replaced by their counterparts in the parallel minor, a practice that became ever more common through the nineteenth century. But mixture extends beyond these details and influences tonal movement as well. The waltz by Schubert, 130E, has as its overall tonal direction I–III–V–I. But III is A♭, which is the III of F minor, not the major which is the mode of the piece. Fauré's song, 154, moves back and forth between C major and C minor for its entire duration. Mode mixture over a pedal point constitutes one of the main features of the piece.

By the nineteenth century, musicians were completely at ease with the variability of mode that we call mixture, and it permeated the fabric of music increasingly as composers used it in their search for ever-more colorful and expressive sounds. The natural extension of the concept comes when a twentieth-century composer like Bartók or Hindemith writes music that has a definite center of tonality but is in what we might well describe as a major-minor mode—highly chromatic, still tonal.

CHROMATIC NT AND PT While chromatic NT and PT can be found in folk song and even occasionally in Renaissance music, their use developed far more in Baroque music. Chromatic embellishing notes generated chromatic chords, which, in turn, could be embellished by additional chromatic embellishing notes. The second chord in 130B is the sum of the NTs—two of which are chromatic—around the C-major triad. The result is a chromatic neighbor chord, the same one that we hear in the opening of 153. Chromatic NTs and PTs do not always generate chords, but their use does increase the level of activity, which happens throughout 130F.

TONICIZATION Looking at a piece of tonal music as a whole, the unity of the pitches stems from the controlling power of one note, the tonic. As a rule, a piece has only one tonic. There are a few rare exceptions, such as the Chopin *F-Minor Fantasy*, which begins in F minor and ends in A♭ major. But in the vast majority of pieces, tonal unity is one of the most powerful organizing forces. Within that large unity, any note on which a major or minor triad can be built may act as a temporary tonic. That tonicized note, however, still is subordinate to the overall tonic in the view of the entire piece.

The applied dominants and leading-tone chords, which are necessary to effect tonicization, bring in chromatic notes. 144E has V⁷ of IV as early as 4, with G♭ sounding as the 7th, a chromatic note. In 8 we hear V⁷ of II. The leading tone of II is A, another chromatic note.

MODULATION Tonicization is a matter of detail. Modulation affects the large tonal movements of a piece. Modulation need not involve much chromaticism if the pivot chord is diatonic. If the pivot chord is chromatic or if it is tonicized, chromaticism will be involved.

VOICE LEADING BY HALF STEP In diatonic music we speak of stepwise motion, meaning motion through the notes of the scale. In a chromatic context, motion by half step may begin to undermine the scale. In such a piece as the Chopin *Prelude in E Minor*, 144B, half-step motion is the norm. Only half steps are used in the motion within the chords of 167C; half-step motion characterizes the connection from one chord to another, too, although octave displacement disguises the fact. The sketch on page 108 shows the basic counterpoint behind the music.

ENHARMONIC CHANGE As the use of chromaticism increases, problems in spelling arise. What is the difference between C♯ and D♭? On the piano there is none. String players will not agree. The tempered system divides the octave into twelve mathematically equal parts, but performers bend the pitches in accordance with their melodic tendencies. Looking at a piece of music, we normally expect a sharp to denote an upward tendency, a flat, downward. But composers were not always consistent. They wanted to show the direction of a line, but also wanted the chords to look logical and familiar. For example, chords with both sharps and flats are unusual. The result is that chords usually are spelled in a way that is the simplest to read but may not show the tendencies of the voices. In 167B, the second chord in 16 has as top note a PT between C and B♭, which should be spelled C♭ to show that it will move down. It is spelled B because the B-major triad looks simpler than the C♭-major triad. Change in spelling without change in the actual sound is called *enharmonic change*.

SUMMARY The techniques of chromaticism are the techniques of diatonicism carried further. The same linear devices—namely, PT, NT, and SUS—are used both to elaborate chords and to invent new ones. The increased use of those techniques and the more intensive use of mode mixture and tonicization make the vocabulary of nineteenth-century music more chromatic than earlier music. To be sure, there are individual examples of chromatic music from the mid-sixteenth century on. The deliberate exploitation of chromaticism, introduced in the late Middle Ages and the subject of limited but quite remarkable experimentation in the sixteenth century, became an occasional feature of tonal music in the seventeenth century. Yet music remained largely diatonic, even the music of composers who wrote some highly chromatic works, such as Frescobaldi, Purcell, Bach, and Mozart. In the early Romantic period, the impulse toward greater (or more obvious) expressivity found a vehicle in the use of chromatic chords and lines. Even later, in such works as *Tristan* and *Parsifal,* Wagner reached the point at which all twelve tones were about equally available at any time, no matter what the key. By the end of the nineteenth century, it seemed that the possibilities of triadic tonality were on the way to being exhausted—or at least turned over to composers of operettas and musical comedies. Many composers who wanted to continue writing tonal music without following Wagner reversed the trend toward increased chromaticism and worked within a relatively diatonic vocabulary.

81

Mode Mixture 1

Variability of mode has characterized music of many kinds, from folk song through art music of recent times. Now we concentrate on that intensive use of mixture which is an important ingredient in chromaticism. We begin by distinguishing between long-range use of mixture (between phrases or sections) and those involving details (a chord or a tonicization).

BETWEEN SECTIONS One of the clearest ways to signal the start of a new section is to change mode. Haydn was one of the first to see this possibility and to use it to good advantage. In 147A , he tells us that the second section is under way by switching from E major to E minor, changing texture and register at the same time. When the motion within E minor has been completed, E major returns as does the material of the first section.

Many slow introductions to symphonies in major either begin in minor or soon move into it, usually ending with a cadence on V;. The ensuing fast movement gains freshness from the contrast of modes. A minuet or scherzo in minor will almost always have a trio in major, as in 135 . The reverse is less often the case. A set of variations in one mode will usually have at least one variation in the opposite mode, which is true of both 145 and 146 . A piece in ternary form can make good use of mixture to differentiate the middle section from the first and third sections. In the aria 158 , which is in ternary form, the change from G major to G minor lets us know that the second part is beginning. When G major returns, we know that

the first part is also returning. Such large contrasts of mode do much to articulate the large divisions of a piece since they are easy to perceive.

WITHIN A PHRASE Seeing in nature the reflection of his own life and feelings, the poet of 150 asks the brook (22) why it is so still. This is the projection of the poet's uncertainty about the feelings of the maiden whom he loves. At the question, the composer shifts mode—the serene B major suddenly gives way to B minor. The two replies that the girl might give are considered. "Yes" is in the major; but at "no," the line swings to D♮, and a sudden tonal shift brings the music to G major, which is VI of B minor.

Another song, 153 , begins with a prolongation of I and modulates to a cadence in V. But the first appearance of that V as tonic, in 11 , presents it in the minor mode, which continues the melancholy mood of the previous measures. Only as the vocal phrase is finished does the piano arrive at a G major whose effect, in this context, is calm and reposeful, leading into the second verse.

IN A CHORD The scale degrees that parallel major and minor do not have in common are 3, 6, and 7. Any of these may be appropriated for use in the opposite mode. Of the three, the major version of 7 is used in the minor as leading tone, and the major version of 6 is often attached to it. The minor version of 6 is frequently used in the major, where it is referred to as the *flat (or flatted)*

69

6. We examine its uses as root, third, fifth, and seventh of a chord.

In its second phrase, 130C has a melody built on a NT motion, E♭–F–E♭. Between the F and the E♭ there is a chromatic PT, F♭. Or is F♭ an instance of mode mixture? Both. The chord under the F♭ is VII⁴. Flat 6 is the seventh of the chord.

Flat 6 is the fifth of a chord in 162, 24, where a forceful II² chord leads back from the tonicization of II to the dominant in a large I–II–V–I motion. To undermine the tonicity of II, which lasted for five measures, Beethoven uses A♭, pulling the motion down from A to G and guiding it toward the dominant.

Flat 6 as the third of a IV chord is a familiar ingredient of Romantic music. But it also appears in earlier works, of which 158, 68, is but one instance. A more extended example is in the swift-moving song by Mendelssohn, 152. On the way from the opening tonic prolongation to V the motion stops off at VI in 24–39; for the moment, we think in D major. In this long tonicization D's dominant is not used, but its subdominant is. IV functions as a neighbor chord, guided by the top line's move from A to B♭ and back. B♭, to be sure, is taken from D's parallel minor, and it is the third of the IV chord, its unexpected color adding much to the atmosphere of the song.

When flat 6 is the root of a VI chord in the major mode the chromaticism can rise to a high level, for flat 3 also joins it. To start the second phrase of 161 with a fresh sound in 9, Bizet launches it with VI, not of the D♭ major heard in the first phrase, but of the parallel minor. The common tone is the tonic, D♭ (C♯). Enharmonic spelling is used to avoid writing B♭♭ major, since A major is much easier to read.

As early as the eighteenth century, composers were quite aware of the possibilities of flat 6 as a root. In 147, Haydn moves from I to V via a simple pivot chord, I/IV. This is followed in 8 by a chord built on the flat 6 of B major, which lasts an entire measure before melting into the cadential I⁶₄. The move is as surprising as any in the work of this surprising composer.

Flat 6 usages in Brahms's piano music

Op. 119 No. 4

Flat 6 as the root of a triad. It is embellished in the top voice by a NT, in the bass by arpeggiation. The resulting I chord does not function as tonic.

Op. 76 No. 4

(Reduced)

Flat 6 as the third of a IV⁶₄ chord. It is also a long NT.

Op. 119 No. 7

Flat 6 as the fifth of a II⁶₅, then as the third of IV.

Op. 119 No. 2

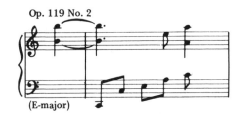

(E-major)

The suspended B (from a B-major triad) is in sharp relief with the flat 6, here the third of IV⁶.

Op. 116 No. 4

Flat 6 as the fifth of a neighboring II⁶₅.

Op. 118 No. 2

Flat 6 as the seventh of VII².

Op. 76 No. 3

Flat 6 as the ninth of V⁹. Notice the displaced resolution.

82

Chromatic Chords; More Vocabulary

Chromatic voice leading makes a few new chords possible and suggests many new ways of using old chords. Such contrapuntal chromatic chords function in the same ways that contrapuntal diatonic chords did. They also increase the level of dissonant tension and heighten the excitement of the music, which is why they became an important part of the vocabulary of Romantic music.

DIMINISHED 7TH In the minor mode, a 7th chord built on the leading tone (taken from the major) has as its outside interval a diminished 7th. This is a strong dissonance and actively demands resolution. As a leading-tone chord, based on the leading tone of almost any scale degree, we observe it in ⌐138¬, 1 ; ⌐150¬, 2 ; ⌐150¬, 50 (third beat); and VII⁷ᵇ appears in the major in ⌐150¬, 53 , over a tonic pedal. Three diminished-7th chords within five measures, in ⌐162¬, 93–97 , add much to the drive toward the end of the exposition.

We also saw that the diminished 7th may act as a chromatic neighbor chord. Examples include ⌐130B¬; ⌐153¬, 2 , 19 , and 27 . Other contrapuntal usages might be described as passing chords, as in ⌐130F¬, 13 ; ⌐132¬, 7 ; ⌐139A¬, 7 . But many of these function as applied-leading-tone chords as well as passing or neighbor chords.

Octave displacement of one or more voices can make the contrapuntal motion less obvious, but also more interesting. Compare the example below with ⌐147A¬, the last beat of 17 through the first beat of 20 .

Also compare the example with the same phrase in the reprise, from the end of 54 through 57 , to see how Haydn extended the lines in musical space in elaborating the repetition.

AUGMENTED 6TH Reduction of ⌐142A¬, shown in the example below, tells us that the single phrase that constitutes the·theme of Beethoven's *C-Minor Variations* is built on contrary motion between the outer voices, leading to a stark unison cadence. Heightening the drive to the dominant is a chord that has F♯ in the top line, A♭ in the bass. Both notes have a tendency to move to G; the interval between them is an augmented 6th. The chord that has that interval between bass and soprano, in root position, is called an *augmented-6th chord*. In this example it is a passing chord.

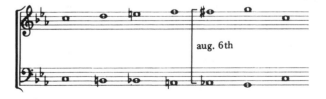

aug. 6th

The augmented sixth comes in three types: Italian, French, and German,

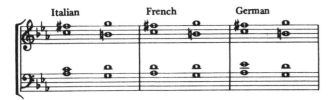

Note that when the German 6th moves directly to V, parallel 5ths result. In a musical composition, these parallels are usually avoided since the augmented 6th chord moves to I_4^6 more often than not. But in the excerpt from the Franck symphony 166, 13, parallel 5ths do appear.

A comparison shows that three of the four notes are the same in all forms of the chord. Inner-voice details account for the differences, which affect the color but not the function; all three resolve in much the same way. The labels ("Italian," "French," "German") that are associated with them are handy for reference, but have no other significance.

The "6th" in an augmented 6th is an interval. It does not in itself imply a VI chord. But in fact most augmented 6th chords are built on the note one half step above the dominant—i.e., 6 in minor, 6♭ in major.

AS A PASSING CHORD The augmented 6th is used most in the approach to a cadence as part of a passing motion. 142C reaches the dominant in 6. Preceding that, we heard an augmented 6th outlined, its resolution delayed by a SUS in the top line.

Another, milder use of the chord occurs in 130F. The piece starts in F major, slips into F minor, and is on the way back to the major in 13. A bass ascent from 1 to 5 starts on the last beat of 11. At 13 it reaches A♭. Over the A♭ we hear first a diminished-7th chord, then an augmented 6th. The inversion is $VI_{2\sharp}^4$. The augmented 6th is inverted to produce a diminished 3rd between B and D♭. With the doubling, an augmented 6th is heard, too.

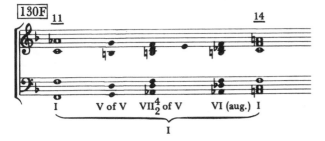

These five chords add up to a prolongation of I, the mode variable. The fourth chord includes both

an augmented 6th and its inversion, a diminished 3rd. This is because of the doubling, which adds to the richness of sound. Follow each voice: soprano fills a 3rd; bass moves from 1 to 3; alto (C–B–B–C) prolongs 5 with its neighbor; and tenor moves from 1 to 5. Other notes are doublings.

AS A NEIGHBOR CHORD The augmented 6th often is involved with NT motion. The melodic tendency of 6 to descend to 5 is part of the chord's tendency to move to the dominant; so is the tendency of the leading tone of the dominant to step upward. Often, the dominant appears first in the form of I^6, which absorbs the tendency tones and sets up V^7. The introductory phrase in 152 moves to an augmented 6th in 8, guided by the NT motion C♯–B♯–C♯. Under the B♯, an augmented-6th chord in root position leads into I^6.

150 moves from B major to the key of the flatted 6th, G major, in its middle section. The cadence in VI falls on the first beat of 41. Schubert moves through the cadence in two ways: by resuming the sixteenth-note motion heard earlier; and by adding an E♯ to the G-major triad, converting it into an augmented 6th. What had been the temporary tonic becomes a dissonant chord. Resolution of the two active notes in the interval of an augmented 6th guides the motion back to B major with I_4^6–V^7–I.

The last inversion of the augmented-6th chord can be as powerful as root position, since the leading tone of the dominant, in the bass, is a very active note. 144G, in its final phrase, builds a crescendo to 39, where a widely spaced VI^2 is an augmented 6th. A moment of silence clears the air for the final I_4^6–V^7–I.

PROLONGATION OF AUGMENTED 6TH Itself a contrapuntal chord, the augmented 6th may be elaborated with other linear chords. In 135, bringing the activity to a focal point that will lead back to the tonic, Mozart aims for VI in 27. Then the first violin moves to a NT, G♯, creating an augmented 6th with the cello and intensifying the push to V. In 28, the outer voices maintain the augmented 6th; the inner voices move from the German 6th through a contrapuntal chord to the Italian 6th. The contrapuntal chord is part of the prolongation of the augmented 6th, whose two forms here seem quite interchangeable.

NEAPOLITAN 6TH   The II chord in minor has never played the important role that it has in major because it is a diminished triad. II⁶ is used quite often, of course, but neither it nor the root position is a satisfactory goal for tonicization. A more stable version of II emerged in the seventeenth century. It is built not on the diatonic 2, but on the flat 2, perhaps a vestigial remnant of the Phrygian mode. This version of II usually appears in the first inversion and is known as the *Neapolitan-6th chord* (N⁶). While it never replaced the diatonic II, it became a significant addition to the vocabulary of chromatic chords, first in the minor mode, then in the major.

N⁶ as a version of II in the cadence is illustrated in 138, 5–6. The cadence is II⁶–I⁶₄–V⁷–I, or would be if Clementi had written F♯ in the top line. Instead he uses F, delayed by a SUS but still part of the N⁶.

Not all cadences are built on dominant-tonic motions, and the song by Fauré, 154, has no dominant at all. The long opening phrase, with an introduction of two measures, only draws breath in 14. In 7–8, there is a III minor–I progression, elaborated into III–II–I in 11–13. The effect is that of a cadence in which passing motion replaces the harmonic progression. The passing chord is N⁶. We should also be aware that the entire phrase is built over a tonic pedal.

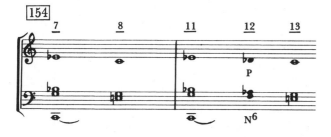

By the nineteenth century, composers were familiar enough with the Neapolitan chord to use it in positions other than ⁶₃. In 144F, we hear a major triad on the flatted supertonic at the last cadence. The same piece can help us find the answer to the question of whether every major triad based on the flat 2 is a Neapolitan chord. We look closely at the function of the second chord in 2 for the answer. The D♭-major triad is in C minor, but it is part of a tonicization of VI. It acts as IV of VI.

Thus it is not a Neapolitan chord. Once again, the same chord, in a given key, has different meanings in different contexts.

THE AUGMENTED 6TH AS THE DOMINANT OF THE NEAPOLITAN   Out of context, a German 6th sounds exactly like a dominant-7th chord even though they look different on paper because of enharmonic spelling. If a German 6th is resolved as a V⁷, where does it go?

The same sound that functions as a German-6th chord can also function as the dominant of the Neapolitan. This is what happens in 144G. In 17, on the second beat, the chord is V²₂ of the Neapolitan 6th, which indeed follows. Exactly the same chord appears in 39. But the note that was spelled D♭, indicating a downward tendency, now is C♯, a leading tone, which resolves up.

A famous augmented-6th chord

A♭ major: VII⁷ of II?   VII⁷ of IV?   C: VI⁶♯   I⁶₄   V⁷   I major!

HALF-DIMINISHED-7TH CHORDS   There are two chords that have the curious label "half diminished." Perhaps the name is an attempt to say that the lowest three notes of each make up a diminished triad. To this we add a major 3rd or a perfect 4th. If the overall range of the chord is a minor 7th, we call the chord *half-diminished minor*. If the total size of the chord is a major 7th we call the chord *half-diminished major*.

Half-diminished minor   Half-diminished major

The linear origin of both is similar. They are derived from embellishments of the diminished-7th chord. The following excerpt from César Franck's

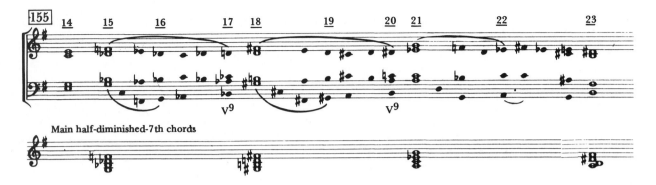

Main half-diminished-7th chords

Prelude, Chorale, and Fugue includes both forms. This is the opening of the chorale:

Half-diminished-7th chords

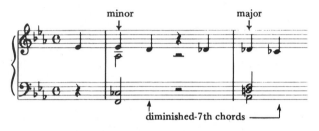

diminished-7th chords ⟶

HALF-DIMINISHED 7TH MINOR Used increasingly in the course of the nineteenth century, the half-diminished 7th minor is built of two minor 3rds and a major 3rd. The outside interval is a minor 7th. This chord type, with a diminished triad contained within, originates as VII⁷ in the major and II⁷ in minor. 147A , 4 , shows VII⁷ in E major, the third omitted and the fifth doubled. Here we have a neighbor chord to the I of the next measure, part of a tonic prolongation. In 152 , 48 , we hear II⁷ of the B minor, which is tonicized from 94–102 . Again, the 7th of this dissonant chord resolves down; it may be heard as both an IN and an indirect SUS from the previous measure's B in the bass.

The minor form of II⁷ is used frequently in the major. One instance is in 144H , 13 , where II^6_5, disguised by the embellishing notes E–D–C♯, is a neighbor chord to the A-major triad being tonicized. A similar use of the chord is in the first measure of 141 , where II² minor elaborates I. In 158 , 34 , the E♭ in the bass is both a chromatic PT and a minor-mode note used in the major. The chord is II^4_3.

Freed from its original functions, the half-diminished-7th chord is used as a contrapuntal chord in a chromatic context in much late Romantic music. It is, for instance, an important part of the vocabulary of 155 . The first half of the song, a description of a peaceful landscape, includes a C♯ in the E-minor context so consistently that the Dorian mode lives once again. This means that

VI⁷, a passing chord in the motion from I to V, is a half-diminished 7th in 3 , 6 , and 12 . The second half of the song, an exclamation of despair at the young man's loss of his freedom, takes off from the VI⁶, which replaces the expected I in 14 (see above). Three half-diminished-7th chords, in 15 , 18 , and 21 , provide the framework of an ascending chromatic motion, with contrapuntal chords leading from one to the next. The language of tonal music has evolved from the point at which half-diminished 7ths were contrapuntal, elaborative chords to the point at which they are the structural chords that other, more dissonant chords elaborate. The succession leads to V in 23 , as the E♭ turns into D♯. In the elaborated resolution of V⁷, one of the contrapuntal chords, on the last beat of 24 , is another half-diminished 7th, and the same chord returns as part of the closing tonic prolongation over the pedal E, on the last beat of 27 .

Probably the best-known use of the half-diminished 7th is in Wagner's *Tristan*. Indeed, the particular inversion used in the first chord of the opera has been called the "Tristan chord." A few of the multiple interpretations of that sound are shown below, taken only from the *Prelude*, 167D , and the *Liebestod,* 169 .

Prelude

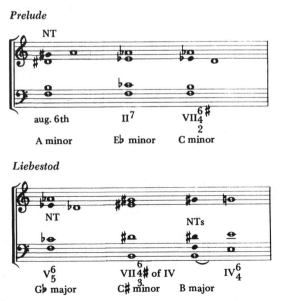

Liebestod

HALF-DIMINISHED 7TH MAJOR Another version of the half-diminished-7th chord is also built with two minor 3rds; but to this a perfect 4th is added. The outer interval is a major 7th. The difference between the two is:

Half-diminished 7th minor   Half-diminished 7th major

F major: VII⁷
D minor: II⁷   Embellishment of diminished-7th triad

This chord has no diatonic origin, and not until late in the nineteenth century did it come into common usage. It originates as an elaboration of the diminished-7th chord. In 166 , 7 , the main chord in the second half of the measure is a passing diminished 7th. The first violins, which have been elaborating the passing chords, reiterate the G, in a SUS, to form a half-diminished 7th major. The resolution is not to a consonance, but to a less tense dissonance, the diminished 7th.

A similar use of a half-diminished 7th occurs in 157 , 25 . Over a prolonged A in the bass a stream of contrapuntal chords flows. The right-hand part of 25 begins with a half-diminished 7th major, whose 7th is resolved stepwise down to a diminished 7th.

The half-diminished 7th major became a more important member of the chord vocabulary in the early years of the twentieth century. One instance is in 175 , 24–26 . The two chord types heard are V⁷ and half-diminished 7th major. The first half-diminished major is a neighbor chord between two statements of a V². The other is also a linear chord, part of the prolongation of the V².

MAJOR-MINOR DOMINANT 7TH Closely related to the half-diminished 7th major is a five-note chord with both a major and a minor 3rd.

Major-minor V⁷

V⁷ [ ]   half-diminished 7th major

The linear origin of this chord goes back to Renaissance polyphony. Even in the nineteenth century it was not approached directly, as we can see from 141 . 7–8 are busy prolonging B major's V⁷, at the end of the first phrase. The second violin embellishes F♯ with a SP, reaching up to A. That note clashes with the A♯ of the first violin. The sound of the major-minor V⁷ is only touched on, but the process is clear—a dissonant sound generated by linear motion may be taken into the vocabulary and may achieve identity as a chord.

AUGMENTED AND DIMINISHED 5TH Another version of V⁷ involves chromatic displacement of the fifth of the chord, either a half step up or a half step down. 151 , 20 , shows an augmented 5th as a chromatic PT. The chord is used for its own color again in 23 .

The dominant of E is prolonged through the opening of 172 , although B is not always to be found in the bass. In 4 , E♯ is a chromatic NT. That sound, now spelled enharmonically as F, becomes the root of a minor triad in 5 . The chordal support drops out in 6 , and in 7 the note resumes its role within the controlling sound. But the F is absorbed into the chord, and we hear a V⁹₅♭. Only with the next phrase does F♯ return.

DOMINANT 9TH The dominant 9th became an autonomous chord a good deal later than the dominant 7th, but in the same way. For eighteenth- and early nineteenth-century composers the 9th was a linear embellishment of the dominant 7th chord, as in 130B , 12 . Here the 9th is being used for its own color value, as the placement on the strong beat and the accent show. Somewhat similar is its use in 144E , 4 , where we suspect that the V⁹, despite its linear origin as NT, is coming into its own. A SUS is the origin of the 9th in 165A , 190 , mode mixture coloring the 9th minor.

A straightforward use of V⁹ is found in 149 . The opening progression is I–VI–V⁹–I. We observe that VI is mixed, being not the expected major triad, but a minor one. The 9th is now an integral part of the dominant chord, and V⁹ is itself elaborated by a SUS in the melody. A similar situation occurs in 25 . When a chromatic version of the familiar progression in 5ths begins in 33 , V⁹ takes its place with V⁷ in the progression. When the motion in 5ths begins again, starting in 36 , the chords are all V⁹s, major and minor. These, in turn, are elaborated by still more dissonant SUSs.

The dominant 9th, like any chord, may be liberated from its original function and be treated as a contrapuntal chord rather than a harmonic one. The name, dominant 9th, persists even though the dominant function may not survive. 154 , 31–33 , prolongs a minor form of I⁷, a version of the tonic. The top line has NT motion, B♭–C–B♭; the bass has C–F–C. The inner voices are so chosen as to form a dominant-9th chord, whose role here is that of a neighbor chord. In another song by the same composer, 155, another linear use of the chord appears in 9. The motion from VI⁷, on the last beat of 8, to the V⁷ in 10 is elaborated with linear chords in 9. The first two are dominant-9th chords, leading to a chord that sounds like a dominant 7th but functions like an augmented 6th of the upcoming dominant.

AUGMENTED TRIAD The contrapuntal origin of the augmented triad may be seen in 161, 17. A is a chromatic PT between the A♭ of the preceding measure and the B♭ of the next. Stretching out the PT over a full measure, the composer makes us hear it in relation to the other notes, D♭ and F. Thus the augmented triad begins to have a life of its own. The augmented triad is used in much the same way in 149, 9, but this time the active note, D♯, is a NT. The same sound is heard again in 11. Enharmonic change is a clue that the

line that moved up in 9 will now move down, and E♭ does eventually go to D. The music that starts with the upbeat to 14 is the same as that which starts with the upbeat to 9, now transposed a minor 3rd higher. The augmented triad of 14 is the augmented triad of 9 a minor 3rd higher. All of these augmented triads are accented, calling attention to their particular color and dissonant quality.

SUMMARY The chromatic chords that became part of the vocabulary of tonal music grew out of triads. Their linear origin shows in the way they resolve to consonant chords. Once a dissonant chromatic chord is absorbed into the language of music, two things happen. First, each of those chords may be further elaborated into more dissonant chords, adding to the vocabulary again. Second, the dissonant chords may be used with less connection to their original function.

Some linear origins of dissonant and chromatic chords

☞ Worksheet 43

PART FOURTEEN
MUSICAL FORM AND FORMS 2

83

What Makes the Form of a Piece?

Many forces interact to shape the form of a piece of music. In tonal music, the tonal structure is probably the most important single factor. If all the notes of a piece are related to a single tonic, as they are by definition in tonal music, the embodiment of that network of relationships is, in a sense, the piece. Those relationships include, at the least, directed motion within, away from, and back to the tonic, the bass-soprano framework of the polyphony, the interplay of consonance and dissonance, and the punctuations, both large and small, that organize the music into phrases and sections by means of cadences of varying degrees of closure.

The rhythm of the music—how it flows through time—is also of decisive importance: the rhythm of the motive and its development, of the phrase, of phrase groups, of whole sections—indeed, all aspects of duration in time. The deployment of the notes in musical space can be a vital element in giving a piece its particular form as can the use of tone color, articulation, and dynamics. All these elements function together with the tonal structure to give a piece coherence and to articulate the several parts of the piece. It is clear that if we describe form only in terms of themes we are missing much of what is happening in a piece of music. Our view must be comprehensive.

Title page of the original edition of Haydn's oratorio *The Seasons*, published in Leipzig in 1802.

84

The Single-Idea Piece

A piece based on a single musical idea is usually short, but may be quite concentrated. Early Baroque organ toccatas such as 64 and most preludes fall into this category, as do the Bartók pieces 51A, 51B, 51C, 51D. An overview of the prelude of 128 shows that, as in much Baroque music, we must speak of figuration rather than motivic development. A single figure, a single texture, runs through almost the entire piece. When a change occurs, we know that the prelude is near its conclusion.

Since there is little variety in the texture of 128 and none in the figure up to the presto (28), our attention is focused on the tonal movement and on the details of the consonance-dissonance interplay. Four measures establish the tonic. A move through V leads to III in 11. But that point is not confirmed, and there is no punctuation or breath. The continuity is unbroken as the movement finds its way back to I in 18 and moves through the tonic to the dominant. V is prolonged from 20 through 33, arriving, at the adagio, not at the expected I, but rather at V^7 of IV. But the bass holds on to C, and the emphasis on the subdominant is brought within the orbit of the tonic for the conclusion. All is motion, activity, continuity.

There are few composers who took up the challenge of condensing so much into so little space. Chopin, a great admirer of Bach's music, wrote a set of preludes which, like the Baroque master's, include one in every major and minor key. Some are based on figuration, others use motives; sometimes the difference is hard to define. The pieces themselves have nothing of the spirit of the Baroque about them; they are Romantic miniatures.

The first, 144A, is the closest to Bach. A comparison with the model, the first prelude of the *Well-Tempered Clavier,* shows that both are figurative and continuous. The eight-measure phrase that begins the Chopin prelude hardly breathes at its end; the sixteen-measure phrase that follows runs directly into the concluding ten-measure ending.

The one-measure figure begins with a tiny rest (like a breath) that is kept for the first seventeen measures. Then, as if eager to reach for the climax, the figure pushes onto the downbeat, then returns to its offbeat articulation. The final phrase has both versions. This small, but significant variant is typical of Chopin's meticulous attention to detail.

The texture of 144B consists of a single-line melody over continuously moving chords. The tonal structure of the piece is discussed on page 111. There are but two phrases, each quite long. 1–12 is a single thought, a long lyric line that breathes at the cadence on V^7, where the texture opens for a moment. The repetition pushes to a climax in 17, then falls rapidly. After all the chromatic motion, Chopin stabilizes V with a long prolongation that ends with a moment of silence and the only V–I cadence in the piece. Much of the musical interest in the piece comes from the subtly colored chords generated by the chromatic lines, weaving a rich and complex web of sound.

The texture of 144D has three layers: a melody and an accompaniment figure in the right hand, and a bass line, sometimes in octaves, in the left. Three four-measure phrases comprise the piece. The first is statement, the second continuation, the third an intensified restatement. Since there is no change in the figure or the texture and the entire piece stays in the middle and low registers, tonal movement must provide the activity, supported by a crescendo and an implied accelerando. The tonal structure is sketched on the next page.

Pianists who have been struggling to play the sixteenth note in the melody just after the third note of the triplet are invited to study the reproduction of Chopin's manuscript facing 144D. It can be seen that the composer took great pains to line up that sixteenth note *with*, not *after*, the last note of the triplet, just as Bach would have done. When Chopin wants a note after the triplet, he writes it as a thirty-second note.

The shortest prelude in our group is the C

Tonal structure of 144D

minor, 144F. It consists of three phrases, the third of which is identical with the second. This piece is built on a one-measure motive, whose insistent repetition in every measure gives this short work a surprising weight.

The longest prelude in our group is 144E. It is in five sections, all based on similar material with no significant changes in texture or tempo. A two-measure motive is used consistently. The first, third, and fifth sections are alike, while the second and fourth are continuations.

Outline of 144E

section	measure	description
first	1–18	two nine-measure phrases, antecedent and consequent, ending with V^7–I
second	19–34	a nine-measure phrase and a seven-measure phrase, leading to a cadence in VI flat, then returning through V to
third	35–42	a repetition of the antecedent phrase of the first section, ending on V. Instead of the consequent phrase, the music goes directly to
fourth	43–64	two similar four-measure phrases, a different four-measure phrase, and a six-measure phrase that goes on to prolong V for four more measures
fifth	65–90	repetition of the first period. 80 is both the last measure of one phrase and the first measure of a four-measure phrase. The concluding seven-measure phrase begins in 84. The entire section is over a tonic pedal.

How does Chopin differentiate between the sections? Again, the design material is similar throughout the entire piece. Changes of tonal direction and variants of the basic melodic material are the means used to let the listener know that a new section is beginning. Thus, in 18, the note that was tonic, Ab, becomes the G♯ (in 19) that is the 3rd of VI^7 minor, an augmented 6th that immediately turns into the dominant 7th of the Neapolitan 6th. This starts the tonal movement toward E major (Fb major), which is the tonal center of the second section. The return to the Ab is managed neatly with a shift from E to its III, G♯ minor, in 32, and enharmonic spelling shows Ab minor in the next measure. VII⁷ of V leads into the dominant that starts the reprise of the initial phrase, without the introductory measures.

The fourth section ends with V;. The V⁷ of VI flat that follows has the same relation to E♭ that the V⁷ of A had to A♭.

A♭:   I   VI flat   V   VI flat of V

This is the most unstable section. It is the most chromatic, and no one tonal center emerges. The goal, however, is E♭. The prolongation of that becomes the dominant preparation for the concluding section. But what creates the character of a concluding section? For one thing, the repetition of the first two-phrase period. For another, the tonic pedal, which answers the fourth section's instability. Another important factor is the way in which the activity is gradually reduced, starting in 81 . A short fragment of the motive is repeated, echoed, and dies away. Nothing is left but NT motion within the tonic chord. But that persists, with a diminuendo, long enough to exhaust the musical momentum.

One link between sections that may not be readily apparent is in 57–60 , where the prolongation of E♭ is colored by C♭. This may be heard as an aural link with the B that had played an important role as 5 of E major in the second section. In 79–82 , the F♭ refers back to the E that had been conspicuous in both the second and fourth sections. Thus the last measures form a link with earlier sections of the piece and draw threads together to create a convincing sense of finality. It should be understood that the piece does not end on a $\frac{6}{4}$-position chord, as may appear to the eye. Any pianist knows that the bass A♭ of 88 sounds to the very end, held by the pedal.

For further study

Listen to the preludes of the *Well-Tempered Clavier,* paying particular attention to the chromaticism.

An analysis of the tonal structure of the first prelude may be found in *Five Graphic Music Analyses* by Heinrich Schenker, which also includes an explanation of Schenker's graphic symbols. The same music is discussed at length in Richard Goldman's *Harmony in Western Music.*

You should listen to all of Chopin's *Preludes,* and spend some time with those that seem to have particular interest for you.

Two composers who carried Chopin's conception of the prelude forward are Scriabin (Opp. 11, 13, 15, 16, 17, 22, 27, 31, 35, 37, 39, 48, 67, and 74) and Fauré (Op. 103). Later preludes by Debussy and Rachmaninov go beyond the notion of a single-idea piece to a larger form, such as ternary.

☞ Worksheet 44

85

Comprehensive Analysis of Mozart's Variations on *Ah vous dirai-je, Maman,* 145

BACKGROUND The practice of writing—originally, improvising—variations on well-known tunes is as old as keyboard music. We have seen in Baroque music examples based on folk songs and chorales. Some variations, not usually based on previously existing melodies, but on invented chord or bass patterns, are continuous, with little or no pause between variations. Other types make each variation a complete entity in itself. In the late eighteenth and early nineteenth centuries this latter type flourished. Composers endeavored to give each variation its own distinct character, and the type is sometimes called *character variations*. Such variations were written well into the twentieth century.

Mozart's variations on a French folk tune, 145, written while he was visiting Paris, were designed to show his skill in elaborating a melody he knew was familiar to his audience. The piano setting that constitutes the theme is Mozart's own.

TONAL STRUCTURE Since variations are built as much on the tonal structure of the theme as on its thematic design, a reduction of the theme is helpful in studying the piece. Each variation should be compared with the reduction to uncover the many ways in which the basic material is manipulated.

145: **Reduction of theme**

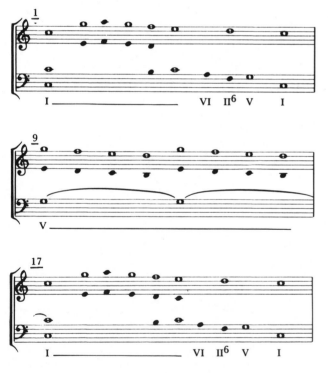

THEME The setting of the theme is simplicity itself, yet it contains the seeds of the entire composition. The right hand plays the melody in single notes, the left a bass line and inner voices. The harmonization stresses the tonic in the first eight-measure phrase, the dominant in the second, and the tonic in the third. The limited range of the melody is matched by that of the accompaniment.

But Mozart does touch on the low C at phrase beginnings and endings. These low notes stabilize the tonic. They also open up the low register and create octave skips that will be exploited in the variations.

VARIATION 1 With virtuosity always in the picture, we are not surprised to find the melody immediately broken into sixteenth-note filigree work in the first variation. At once we have the feel of keyboard music, which depends so much on active movement. NTs predominate, some chromatic, and we hear one chromatic PT. But the melodic elaboration of 3 brings in a new element. We may understand it better with the aid of a reduction in reverse—i.e., a synthesis.

The fourth measure uses still another technique —inversion. The implied inner voice is tossed up an octave, and the resulting 6th is filled in with PTs.

The same device is repeated twice, creating a sequence that leads to the cadence. Looking back at the theme, we can see that Mozart considered the IN in 7, E, as an embellishment, not as an essential part of the theme. In variation 1, 31, he chose to replace it with a more melodious turn. Variation technique does not mean following slavishly the notes of the theme; but it does involve retaining the structural notes as a firm foundation. The animation of this phrase owes much to the rhythmic activity, of course, as well as to the opening up of the upper register and the way in which the simple tune is elaborated into a polyphonic melody.

Returning to consider the left-hand part of the phrase, we find that it starts with the same notes as the original. But by the end of 28, the rhythm is intensified by sixteenth notes that replace the second quarter, and C is replaced by a chromatic version of the same scale degree, the dissonant C♯. In both first and second endings (32), the left hand fills up its octave with motion, the first ending with eighth notes that lead back to the repeat, the second ending with two quarter notes that have more finality.

In the theme, the two four-measure units making up the second phrase are identical except for the grace notes and NTs in 15 and the PT in 16 . But in the first variation, Mozart treats those four-measure groups differently. While 34–37 are in the manner of the opening of this variation, 38–41 use the technique of polyphonic melody again. The third phrase is identical with the first. Thus, although Mozart uses two techniques of melodic embellishment—simple figuration and polyphonic melody—in one variation, both are heard in all three phrases. Their variety does not weaken the unity of the variation.

VARIATION 2 As in many Baroque variation sets, the variations may come in pairs. Variation 2 is the partner of variation 1, the sixteenth-note motion now in the left hand and the quarter notes now in the right. The top line has the theme, much in the manner of a *cantus firmus*. In the course of this variation, inner-voice implications are made more explicit, and we have something close to a four-part texture.

The left-hand figuration takes its cue from the octave skip of the theme and the NTs of variation 1. When the figure is condensed to four notes, the skip remains, occurring twice as often and helping to drive the music toward its goal in 57 . To stabilize after all this activity, the lowest available C is sounded.

The neighbor chord of 52 , now IV instead of IV$_4^6$, creates the possibility of a SUS, which Mozart takes advantage of and uses to begin a chain that will be heard again. In consequence, the texture grows more dense and more dissonant. At the same time, the chromatic NTs add their own interest and dissonance.

Four parts are heard rather explicitly, with the suggestion of five in the second phrase. The SUSs are heard in the alto; tenor and soprano are also quite dissonant. The pair of four-measure units are almost identical. The third phrase starts like the first, but the piece has picked up too much momentum for a literal repeat. The melodic descent is enriched with chromatic PTs, and the bass adds chromatic leading tones of its own. Between the SUSs and the N̂Ts, every strong beat from the

second half of 67 into 70 is dissonant. Eleven of the twelve notes of the chromatic scale are in the last five measures of the phrase.

VARIATION 3 A new triplet figuration elaborates the structural notes of the melody in the right hand. The initial melodic interval of a 5th is expanded into an octave and a 5th, and the G has a chordal skip, adding up to a two-octave arpeggio that quickly opens up the musical space. Starting with 77 , inner-voice notes begin to appear an octave higher, the inversion again converting 3rds into 6ths. These, in turn, are elaborated with SUSs, which are the inversion of those in the previous variation. We see, in a detail like this, how Mozart used his training in Baroque techniques to make much of a small amount of material.

The melody is supported by a left-hand part that uses the pitches of the original setting, but spreads them out in a more sonorous way. Inversion continues in the second phrase, whose two parts almost match, but not quite. Again, C is replaced with C♯, in 86 , and the dominant prolongation picks up an applied-leading-tone chord (VII⁷ of V) in 88 , thus bringing that prolonging motion to a focal point where it can release its energy on the tonic more emphatically to start the last phrase. The third phrase is a carbon copy of the first.

VARIATION 4 This variation is paired with the third. The triplet figuration is now in the left-hand part. This means that the low register is explored more actively than in the previous variations. Mozart's piano probably went no lower than F, and the bass line descends to that note twice. The right hand presents the melody as *cantus firmus*, with a few elaborations in the second phrase. Inner voices continue the SUSs of the previous variation, but the chromatic PTs are taken off duty.

VARIATION 5 The variations that precede and follow this one have a rather full sound, with much activity in the lower range and chords in the upper. By contrast, variation 5 has a thin texture and keeps to the middle register. It is the quietest of the variations. Both hands take up a short-long figure, whose short (eighth note) is divided into two sixteenth notes in the right hand for the second phrase and in both hands for the third. The second phrase's melodic descent from 5 to 2 is almost completely filled in with chromatic PTs. With but a few notes, Mozart keeps the SUSs in the first phrase in a syncopated rhythm.

VARIATION 6 The most interesting features of this variation are the use of space and register. The C in the bass has always had the same location in the fourth measure as in the first. Now they are an octave apart, and the octave is filled with sixteenth-note activity. Within the first phrase, the left hand moves through more than two octaves. The second phrase begins with the sixteenth notes still in the middle register, but now they are the highest voice. This leaves them free to rise, and by 161 they are more than two octaves above their starting point. Their rise is in contrary motion to the melody, which starts from the same G as the figuration, then descends. The drop of two octaves in the sixteenth-note figuration signals the end of the second phrase and the beginning of the third, which repeats the first. Looking back, we see that the right-hand part was much like that of variation 4, the chords now separated by rests.

VARIATION 7 As if keeping up the previous variation's momentum, the right hand fills more than two octaves with its initial sixteenth-note rush. Then the inversion-plus-SUS technique reappears. There are no PTs to fill in the skips, and the polyphonic line is quite apparent. The bass supports with octaves. The space-filling VI in 175 gains more emphasis by having its dominant precede it; the sequence of which that tonicization is a detail sweeps to the cadence. The melodic elaboration in the second phrase fills, again, two octaves, and the same four-measure unit is heard twice. The third phrase is the same as the first.

VARIATION 8 This variation has a distinctive character. What sets it apart from the others? The change of mode, which Mozart officially announces by the word "Minore," creates an immediate impression of change. But so does the new texture. The figuration of the preceding variations is replaced by imitation. The subject of the imitation is a variant of the theme, the opening skip of a 5th being filled in with PTs. The tune appears as a *cantus firmus* in the top line from beginning to end while imitation opens up one register after another. The SUSs continue to add their tension and color, sounding just a bit different with the change of mode.

The second phrase seems more like a single unit than ever, with imitation carrying across what had been a light punctuation mark in previous variations. The dominant prolongation underpins the imitative entrances, and inner voices add contrary motion. Eighth notes return to the melody in time

for a smooth transition to the third phrase. This is like the first, with the addition of the chromatic PT.

VARIATION 9 Again, variations come in pairs. This time the pairing is on the basis of contrast rather than similarity. The cheerful "Maggiore" dispels the serious atmosphere of the "Minore." But once Mozart has started to work with a technique, in this case imitation, he does not let it drop easily. The imitations cover the full range of available musical space, not overlooking the final notes of the first and third phrases. The third and fourth entrances remind us of nothing so much as tonal answers. At the end of the second phrase, in 233, the melody has climbed up into the "wrong" octave. How to get down? By inversion, which, in turn, combines with the tonal answer to bring forth a new shape for the imitation of the motive. We hear the descending 4th twice, then a descending 5th, and finally the rising 4th that ended the first phrase.

VARIATION 10 The new accompaniment figure that occupies the middle register is based on arpeggiation. The melody sails above it for four measures. Then the top line is worked into the figuration as the left hand becomes busy with its octaves. II^6, which had led to the dominant in the cadence, gives way to the more dynamic VII^{7b} of V.

In the second phrase the chromatic descent of the melody is repeated by the bass, again surrounding the accompaniment with melody. The third phrase repeats the first. In all the phrases, the use of E♭ and A♭ reminds us not only of the minor mode, but also of how close major and minor can be. The contrast of texture between this variation and the preceding ones makes a strong impression on the ear. Three registers seem to be in play at the same time.

The last two variations are a pair. Again, the grouping is on the basis of contrast, this time in tempo. As he often does, Mozart precedes a lively concluding variation with one that is much slower and quieter.

VARIATION 11 The opening melodic 5th is elaborated into a triad. The resulting melody is presented imitatively, woven into the tonic prolongation. But in the second half of the first phrase, starting in 270, the texture changes. Still another form of the inversion plus SUS takes over the right-hand part, supported by the left with chords. But not quite the same chords. The VI that had filled the space between I and II^6 has been replaced with I^6, extending the sway of the tonic.

The texture is different again in the second phrase. The left hand's bass and repeated chords accompany a continuation of the florid version of the tune, suggesting the character of a Rococo aria. Before descending, the initial **G** of the melody moves to the next chord member, **C**, by means of PTs, and curves back to start the downward move. Perhaps there is enough activity for us to think of four measures as a phrase, or perhaps we should keep eight measures as the unit. The dominant is elaborated with VII^6 of V, held under a *fermata*. The last phrase is the same as the first, after the few notes that lead into it. There is something a bit operatic about this variation, and the pauses are partly responsible.

VARIATION 12 Virtuosity comes to the fore in the last variation. Sixteenth notes fill every measure and almost every beat. Using triple meter for the only time, Mozart invents still other ways to elaborate the basic notes of melody and bass line, with the left hand busy shooting off keyboard pyrotechnics. Both hands join in for the second phrase, which uses inversion in its latter half to vary the series of NTs. When the first phrase has been repeated in the third, the second ending carries the piece on to a short coda. This begins by echoing the previous phrase ending. Then it prolongs I harmonically, the tried and true way of bringing a Classical work to a convincing conclusion. The arpeggiation plus NT of the right hand stretches the last chord over four measures and through two octaves. Freed from the phrase structure of the theme, Mozart slyly condenses two four-measure phrases into seven measures, with 3̲2̲1̲ doing double duty as the end of one four-measure unit and the beginning of another.

SUMMARY The variation form affords us an opportunity to see how a resourceful composer can get a great deal out of very little. Each variation is based on the tonal structure of the tune and its setting as the theme. Contrapuntal chords are added and omitted from one variation to another, but the basic framework is never altered. Elaborative techniques used include virtually everything Mozart knew about counterpoint.

Each variation has its own characteristic rhythmic figuration and texture. These are kept fairly constant within the variation, but not as constant as in a Baroque work. Dynamic levels are also fairly consistent within a variation, but there are exceptions. If those exceptions are authentic, they imply that the piece was written for piano rather than harpsichord.

Variations often come in pairs. The second variation of the pair often reverses the roles of the two hands, a continuation of Baroque practice. But pairing is also based on contrast of mode or tempo.

More than in most forms, theme and variations allows us to look over the composer's shoulder and see him organizing his ideas into a musical structure. We see how he starts with rather straightforward material and builds it up a step at a time. There is some kind of analogy between this progressive elaboration of musical material and the concept of structure and prolongation. For this reason, the study of theme and variations can be particularly rewarding.

It remains to be added that most of the elaboration seen in the Mozart piece was melodic. Although there was some development of new contrapuntal chords, the main interest of the piece lies in the various figurations spun out of the tune and their deployment in musical space. These generalizations apply to most of Mozart's variation sets. Other composers, starting with Beethoven, have taken the harmonic structure of the theme as an important basis for the variations.

For further study

One of the most remarkable sets of variations in existence is that by Beethoven, Op. 120, on a theme by the Viennese publisher Diabelli. The theme and five of the variations comprise $\boxed{146}$. Although the theme may seem rather simple, it is full of developmental possibilities: the prolongations of I and V gave Beethoven scope for expanding those chords in a variety of ways; the applied dominants also lend themselves to expansion in time and space; the offbeat accents, so like Beethoven's own; and the two divisions of the theme, balanced but not identical. A detailed study of any or all of the variations will richly reward any student of music. Since the variations are based as much on the tonal structure as on the melody (unlike Mozart's set, $\boxed{145}$), a reduction of the theme in four parts is given below. The many ways in which this framework is "realized" are the center of interest in the piece. One way to start the study is to see how the opening I–V is set forth in the theme, then compare it with the same prolonged chords in each variation.

C: I   V;   IV⁶   V/I   II⁶   V   I/V
                  G   C

V⁷   I   IV⁶   V⁶   I   II⁶   V⁷   I

Variations flourished in the Classical period, and the Romantic composers who were most successful with the form were those who retained aspects of the Classical style within the nineteenth century. Brahms modeled his variation sets after those of Beethoven, and his *Variations on a Theme by Haydn* constitutes one of the high points in the form. Twentieth-century composers who continued the tonal tradition added to the variation literature. Aaron Copland's *Piano Variations*, the second movement of Béla Bartók's *Violin Concerto*, and the second movement of the Stravinsky *Octet* are notable examples. But atonal music found the variation form useful as well. Schoenberg and Webern both wrote variations for orchestra, as did Elliott Carter. See also 186.

☞ Worksheet 45

86

Rounded Binary Form

BACKGROUND By the middle of the eighteenth century the forms that had served so well in the Baroque period were unable to contain the musical impulses that were in evidence everywhere. A new middle-class audience demanded a straightforward, appealing type of music, which was found above all in Italian opera. Instead of melody built on continuous figuration, composers began to invent tunes with clear-cut motives, with regular patterns in which phrase and period were articulated for all to hear. Hand in hand with the salient motive went the desire to do something interesting with it. The division of a dancelike piece into two equal sections did not satisfy the urge to develop ideas. Yet composers were apparently reluctant to do away with the time-honored binary form. Instead of abandoning it, they expanded it, giving more weight to the elaborative section after the double bar and rounding it off with a repetition of the opening material. The minuets of Mozart that were composed in the 1760s are still strictly binary; those written a few years later are

rounded off with at least a mention of the opening melody; and before long, the section after the double bar is a good deal longer than the first part of the piece. Although the melodic shape of the piece is now threefold—statement, elaboration, and restatement—the tonal movement is still in two parts, and the form is known as *rounded binary*. This proved to be a highly useful format for minuets and scherzos and later, in the nineteenth century, for short piano pieces.

TONAL MOVEMENT AND FORM The added emphasis on the latter part of the form comes not only from the return of the opening melody, but also from the reaffirmation of the main key. Both can be and are dramatized in Classical pieces. Thus the underpinning of the rounded binary form is often a tonal movement from I to V or, in minor, possibly I to III. The initial move away from the tonic may start in the first section or at the beginning of the second section. In either case, such a modulation creates a desire for the return of the tonic, which is embodied in the return of the opening musical material and creates a satisfying sense of closing the circuit.

A clear-cut use of the form is seen in Gluck's noble "Pantomime," 131. The opening eight-measure period concludes in the tonic, and the second section begins anew in the same area. But in 10, I/IV. The V of G is then prolonged for five measures. Observe that in order to make us feel that C is tonic Gluck prolongs not C, but its dominant, so that we wait expectantly for C to arrive. This it does in a simple cadence. The reinstatement of B♭ in 20 smoothly prepares the reprise of the initial idea, which, of course, reaffirms F and reminds us that although C was tonic for a few measures, C is still V of F major.

MINUET The courtly dance known as the *minuet* originated in France, probably in the seventeenth century. In the Baroque suite it is optional, in binary form, and rather easygoing in character. Haydn and his contemporaries used it as the third movement in the four-movement cycle of string quartet and symphony. As compared with the Baroque minuet, the Classical version is faster, more dramatic and vivacious, and the form has expanded into the rounded binary. Originally the minuet was followed by a second minuet performed by three instruments, after which the first minuet was played again but without its internal repeats. Although the limitation to three instruments soon disappeared, the second, smaller minuet was still called a *trio*.

The young Mozart wrote the minuet 134 without a trio. It is a small-scale piece, but there is a good deal to be learned from it. The opening eight-measure phrase begins with simple imitation, setting up a harmonic prolongation of I. With the reach up to the highest register in 5, VI/II, the favorite pivot chord in modulations to the dominant in the major mode. Then A is avoided in the bass until the cadence (8). The second phrase is a dominant prolongation with mode mixture and a varied texture, discussed on page 52. The third phrase (16 , third beat) starts again from the beginning and thus poses the typical compositional problem of a rounded binary piece whose first section modulates. This time the music need not modulate, but rather must reaffirm the tonic. Mozart goes back to the first four measures of the phrase, which are firmly in I, then steers the tonal movement so as to retain the contour and rhythm of the first phrase while remaining in the tonic.

Far more complex is the minuet from Mozart's *String Quartet in D Minor*, 135. The opening ten-measure phrase is discussed on page 52. It does not modulate, which means that it can be—and is —used literally in the reprise. The second section of the piece is in two subdivisions. The first is twelve measures long, moving immediately to the dominant and prolonging its dominant. In this phrase, three four-measure units are woven closely together from the opening motive. Just as the V⁷ is about to resolve to I (of A) in 22 , I turns into V⁷ of IV, leading directly into the second part of the section. Here all parts toss the motivic idea back and forth. The bass line moves in 5ths, shared by viola and cello, while the top line and alto work their way down in parallel tritones (see *Gradus* I, page 79), moving chromatically. The motion is slowed in 27 by the arrival at VI, which prepares the dominant. The repetition of the opening is literal, which is rather unusual for Mozart.

The trio shows the Classical principle of contrast in an extreme way. The intense minuet, darkly colored by chromaticism, is followed by music so cheerful that the listener may be surprised even after repeated hearings. The trio is as diatonic as can be; the phrases are all eight measures long; the texture is simply melody and accompaniment; the chord vocabulary is limited to I and V⁷ and very little more. The repetition of the minuet is, again, a stark contrast.

SCHERZO In his later string quartets, Haydn sped up the minuet to the point where the pulse is actually one beat to the measure. Then the piece ceased to be a minuet, and Haydn called it *scherzo*. Beethoven gave the scherzo its most decisive formulation, using it not only in quartets, but also in symphonies and sonatas, where its rhythmic surprises and broad gestures fitted his large-scale concept of instrumental music. As music generally slowed down during the nineteenth century, the scherzo lost favor; but there are good examples by Mendelssohn, Berlioz, Chopin, Schumann, and Brahms, most of them taking as their model the Beethovenian prototype. Modern adaptations of the scherzo are found in the string quartets of Debussy, Ravel, Bartók, and Berg.

The short piece by the Czech composer Reicha, 137, shows one of the characteristic attributes of the scherzo: fast rhythmic activity over a slow rate of chord change. The reason the first phrase takes sixteen measures to unwind itself is the deliberate rate of chord change: four measures for I, four more for IV. Then, in two measures, II/IV, and a modulation to a cadence in III brings the music to an unexpected goal. As the cadence nears, the rate of chord change speeds up, helping the drive to the end of the phrase. The second section is in the orbit of E until 33 . Then II/VII, the diminished triad making a rare appearance as a pivot chord. That triad is arpeggiated down to 39 , where we finally hear the D that will guide us back to G. It does that through a scale that is almost entirely chromatic, prolonging D and leading back to the restatement of the opening idea in 43 .

Again, the problem is to redirect the tonal course of the phrase and keep it centered on the tonic. 51 pretends to move toward E again, but soon E is put in its place as 6 of G. The tonal equilibrium has not been entirely restored, and a sixteen-measure period, in two symmetrical phrases, balances the tonal forces with tonic prolongation and clear motion to the dominant. Throughout the piece, the chromatic NT, often in 3rds, had had a motivic status, its rhythmic placement shifting about and giving the most emphasis in the last period.

The scherzo from Beethoven's *G-Major String Quartet*, 136 , shows the composer's typical preoccupation with motivic development. A four-note motive, sometimes condensed to three, commands the listener's attention in much of the piece. An overview of the work shows that the first, expository section is only eight measures long, while the rest, including development of the ideas, restatement, and a lengthy continuation and ending, comprise thirty-five measures.

The pithy opening section is a period composed of an antecedent phrase and a consequent phrase, anchored securely in I. The tonal movement in the second section begins with a tonicization of III, mode mixture making that a major sound. Some kind of a surprise is usually in store after the double bar, and the B-major triad certainly was not what was expected. Just as in 132 , what seems like a quick return to I proves to be a move through I to V⁷ of IV. Then IV serves its customary purpose of being a stepping stone on the way to V, and the eight-measure period ends on the dominant in 16 . Another eight-measure period would end the piece neatly. But we suspect that something different is brewing by 21 . The repetition of the opening phrase has been expanded spatially, all instruments becoming involved with the main motive in the antecedent phrase. The consequent phrase is altered even more: it is opened up; the texture changes to a unison insistence on the motive; the duration is extended to six measures; and the motion is redirected to IV. The remainder of the piece is a forceful ending, using new material. The four-measure phrase that begins with the upbeat to 27 ends on the first sound in 30 . But the rest of 30 has the air of a new phrase, four measures long and repeated with the instruments exchanging roles. This phrase ends on the downbeat of 34 and is repeated; expanded spatially. The final phrase begins in 38 and is six measures long. It uses imitation based on the main motive. The first note is anticipated, creating a SUS, over a harmonic prolongation. In the bass, the scurrying cello fills 1–5–1 with PTs. In the last two measures of the phrase, the first violin sweeps through three octaves, a strong spatial gesture that combines with the concluding tonic for finality.

The trio is simpler, as we might expect, but no less concerned with motivic development. The proportions of the sections are quite similar to those of the scherzo. One reason that C major sounds so familiar is that IV played such an important role in the G-major scherzo. Another reason is that the tonic that ended the scherzo sounds, in retrospect, like the dominant of C major.

The first phrase is eight measures long, punctuated in the middle more by the rest than anything else. The contrary motion of the outer voices reminds us of the theme of the *C-Minor Variations*, 142A . When G is reached after the chromatic descent from C, it is stabilized with its own dominant to make a short cadence in V. This concludes the first, brief section of the trio. Prolongation of V underpins the next part, which consists of two four-measure phrases and a three-measure extension. Interest centers upon the first-violin part, which moves from one register to another with great fluency. A triplet figure emerges in 54 and becomes part of the rhythmic vocabulary of the rest of the trio. The reprise, starting with the upbeat to 63 , is an object lesson in heightened repetition. The first violin plays the melody an octave higher than at first. This leaves space for the lower instruments to be active. The second violin and cello take turns with the triplet figure in a simple kind of imitation. Against this, the eighth notes of the viola pursue their independent course. To bring the trio to a close, Beethoven draws the motivic elements closer together over a harmonic prolongation which is sharpened by V⁶ of V. The last phrase is pushed off by the cello's arpeggiated ascent in 70 , and at the end, the first violin sweeps through three octaves to the highest note in the movement, the very opposite of the gesture that ended the scherzo. One force that gives the trio its shape is the expansion in space from the first C-major sound, in 44 , within one octave, to the last C-major sound, spread over five octaves.

At the second ending the composer finds himself in the wrong key. Quite possibly the scherzo could have resumed without any further ado, but Beethoven chose to make a short transition back. Still in C major, the cello moves from 1 to 2, not as a step but as a 7th, and the viola joins in parallel 10ths. It also sustains the C, whose meaning changes from tonic to subdominant as the modulation back to G unfolds. Over the slow-moving lower instruments the violins anticipate the scherzo motive, telling us clearly what the transition is all about. At the end of the transition, G is not entirely stabilized; that is left to the repetition of the scherzo.

PIANO PIECE Although Clementi is remembered today as the composer of easy sonatinas, he was one of the important musicians of his day. He played a decisive role in the development of piano composition, and his sonatas show the early Romantic style that so impressed the young Beethoven. $\boxed{138}$ projects an almost melodramatic gloom. Its use of the piano is quite idiomatic. It is also an early instance of rounded binary as a short piano piece. The customary repeats are not found in this piece.

However, the first phrase is repeated, but varied —a good example of the Romantic attribute of extending a form while keeping its general outlines. The opening six-measure phrase is built on a two-measure motive; the tonal movement is from I to V. The progression of the bass ties the phrase together as it moves stepwise, with octave shift, from the beginning to the cadence. A short linking motive, an upbeat of three eighth notes, leads from the end of $\underline{6}$ to the varied repetition; the motive will be heard again. Indeed, it is soon woven into the repetition of the phrase in inner voices. The first section ends in $\underline{12}$. When that motive appears at the end of the phrase, it sets off a series of imitations which vary the texture drastically. In the second part, an eight-measure phrase is centered around IV, then V, prolonged in $\underline{17}$–$\underline{19}$. Perhaps the resolution to I in $\underline{20}$ takes away some of the impetus toward the reprise. In $\underline{21}$, a sudden crescendo brings the restatement of the first idea. But it begins with another texture and, of course, does not move to V. It moves chromatically through three diminished-7th chords, arriving at the dominant in $\underline{24}$. But there has been too much activity for a simple cadence. Clementi prolongs the dominant with its neighbor chord, VII^7 of V, and devotes all of $\underline{25}$ to the dominant, after which the dissonances gradually resolve in $\underline{26}$. The upbeat motive which had dominated the design of the middle section and had then withdrawn in the reprise, makes a final appearance in the last measure, tying all motivic elements together.

Beethoven also omits the repeat in the first part

of $\boxed{132}$, but calls for it in the second part. This excerpt is a theme, to be followed by a set of variations. Rounded binary was frequently used for themes in the Classical period. Two four-measure phrases comprise the first section, leading from I to V. The next four-measure phrase leads to IV, balancing the emphasis on V. But IV and II do lead back to V, then the I that begins the restatement. Two four-measure phrases are welded together as the punctuation between them is overridden by the anticipated G. The four-measure phrase completes the tonal journey, and the piece could almost end with $\underline{16}$. But not quite. The main reason is that $\underline{16}$ ends in the wrong register. $\underline{17}$ promptly returns to the original register and ends the piece there. The last four-measure phrase combines registral emphasis, motive, applied dominants, and rhythm to make a convincing close.

The three piano pieces by Schumann, $\boxed{139A}$, $\boxed{139B}$, and $\boxed{140}$, are in rounded binary form. Motivic development is almost obsessive in all three. $\boxed{139A}$ is a short interlude in a long set of pieces, which may explain why it begins in F minor and ends in A♭ major. The melodic structure of the first phrase is sketched on page 53. The second phrase is a study in contrary motion between the outer voices, leading to the dominant that sets up the tonic. This tiny, concentrated piece shows the most intimate aspect of Romanticism.

The contrapuntal background of the first section of $\boxed{139B}$ is shown on page 63. Lines are Schumann's preoccupation, and he weaves them into a passionate utterance that is remarkably personal. To lighten the tension, the short section following the double bar moves to the major, to III. But that is tonicized only by its dominant and a neighboring II². III never appears as tonic in this restless piece. Soon III's leading tone turns off into a downward motion, goes through D♭ and C to the leading tone of C, and the reprise begins. The only harmonic progressions in the piece come at the end of the two sections. All other chords are linear.

$\boxed{140}$ was discussed on page 45. The treatment of the motive is not as compulsive as in the previous two pieces, since the second part has a new formulation of the basic idea. One detail, relating to the piece as a whole, remains to be discovered. The first three notes of the melody, E–F–E, contain within themselves the seed of the NT motion that generates the chords heard over the pedal in the first eight-measure phrase. The same motion begins the melody of the second section, in a varied rhythm. The F is prolonged with a triad. Now we hear E–F–E not as 5–6–5 as we did at the beginning, but in terms of the tonicized III, 3–4–3.

87

Comprehensive Analysis of the Minuet from Haydn's *London Symphony*, [133]

BACKGROUND The last set of symphonies written by Haydn, twelve in number, was composed for a series of concerts in London in 1790–95. These are the works that made Haydn's reputation as the greatest composer alive (the British press called him "the Shakespeare of music"). The last of the twelve, No. 104, is called the *London Symphony*. The minuet, [133], is the third movement.

The movement as a whole is in three sections—hence *ternary* in form. Each section, in turn, is an rounded binary form. The musical line is spacious and clear, the rhythms strong and more suggestive of folk dance than of the court.

Outline of [133]

section	measure	description
minuet, first part	1–8	I–V⁷–I, tutti, *f*
	9–16	the same music, light scoring, *pp*
minuet, second part	17–20	four-measure phrase, tonicizing VI
	21–26	six-measure phrase, VI/II in a move to V;, strong tonicization, but not a modulation
	27–34	eight-measure phrase, prolongation of V⁷ with mode mixture, starts *p* and builds to 35–46
	35–46	rounds off the binary with a repetition of the opening in the form of an eight-measure phrase and a four-measure extension which includes two measures of silence
	47–52	concluding six-measure phrase, two measures of V⁷, four measures of harmonic prolongation
trio, first part	53–64	two measures of preparatory movement through D minor to B♭ major, then a ten-measure phrase beginning with a harmonic prolongation, then modulating to a cadence in V
trio, second part	65–72	continuation, using the two trio motives simultaneously in an eight-measure phrase which moves to a tonicization of II (C minor)
	73–80	another eight-measure phrase, which continues the tonicization of II, then goes to V–I; the last two measures of this phrase are the two preparatory measures that began the trio
	81–88	the initial ten-measure phrase, now shortened to eight, the last of which is silence
	89–94	a concluding six-measure phrase (but it ends in B♭, and the minuet is in D—what to do?)
transition	95–104	a ten-measure phrase, using only the first trio motive, modulating back to D, aiming at D's dominant; in the modulation, I/VI, the motion heightened by the reiterated augmented 6th

The sketch (right) shows the tonal structure in terms of bass and soprano. Before examining it in detail, we should remember what such a reduction can tell us about activity and stability, the interplay of which is one of the forces that shape any tonal piece. Every motion is either a prolonging motion, stabilizing one basic sound, or a movement from one point to another. Many phrases, of course, begin with a prolonging motion and are then directed to another point, or begin in motion and arrive at a stable point. Keeping these general considerations in mind will clarify the underlying drives of this piece.

The first phrase is a clear-cut example of the single-idea phrase. It prolongs and stabilizes the tonic for four measures, then moves through contrapuntal chords to V⁷–I. The offbeat accents highlight the neighbor chords. The melody has the

Sketch of the minuet of 133

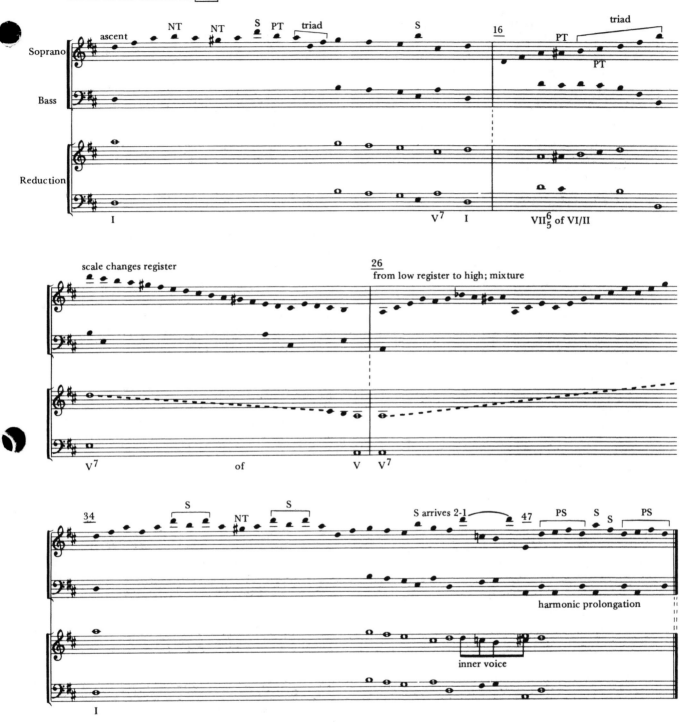

familiar quick ascent; 5 is prolonged over the tonic and the phrase ends with the descent from 5 to 1.

Since the first phrase is completely in I, motion away from the tonic begins at the start of the second section. As we observed in both the Beethoven and the Reicha scherzos, the rate of chord change is slow, the surface movement fast. Haydn takes four measures to arrive at VI and stabilize it. The VI then continues into the six-measure phrase in

which the motion to V; takes place. The dominant prolongation has several interesting features: the movement from low register to high, mode mixture, the overlapping with the end of the previous phrase in the horns, and the gradual addition of the instruments in the large crescendo.

The full-bodied restatement of the melody is elaborated with figuration invented during the crescendo, but the overall effect is much the same as

91

the opening, and the structural notes, of course, are identical. However, 41–42 do not exactly match 7–8 , and we realize that Haydn is avoiding the melodic 3–2–1 with its finality. The end of the eight-measure phrase is opened up, and the four-measure extension leaves us in the air as I becomes V_5^6 of IV. An upbeat remains poised in the air for two measures of silence—one of Haydn's favorite devices. Then the dominant trills its way in, and a strong harmonic prolongation, with the melody restored to its original register, ends the section. The basic tonal movement, stressing tonic and dominant with a move to the subdominant at the end for balance, could hardly be simpler; the detailed working out could hardly be finer.

Seizing upon the single note, D, which we just heard as tonic, Haydn turns it into the 3 of B♭ major, whose link to D major is through D minor. Indeed, the opening of the trio sounds for a moment as if it were in D minor, and not until 55 are we clearly in B♭ major. 53–54 are introductory, with a two-note motive that will be used again. The phrase that begins in 55 has a momentum that counteracts the hesitation of the trio's opening, and the phrase runs on for ten measures, modulating to a cadence in V. The coloration of the trio suddenly darkens as II is prolonged for the next eleven measures. V–I is followed, as usual, by V–I (75–76).

II

Then a larger gesture, through the dominant of V, leads to the reprise. The tonic comes in the form of the introductory measures, and the opening material starts to repeat on the upbeat to 79 . The phrase cannot modulate to V this time, of course. It heads for the cadence in the tonic, but only seems to get as far as IV. The last two measures of the phrase are silent, paralleling the silence at the same point in the minuet. The final movement is left up in the air. Then the unexpected F♯ starts the final six-measure phrase. It picks up where the previous phrase left off, ending with the harmonic cadence itself.

After the repeat, Haydn calmly moves from the B♭ triad to an A-major triad, which means that the bass does not have far to go. The top line moves chromatically from F to A, and the two lines thus generate an augmented triad as passing chord, IV⁶ (in D minor), and the augmented 6th in an unusual example of oblique motion. The flute picks up an inner voice and reflects it an octave higher, adding to the interest of the texture.

MOTIVIC STRUCTURE The main rhythmic motive of the minuet consists of the first four notes

of the melody. The first two eighth notes are replaced by a quarter note at times, and the fourth note is omitted occasionally. The rhythmic impulse starts with an upbeat throughout the piece, and the unit might well be thought of as "three-one-two" rather than "one-two-three." The upbeat is accented quite often. In the phrase that starts in 20 a shortening of the motive makes it into a two-beat group, two eighths and a quarter, which crosses the three-beat meter and creates what might be called a rhythmic dissonance—that is, disagreement. Instead of two threes, we hear three twos, first in the violas, then in cellos and basses, all doubled by bassoon.

In the dominant prolongation that starts in 26 , the motive takes new forms. As the crescendo builds, the violins cannot wait for the two quarter notes of the motive, and these are sped up into four eighth notes. Once the eighth notes have started, they build a momentum of their own, and the motive appears in the restatement with much of that figuration. The final measures reiterate the motive insistently, centering it on the tonic.

Rhythmic motive in the minuet of 133

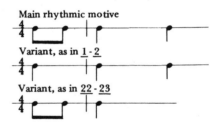

Main rhythmic motive

Variant, as in 1 - 2

Variant, as in 22 - 23

Two motives are used in the trio. The first is heard in the introductory measures, based on the skip of a 3rd; the second fills that 3rd with a PT and goes on into a chain of eighth notes that seem to be as much figuration as motive. In the second part both ideas are combined to give a somewhat linear texture. The reprise presents them as they were in the trio's first phrase. The transition uses only the first trio motive, stretching the 3rd to a 5th, while the inner voice in second violin and second oboe remind us of the 3rd again.

ORCHESTRATION Scored for the full Classical orchestra, the piece has a robust sound. Only the clarinets are not used to particular advantage. Haydn had little experience with them, and included them in his orchestra for the first time in the last six of the *London Symphonies*. There is no clarinet part in the trio.

The strings are by far the most important group here. They play the complete chord content in almost every measure, and the first violins have the melody much of the time. The second violins play in 3rds (or 10ths) or octaves with the first violins for most of the minuet, and join the lower strings in the trio. At the outset, the violas double the first violins at the octave, thus coming between first and second violins to enrich the sonority; this is no S.A.T.B. format transferred to strings. Later the violas help where they are needed, with inner voices (17), with the bass line (22), with doubling the cellos and basses (25). The bass line is played by the cellos and basses in octaves.

For the most part, the winds reinforce and color the strings. Flutes and oboes double violins and violas. Clarinets, horns, and trumpets form a unit that provides the solid sound in the middle register—the orchestral tone. Bassoons not only double the bass line, but, in the trio, also double the melody.

Horns, trumpets, and timpani have background roles. They add to the body of the sound and punctuate the rhythm. The timpani are used to particular advantage in the dominant prolongation, where their roll plays a striking part in the crescendo. Brass and timpani are silent in the trio.

Several details of orchestration merit special attention. The repetition of the first phrase is smoothed out considerably by the legato articulation of the winds. At the end of 14 , the flute flies up an octave. Both it and the oboe play inner-voice parts an octave higher in the cadence, lightening the color.

26 ends a phrase, but in the same measure the horns begin their sustained A. This links the end of one phrase to the beginning of the next, keeping the activity going at the lowest point of tension in the piece.

As is customary, the scoring of the trio is much lighter than that of the minuet. The melody of the first phrase is played by the first violins, doubled first by an oboe, then by a bassoon. The accompaniment consists of simple pizzicato chords played by the other strings. The writing is linear, and the parts are all clearly heard. The contrast with the full sonorities of the minuet is striking. For example, hear how the single flute that enters at 66 stands out against the lower part. The texture grows somewhat denser at the prolongation of II as the strings play arco and the cellos and basses hold the dominant of II. But as V approaches, the texture lightens again, and the reprise of the melody is much like the first statement—not exactly, however. This time the bassoons join the accompaniment, and the flute adds a descending line. In the cadence, an oboe doubles the upper octave of the violins. The transition sees the oboe playing an important role, with both melody and an inner voice.

SYNTHESIS The fascinating way in which these elements interact is not always easy to describe, but we can see that the composer does not rely on any one of them to make his points. Citing specific instances of elements functioning together may be of value. The echoed repeat of the first phrase sounds quieter than the initial statement because only one flute and one oboe are heard in the repeated phrase. Clarinets, bassoons, horns, trumpets, and timpani are omitted; the articulation of the winds is legato; the dynamic marking is *pp* and the accents are left out. Another crucial point: the crescendo on the dominant pedal is effectuated not only by increasing the volume, but also by adding instruments in rising registers and by increasing the activity from quarter notes to eighth notes. A new tone color brings in the surprising new key of the trio with a new texture. The large-scale contrast between minuet and trio depends on change of key, thinner texture, a continuous flow of legato eighth notes against articulated quarter notes or groups of two eighths, a lower dynamic level, and, for the only time in the piece, a tonicization of II in the trio with a sound all its own. The composer uses every available resource to let listeners know where he is in the piece and where he is going.

☞ Worksheet 46

☞ Worksheet 47

88

Ternary Form

TERNARY AND ROUNDED BINARY Statement, digression, and restatement constitute a format that is at least as old as plainchant. We have seen in any number of pieces that the second section provides contrast, while the repetition of the first brings a satisfying sense of unification. But contrast can mean more than one thing. What is the nature of the middle section?

In a rounded binary piece, as in a binary piece, there is but one main musical idea. The second section is a continuation of that idea, with some contrast. But a piece may have two main ideas of a different character and three sections. Then we describe it as being ternary in form. The second section means contrast. It introduces new material and not just a new approach to old material. The familiar cliché ABA form may be applied to both rounded binary and to ternary. Hence, its usefulness is rather limited.

Ternary is the form of *da capo* arias, of many Romantic piano pieces through Debussy, of slow movements in Classical and Romantic instrumental music, and of many works that use the language of extended tonality. The literalness of the repetitions diminishes as composers begin to find such repetition less interesting, and in posttonal music, ternary pieces are few indeed.

The distinction between rounded binary and ternary is exemplified in 133, 135, and 136. Each movement, as a whole, is in ternary form. The trio has different musical ideas from the minuet or scherzo, different textures, different dynamics, and a different mode or key. Each minuet or scherzo or trio in itself is in rounded binary form. The two divisions of those pieces do not contain different ideas, but rather continue the working out of the first section's ideas.

We have previously seen a *da capo* aria by Handel, 93. Contrast between sections was present, but was not very striking. The form persisted through the eighteenth century, often with little change of material in the middle section.

The Mozart aria 158 shows the kinds of contrasts that articulate the form on a small scale. The first section is in G major; the second starts from G minor, then tonicizes B♭ major and B minor before arriving at G's dominant. Long phrases in the voice, with chordal instrumental support, characterize the first section; short ideas are tossed back and forth between voice and orchestra in the second section. Texture and dynamics are fairly homogeneous in the first part, more varied in the next. The level of dissonance is perceptibly higher in the middle section. The rate of chord change is fairly constant throughout the aria. Although none of these by itself represents a startling contrast, probably because the words demand no strong differentiation, together they add up to a clear division between the middle section and the sections that precede and follow.

Not all pieces are as unequivocal in form. Haydn's 147A raises an interesting question to which there can be no certain answer. The middle section differs from the first in both texture and mode. Yet the initial motive continues and dominates the situation as completely as it did in the first section. The feeling that the music is continuing on with the same material is quite strong. Both contrast and continuity are present, and it is difficult to determine which is the stronger.

89

Comprehensive Analysis of Chopin's
E-Major Etude, [148]

BACKGROUND Where the Classical composers had made long pieces out of short ideas, Romantic composers often made short pieces out of long ideas. When composers such as Chopin and Schumann wrote longer pieces, their method was usually to write in a sectional form, such as ternary, in which each section might be fairly short and devoted to one idea. What kind of melodic material did Chopin invent? His melodies are inspired by the human voice—he makes the piano "sing." Such melodies as the one we hear at the beginning of [148] are not material for development; they are complete in themselves. This melody can be stated, repeated, perhaps varied, but it is lyric and needs no working out.

One stylistic source of Chopin's lyricism is in Italian opera. Even a brief comparison of the well-known melody of *Casta Diva,* an aria from Bellini's *Norma* (first performed in 1831), with the melody of Chopin's youthful *Nocturne* Op. 9 No. 2 shows a number of similarities. If Chopin's melody follows the Romantic imperative to "make the piano sing," there is good reason.

Comparison between Bellini *Casta Diva* and Chopin *Nocturne*

Thus the short piano piece, one of the prime vehicles of musical expression in the hands of Chopin, Schumann, Mendelssohn, Brahms, and Liszt, is based on one or more ideas, each of which is the material for a section. In many cases the result is much like the songs of those same composers, and it is significant that Mendelssohn's short piano pieces were called "songs without words."

Each of Chopin's *études* was designed to offer practice in one or more technical problems. The first section of [148] has the right hand doing two things at once—certain fingers "singing" the melody, others playing the inner voices more quietly. The second section affords much practice in playing 6ths and 7ths in both hands. Dynamics and tempo fluctuate a great deal in this music and must be precisely controlled. The musical challenge, however, is even greater than the technical one, for the piece transcends its original purpose as an exercise and is a beautiful work of art.

Overall outline of [148]

first section	second section	third section
1–21	21–61	62–77
	main part, 21–54	
	retransition, 54–61	

The long, arching melody rises very gradually from the tonic. It makes much of the first three notes of the scale so that when it does get beyond them, the notes thus reached are fresh. But at its high point in <u>17</u> it finds those same three notes again, an octave higher. The descent is much quicker than the rise, and at its end we find a sense of completion in 3–2–1 in their original register.

The melodic shape goes hand in hand with the tonal structure. The first four-measure phrase is supported by I–V; the second by I–IV–V; the third is similar to the first. All three are open-ended and linked to each other, creating the long line characteristic of the piece. The three four-measure phrases are answered not by another of the same length, but by an extended phrase eight and one-half measures long. Applied dominants help the melody climb to its peak, and a French 6th, the most dissonant chord of this section, leads to the climactic <u>17</u>. I$^6_4$ is at the top of the crest, but it does not lead to V^7–I. It does set in motion a sequence in which the melody descends scalewise over a bass that moves down a 4th and up a step, until the tonic is reached. The motion is completed without any harmonic progression. I is extended for a measure and a half to add a bit more finality.

Behind the rapid figuration of the melody in the next section there are a few structural notes that circle around B. In contrast to the clear E major of the first section, the second moves back and forth between major and minor, with mixture most conspicuous in <u>30–31</u> and <u>34–35</u>. After that, the passages in diminished 7ths obliterate the mode and perhaps the tonic, too; only if the ear can retain the F♯, which is the dominant of B, is there any point of reference. At <u>42</u>, the B, now as dominant, emerges from the chromatic motion and is prolonged in a way that prepares the ear for the restatement in E. The dominant pedal makes generous use of the minor sound so that the E major sounds fresh by contrast.

From the outline below we can see that Chopin used every resource he had at his disposal to make the second section different from the first. Has the first section leaned on the downbeat? The second starts with an upbeat. Has the bass been heard clearly on every beat in the first section? The bass drops out on the upbeat to the second and moves quite differently, more lightly, throughout the middle section. Has the rate of chord change been rather deliberate in the first part? Then the second section changes chords much less regularly, increasing from two to a measure to eight to a measure. In general, all types of change occur more frequently in the middle section than in the first and third parts. We might well observe that middle sections of ternary pieces are likely to be more active in many ways than the surrounding, more stable parts.

The ending of the piece, the few measures added to the shortened restatement, deserve an additional comment. The last phrase is extended from its original eight measures to twelve. Leading the piece to its conclusion, Chopin thins the texture gradually; reduces the chromatic notes to one which, however, is exploited for all it is worth before it, too, is phased out; slows down the chords from two to the measure to one and finally one to every three measures; quiets the dynamic level; and slows the

Differentiation between sections

	first section	*second section*
1. focus of attention	the "singing" melody	pianistic activity in the form of figuration
2. tonality	E major	B major-minor, melting into uncertain key area, back to B as dominant
3. mode	major	considerable mixture
4. tempo	slow, steady	faster, fluctuating (implied)
5. dynamics	$p < ff > p$	several crescendos to the high point in <u>42</u>
6. interval tension	relatively consonant	increasingly dissonant, many diminished 7ths
7. piano usage	melody plus accompaniment	broken texture with 6ths and 7ths
8. section ending	closure on I	open-ended, with dominant prolongation leading to third section
9. texture	closely knit, full	more open, increasing space between hands
10. vocabulary	diatonic triads, V^7, French 6th	increasingly chromatic triads, diminished 7ths, half-diminished 7th minor
11. phrase shape	three four-measure phrases, one eight-and-one-half-measure phrase	continuous four-measure phrases
12. rate of chord change	regular, two chords to a measure	increasing to eight to a measure, decreasing to one every two measures

tempo—all of which conveys to the listener that the musical momentum is used up. The piece doesn't just stop, it comes to its logical end.

All in all, this *étude* is a study not only in piano techniques, but also in compositional techniques. The aesthetic content is conveyed in a form that is as lucid as such a thing can be.

For further study

Listen to these pieces in ternary form and describe the ways in which the composer differentiates the sections:

1. Haydn, *Symphony No. 101,* second movement (notice the coda);
2. Beethoven, *String Quartet* Op. 18 No. 2, second movement (what is the connection between the first and second parts?);
3. Chopin, *Two Nocturnes* Op. 48 (compare the treatment of the third section);
4. Brahms, *Intermezzo for Piano* Op. 118 No. 2 (what is the form of each section?);
5. Debussy, *Preludes, Book 2 No. 3: La Puerta del Vino;*

6. Hindemith, *Wind Quintet* Op. 24 No. 2, third movement (what is the special feature of the coda?);
7. Bartók, *Piano Concerto No. 3,* second movement.

Project in tonal composition

It is often helpful to choose as a model a particular piece you like and know well. Whether or not you do this, think about the following questions before starting to write a piece in ternary form:

1. What will the key relationship between sections be?
2. What kind of melody should be used for the first part? How can you make a contrast to that in the second part?
3. In what ways will the textures of the two sections be different?
4. Can one section be focused on a certain register while the other moves through several registers?
5. Will the contrasts of dynamics mean that one section is louder than the other, or will the amount of dynamic change itself vary?
6. How will the piece end?

90

Forms Used in Song and Aria

STROPHIC SONG In most folk songs more than one verse (or strophe) is sung to the same music. We say that such a piece is *strophic.* Chorales, too, are strophic. Art songs, sometimes referred to by the German term *Lieder,* may use the same form (many of Schubert's do). But exact repetition of the music cannot transmit any change in the emotion or action of the poem, and strophic form is often modified.

Many poems are in three stanzas, and it is usually the third stanza that requires a change in the music. The result bears some resemblance to the bar form of the medieval German minnesingers, which we also found in many chorales (see page 14). The

song 154 has such a shape. The second section, starting in 15 , is much like the first; but the third, beginning in 28 , is much more continuation than repetition. While the melodic material grows out of what came before, it has quite a different curve, reaching the high point of the entire melody in 35 . The piano part changes chiefly in regard to the bass, which leaves the pedal point for the first time at the start of the third verse. The new quality brought in by the third verse owes its existence to the change in the meaning of the poem. After describing the beauty of the night and nature for two verses, the poet turns to his own feelings; his night, his flowers are not in nature, but in his love. The modifications in the strophic form are an expression of the poem.

THROUGH-COMPOSED When the music does not repeat, but changes to fit the meaning of the words, we say the song is *through-composed,* a none-too-elegant translation of the German *durch-komponiert.* The Schubert song ⬜150 begins with a four-measure introduction, then a four-phrase period that is never repeated. The second part of the song, starting with the upbeat to 23, is entirely different in texture, has a new melody and accompaniment figure, and goes on from where the first part left off.

Something similar happens in ⬜155. The first verse of the poem sets an atmosphere of calm in the countryside; the second verse is an agonized outcry against the fate of the imprisoned young man, cut off from nature and life outside the prison. The music in the two sections is as different as the words. The surprising half-diminished-7th chord in 15 shatters the peaceful mood of the first part, and dissonances in every measure embody the bitterness of the poem.

A different approach to the through-composed song is taken in ⬜157. The poem is in the form of an agitated conversation between the mother of an ailing child and Death. A third party is the narrator, who starts the poem and describes the situation. Moussorgsky's unerring dramatic genius finds the right music for each character; the phrases confront each other, rather than continue. The narrator's first lines, painting the picture of the anxious mother watching over her child, are sung in a parlando style, following the natural accent of the words. This is accompanied by an ominous line of eighth notes in the low register. Suddenly Death appears, and F♯ minor is pushed aside by the parallel major. The mother's protests are sung to a tremolo in the piano. Then Death sings, accompanied by different piano figures. The pathetic replies of the mother bring still other musical ideas. Death insists and, as the F♯ minor melts into A minor, sings "Lullaby" for the first time. Each agitated plea from the mother is answered by a calm, unmoved line from Death. The only music that is repeated is Death's "Lullaby." It is always in A minor and ends on C, except for the last time when it descends to the final A. One would be hard put to find a purely musical logic to this piece. But dramatic continuity could hardly be more convincing, and the piece is a miniature music drama.

Outline of ⬜157

measure	description	key
1–15	Introduction: the narrator	F♯ minor
16–19	Death enters: the narrator	F♯ major
19–21	the mother	unstable
22–32	Death speaks	A major
33–36	the mother	F♯ minor
36–37	Death, "Lullaby"	to A minor
38–41	the mother	unstable, ends in A major
41–42	Death, "Lullaby"	F♯ minor through A major to A minor
43–45	the mother	unstable, ends in A minor
46–47	Death, "Lullaby"	same as 41–42
48–51	the mother's last plea	unstable, moves to A major
51–54	Death, "Lullaby"	again, as in 41–42, F♯ minor through A major to A minor

ARIA Many forms have been used in opera arias, and it is not possible to speak of *aria* as a form. The *da capo* aria of Baroque and early Classical music had a dramatic weakness: the music had to go back and repeat even if the action was going forward. This must have seemed like a minor drawback, if any, in Baroque opera. There, the dramatic action was less important than the virtuosity of the singer, which was displayed especially in the embellished repetition (i.e., the *da capo*). Later generations found the repetition irksome as they began to take the drama more seriously. Arias in strophic form were also used, but they, too, involved musical repetition that held up the progress of the drama. Romantic arias evolved in a number of ways. The Italian composers liked a two-part piece in which a slow section, the *cavatina,* was contrasted with a lively ending, the *cabaletta.* But it is difficult to generalize about the forms of opera in the nineteenth century. The one thing that is certain is that the musicians paid a great deal of attention to the words.

The aria from *Carmen,* ⬜161, is a case in point. Don José's passionate declaration of love is set to a continuous flow of melody in clearly chiseled phrases eight measures long, some of them extended. The musical content is focused in the voice part, supported, inflected, and colored by the orchestra. The music follows the sense of the words, if not their natural accent (the first word is "This," set to a high F on a strong beat), and the vocal line never repeats itself. In the epilogue, the orchestra reminds us of the tenor's first phrase, but there is no dramatic reason for this; it is just too good a tune to waste. The aria is through-composed. The music fits the meaning of the words marvelously and makes a single statement.

ENSEMBLE   The aria features the solo voice; the *ensemble* combines two or more voices. In form—or rather, in adaptation of music to dramatic necessities—they are alike. The quartet from Verdi's *Rigoletto*, 159, takes its shape from the dramatic situation. Each character puts forth his or her own feelings, and the weaving of these different attitudes into a unified whole results in a type of piece that is unique to opera—namely, the ensemble. A survey of the quartet shows one way of approaching the operatic ensemble.

Each character expresses a different idea. The duke woos Maddalena, who responds flirtatiously; outside the room, Rigoletto, the court jester, forces his daughter Gilda to listen to the unfaithful duke, whom she loves. The duke's melody is suave and seductive; Maddalena's quick and light. Gilda's line is expressive, somewhat halting as she struggles with her emotions. Rigoletto's lines are a bit closer to declamation than the others, angry and forceful. The overall impression is a composite of the four parts, embodying that conflict which is the very life of drama and of opera.

The quartet may be divided into two large sections. The first, 1–33, is expository, setting forth the attitudes of the characters. The second, 33–57, deals more with the responses of the characters to each other.

The opening section begins with a spacious eight-measure phrase, built over the progression shown in sketch (a) below. Beginning with 4, the chords change once per measure. Comparing the tenor's line with the top line of the progression reminds us that Baroque music has no monopoly on polyphonic melody; the tenor draws upon notes from the three upper parts in the progression. A continuation of the melody is built over a tonicization of VI, 9–12, in which VI never appears as tonic, but its dominant is prolonged for the entire four-measure phrase. After a dominant any chord may follow, and V of VI leads into V⁷, ending the phrase. The next four-measure phrase repeats the last four measures of the opening. The duke has made his statement.

Still in the expository section, the two female voices answer the duke. Maddalena sings staccato

sixteenth notes, while Gilda sings a broken but more legato part in reaction to what she has overheard. The tonal structure is based on an expanded harmonic prolongation, $I–V_3^4–V^7–I$. Twice heard, this stabilizing phrase makes a good point of departure for the next move, which is more chromatic. As Rigoletto begins his comment, the motion through III minor to V begins, shown in sketch (b) below. The emotional temperature rises with the chromaticism brought about through the mode mixture. Thus the stabilizing four-measure phrase, 16–19, is followed by an active six-measure phrase, 20–25, whose last two measures are the dominant prolonged. All voices join in as four chords are heard for the focal measure, 24, contrary motion between alto and bass counterpointed against unmoving soprano and tenor.

The first section ends with a repetition of the duke's eight-measure phrase, now heard together with the other three voices. The top-line notes not included in that melody are now in the soprano's part. The SUS on the tenor's high A♭ is even more expressive now that the soprano sings a high B♭, an inner-voice note, against it.

At this point the deliberateness of the opening gives way to a more agitated feeling; we are in the second section. Indeed, the last measure of the first section, with the tonic that resolves the dominant and the end of the duke's phrase, 33, is also the first measure of the second section. From this point on, all voices are actively engaged in every measure. The phrases are quite clear, but one blends into the next, and the onward drive is never halted. A four-measure phrase, 33–36 (two two-measure phrases?), is based on a harmonic prolongation. It is answered by a four-measure phrase whose tonal structure is seen below in sketch (c). In quick succession, IV, V, and VI are tonicized, followed by a V⁷–I. But Verdi moves through that I to tonicize II, leading into the cadence that ends the phrase. This eight-measure period, 33–40, is repeated and is the climactic section of the quartet.

It is always fascinating to see how a great composer marshals his forces to build a climax, then gradually slows down the activity to make the end seem inevitable. The four measures starting in 49 have less rhythmic motion, and a tonic pedal brings the stability that prepares the end. Over that, the three upper voices rise stepwise, the baritone descends in contrary motion. The contrapuntal chords generated over the pedal note include the

99

leading-tone chord of II and an augmented 6th. The last five measures are strictly harmonic prolongation.

One interesting detail, for which we must scan the entire score, is the use of the 9th. By no coincidence, that note is the high B♭ so beloved of tenors, as Verdi well knew. In the very first phrase, the highest note is A♭. This is surpassed by the B♭ in the second phrase, which is a $\overset{>}{\text{NT}}$, but very close to being part of a V^9 as well. The

dominant prolongation in 24–25 ends with another 9th of the same type. At the last dominant, in 55, Gilda sings a 9th, now minor and definitely part of the chord.

Verdi has used any number of ways to show the different emotions of the four characters and their reactions to each other. The pacing of the piece depends partly on the ebb and flow of rhythmic factors, partly on the texture that begins with one voice singing and ends with all four active for many measures. It also depends on the polyphony, the contrast between the stabilizing motions that circle around the tonic and the more active motions that drive to the dominant, using chromaticism to increase the tension. The piece serves a dramatic purpose as the focal point of the last act of the opera, but it is also a self-contained and powerfully organized entity in its own right.

For further study

1. Schubert, *The Winter's Journey* (song cycle);
2. Schumann, *The Poet's Love* (song cycle);
3. Brahms, *Four Serious Songs;*
4. Wolf, *Italian Songbook;*
5. Fauré, *Three Songs* Op. 18;
6. Debussy, *Fêtes galantes* (song cycle);
7. Poulenc, *Tel jour, telle nuit* (song cycle);
8. Schoenberg, *The Book of the Hanging Gardens* (song cycle);
9. Webern, *Three Songs* Op. 25;
10. Copland, *Twelve Poems of Emily Dickinson;*
11. Britten, *Sonnets of Michelangelo* Op. 22.

☞ Worksheet 48

91

Introduction to Sonata-Allegro Form

BACKGROUND Both dance forms and operatic forms contributed to the development of what we call "sonata-allegro form" or what Beethoven called "first-movement form." It was, indeed, the form of the first movement of such instrumental genres as symphony, sonata, and string quartet, and of the opera overture. But it was often used for other movements as well. Haydn was one of the first to use this form. Guided by the explorations of K. P. E. Bach, he developed its possibilities and made it the most substantial form of tonal music. Mozart, Beethoven, and Schubert worked within the sonata-allegro framework in the most natural way. Nineteenth-century composers, perhaps awed by the example of Beethoven, tried to adapt it to their expressive purposes with varying degrees of success. The "underground" classicists of the Romantic era, such as Mendelssohn and Brahms, wrote much music that seemed as inevitably shaped into sonata-allegro form as that of the earlier composers; Schumann, Chopin, Tchaikovsky, and Dvořák had problems in accommodating their long, songful melodies to a form that sprang from the development of short rhythmic ideas.

OUTLINE The form is customarily outlined in terms of themes and their development. But we know that musical form grows from an interaction of tonal structure and design, the latter including all aspects of theme and motive. The outline, then, must include at least a minimum description of tonal movement together with the theme groups.

Outline of sonata-allegro form

exposition	development	recapitulation
theme 1: I	based on the material of the exposition, prolonging V	theme 1: I
bridge, modulating to		bridge
theme 2: V or, if I is minor, III		theme 2: I
closing theme or codetta or both, stabilizing V or III		closing theme and/or codetta: I
		coda (optional)

The outline above does not answer many questions concerning the thematic aspect, let alone the ramifications of tonal structure. Is the bridge made of new material, or is it a continuation of the ideas set forth in theme 1? (It can be either.) Why is the "second theme" so similar melodically to the first theme in many works by Haydn? (Because the essential contrast is not melodic, but tonal and textural.) The outline implies that after the second theme there is not much left to the exposition. Why, in many pieces by Beethoven, is that section longer than the total of themes 1 and 2 plus the bridge? (No simple answer to this.) From the outline, one would never guess how much develop-

ment takes place within the exposition in a great many pieces. Questions such as these tell us that each work must be examined as an individual manifestation of the general type. We must not try to fit the music into a preconceived idea of how such pieces should go, but rather try to determine in what ways a given piece fits the norm and in what ways it is unique. Works of art are like people; their general shape is more or less similar, but each one is a bit different from all the others.

TONALITY AND SONATA ALLEGRO The most obvious element of sonata-allegro form is the thematic aspect. What we have to seek out is the tonal structure. Broadly speaking, the tonal structure of sonata-allegro form is built on the main principle of Classical music, which is contrast or opposition. The mainspring of the piece is wound up in the exposition, with the motion from I to V in major or I to III in minor. Tension is maintained in the development, which may be a simple prolongation of V but is more likely to be a far-flung series of tonal moves with V as the goal. This inevitably leads to the reaffirmation of the tonic in the recapitulation, usually at the very beginning but, occasionally, much later.

162 A discussion of the first movement of Beethoven's *First Symphony* sheds light on many corners of sonata-allegro form. Two comments must precede the survey. First, this is not a "typical" Beethoven symphony because there really is no such thing. Beethoven made each symphony different, gave each a character of its own, and each is unique. Second, this piece is not the work of a "follower" of Haydn and Mozart. No doubt Beethoven learned much from the composers who constituted his immediate past; but even in Opus 1, he was entirely his own man. By Opus 21, he was an experienced and successful composer.

THE SLOW INTRODUCTION In almost all the late Haydn symphonies and in many of Mozart's, the first allegro is preceded by a slow introduction, a carry-over from the opera overture. Beethoven uses this attention-getting device in the *First, Second, Fourth,* and *Seventh Symphonies.* This one starts with an unusual tonal movement:

$$V^7\text{–}I\text{–}V^7\text{–}VI\text{–}V^7\text{–}I.$$
$$\underbrace{\qquad\qquad}_{\text{of IV}}\quad\underbrace{\qquad\qquad}_{\text{of V}}$$

The entire progression defines C major without our hearing a single tonic chord. But all the chords are related to C, which is the operational definition of tonality. The dominant proceeds quite deliberately toward the tonic, arriving only in 8 . At once the II[6] carries us off toward the dominant again. V is prolonged with a DN in the bass, elaborated with a chromatic PT that supports VII of VI, VI being one of the two neighbor chords generated. The dominant prolongation lasts four measures and sets up the tonic that opens the exposition.

EXPOSITION A clear, concise motive forms the basis of the first theme; it is the most important motive of the movement. The theme is in the form of a six-measure phrase, four in the strings, two in the winds, with an overlap. Immediate repetition of the theme on II leads to V. The completion of the tonal movement, back to I, starts the bridge. Already the first motive of the theme has been seized upon as a decisive element and repeated with the particular insistence characteristic of the composer.

The bridge begins at 33 , whose tonic ends the previous tonal movement and starts a new one. I is stabilized as tonic and dominant alternate over a tonic pedal. The new melodic material is based on the triad. This is fitted into an eight-measure phrase. Using a version of the main motive, a four-measure phrase moves to V;. The eight-measure phrase that follows, although prolonging V, makes that V sound more like the dominant of C than a new tonic. All the more surprising, then, when theme 2 blithely starts off in G, in 53 .

Contrasts between themes 1 and 2

theme 1	theme 2
melody in violins	melody shared by oboe and flute
emphatic, accented	legato
unison	melody plus light accompaniment
six-measure phrase, then another, then four measures	period consisting of antecedent and consequent phrases of eight measures

The repetition of the second theme, starting with the upbeat to 61 , has a fuller sound because the melody, shared now by violins and winds, is played in octaves. Repetition is not quite the word for what happens, however. The first phrase turns not to the dominant, but toward the subdominant, and the end of the phrase tonicizes IV. To balance this, a vigorous prolongation of I reaffirms G in 69–77 , and the exposition could almost be over at that point. But, still looking for the dramatic contrast, Beethoven plunges into a new realm instead.

We know that something is brewing because of the abrupt change to G minor in 77 . Using the motive of theme 2, the composer unfolds a series of 5ths in the bass, and the ear's attention is focused on the low register. Then the oboe brings in a sustained F and three levels are in operation at once. The motion in 5ths arrives at E♭, from which a stepwise movement brings the bass through G to D. Having changed the mode (and mood) so suddenly, Beethoven has worked his way back to the major and restored the forward drive of the exposition. Both these are accomplished in the course of a crescendo which stresses the dominant.

The section beginning at 88 serves to conclude the exposition. Motivically, theme 1 provides the material; tonally, G major is nailed down, drawing into its orbit the three diminished-7th chords that are available in the twelve notes. Here they are leading-tone chords. It is as if Beethoven quickly passes in review the basic materials of music before bringing the exposition to a close. The harmonic prolongation is effective, as always, in concluding the paragraph. In the first ending, the addition of F to the G-major sound leads back to the repetition of the exposition, which must not be omitted.

Three diminished-7th chords

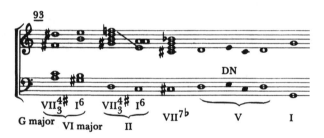

DEVELOPMENT That Beethoven planned his works with considerable care is seen by the tonal structure of the development section, which almost seems to have been mapped out in advance. The sketch below shows the large motions: the progression in 5ths in two gestures, leading to E♭; the stepwise motion in the bass, arriving at G; and the falling 4ths, leading to a tonicization of A minor. Each tonal move is characterized by one texture and one kind of thematic development, so that several of the most important elements of music are coordinated to give each of the four subdivisions of the section its own individual nature. Yet the entire section is continuous as each part flows into the next.

The loud chord that begins the development section is typical of Classical procedure only in that development sections usually begin with a striking gesture of one kind or another. Compare the new version of the theme with the statement in the exposition to see how it is now shortened. When the motion arrives at C, the mode is minor, and the arpeggio part of the theme is now worked over. It moves from one register to another against the tremolo of the second violins. A long prolongation of the dominant of E♭ brings the next part. The very first notes of the motive are developed in many registers as the tonal move proceeds by step to G. Out of this a continuation motive of three quarter notes emerges as the 4ths suddenly fall back to E as dominant of A.

How is the recapitulation prepared? Most often, Classical composers aimed for the dominant, creating a link with the end of the exposition and the tension that would be released by the opening of the recapitulation with its affirmation of the tonic. But in this movement Beethoven does something different. In a move that is both dramatic and humorous, he prolongs the dominant of VI with a large flourish that clearly paves the way for some important statement. Suddenly the ff dies away, and the winds slyly take the E, move to F, and run down the arpeggio of the V⁷, as they did at the end of the exposition. As they go, they build a new crescendo. The resolution of the V⁷ is the beginning of the recapitulation. While Haydn never made a move quite like this, most of his surprises consisted of creating one set of expectations and then doing something different. Beethoven understood that principle very well.

Development Section: Tonal structure and related use of theme 1

RECAPITULATION Comparison of the recapitulation with the exposition reveals some similarity in the first theme, none in the bridge, and fairly literal repetition from then on. Usually, differences between the two versions of the bridge are due to the fact that the bridge in the exposition modulates, while in the recapitulation the tonic is reaffirmed. This often leads to tonally active bridges in the recapitulation, giving the illusion of a modulation but leading right back to the point of departure. However, in the exposition of the *First Symphony*, Beethoven does not modulate, but comes to a cadence on V; and simply continues in V. In the recapitulation he could easily have restated the original bridge and gone on in I. Instead, the composer takes an entirely different path. He takes as his cue the repetition of the opening motive, but moves it up one step, tonicizing II, in 18–23 . Extending that idea, in 182 he begins a move through one tonicization after another, each a step higher. The motion goes through an octave and a half; it is summarized in the sketch on page 112. The winds retain their role of providing chordal movement while the strings concentrate on the sixteenth-note figure that prefixed the first theme (nothing goes to waste here). In the process, the distinction between the first theme and the bridge is lost; the expansion of the theme leads to a prolonged dominant, and the second theme follows.

This time G is indeed V of C, and the second theme is just as it was in the exposition, now transposed to the tonic. The same is true of the plunge into the minor and the return to the major as well as the codetta. Then, from 259 , the descending arpeggio in the winds points toward the subdominant, balancing the emphasis on the dominant in the movement as a whole. A short extension begins, built on IV–II–V⁷–I, which is the last tonal movement of the piece. A version of the theme that emphasizes the tonic serves to stabilize both theme and tonality, preparing the way for the ending. This section is too short to be a coda, and is simply a glorified prolongation of I.

Reviewing the movement as a whole, we might compare sonata-allegro form with rounded binary: each has an opening statement in tonic, coming to a cadence sometimes in the tonic but more often in the dominant or relative major; each has an active, unstable section based on the opening material after the double bar; each is rounded off with restatement of the opening material in the tonic. In many ways, sonata-allegro form is simply a large-scale version of rounded binary form. But, of course, it is more complex. Indeed, sonata allegro is the most ambitious form in tonal music.

PLANNING AND SPONTANEITY Looking at the piece as a whole, we may observe that Beethoven has done two things that may seem contradictory but that form the inner argument of the piece. On the one hand, the overall layout seems almost preplanned, organized into segments that balance and complement each other, areas of greater and lesser tension and activity played off against each other in a way that is carefully calculated. On the other hand, the rhythmic drive and energy of the themes and their development and the tonal moves seem spontaneous and imaginative. Intuitively, one feels that the music had to go the way it did, and yet no one could possibly deduce the piece from the themes themselves. The form grows out of the musical ideas seemingly quite spontaneously; it is exactly the form that Beethoven had inherited from his musical ancestors.

SONATA ALLEGRO IN THE NINETEENTH CENTURY

While the classicizing tendency in the nineteenth century heavily influenced Mendelssohn and Brahms at least, others, such as Schumann and Tchaikovsky, moved in different directions. It becomes difficult to generalize about the nineteenth century because adaptations of the basic form grew more and more individual. In general, as tonal unity weakened in Romantic works, the tensions that made the form work so well in Classical music lost their organizing power. The thematic element came to have a larger part of the responsibility for organizing the entire piece. But we know that the thematic element alone cannot make sonata-allegro form effective. Many Romantic pieces lack overall unity, sacrificing it to increased expressivity of detail. This is the result of an aesthetic choice and does not mean that such works are better or worse than Classical pieces. But they are different, and one of the differences is that tonality gradually ceased to be the central fact of life for music. By the end of the nineteenth century, sonata-allegro form no longer seemed viable, and the list of composers who did did not use it includes virtually all the important names of the time.

SONATA ALLEGRO IN THE TWENTIETH CENTURY

What we have described as the extension of traditional tonality brought a renewed interest in the older forms, including sonata allegro. However, a new outlook on its tonal structure was needed since the dominant had lost its role as the lightning rod that attracted tension to be discharged at the tonic and complete the tonal movement in a satisfying way. Since the harmonic motion was no longer used, linear chords took up virtually all the roles in the tonal drama.

177 One example of such an approach is the first movement of Hindemith's *Sonata for Flute and Piano*. The particular kind of polyphony used here is discussed in Part Sixteen, pages 126–127. The overall shape of the piece, including the thematic aspect and the broad tonal structure, are taken up here.

TONALITY The piece is in B♭, with major and minor mixed. The interval of a 5th is conspicuous in all the themes, both melodically and chordally. The music slips from one tonal area to another through chromatic motions, and many triads are stabilized briefly within large tonal areas.

EXPOSITION The phrase structure of the first theme is much like that of Classical and Romantic music. A clear four-measure phrase in the piano is answered and extended by the flute in an eight-measure unit whose last measure is also the first of the next phrase. The third statement of the idea begins in imitation; but the flute soon goes its own way and, in dialogue with the piano, works out a phrase that runs to the first beat of 18. By that time the key is A.

BRIDGE The end of the first theme is elided to the beginning of the bridge at the start of 18. In the piano, a new idea appears in units of three beats, cutting across the prevailing four. Against the piano's development of the rhythmic motive, the flute spins out a long and active line, moving through more than two octaves. The seven-measure phrase centers around A, ending in 24. Then a digression through F♯ develops the material of the preceding phrase. This six-measure phrase leads into another, similar phrase of five measures, again centered around A. Its open end ushers in the second theme (35).

The new melody is in G♯, and we now see something of the large tonal movement that has brought the music to that point. The first theme is in B♭; the bridge is in A; another half-step motion arrives at G♯. In addition to a new key there is a slower tempo and a lower sound in both instruments. The use of the bottom notes of the flute gives the second theme a special color. The idea is short, consisting of three units of two measures (more or less)—hardly phrases. The more serious mood is chased away by three measures of cheerful music that serve to end the exposition. One can hardly speak of either a codetta or a closing theme, but the three measures, which move back to A, are adequate for the scale of the composition.

DEVELOPMENT A new key, C♯, and a new motive in the piano (a new version of an old motive) begin the development section in 44. The music starts in the low register, making possible a large-scale ascent as the section progresses. Together with the ascent we expect a crescendo since the dynamics are quite soft (*ppp*)—indeed, the softest of the piece, at 44. The piano starts with a five-and-one-half-measure phrase, which is then used to accompany the flute in its expanded version of the first theme. Using the traditional procedure of chamber-music style, the piano, in 55, picks up some of what the flute had just played. The flute precedes its continuing elaboration of the first theme with three upbeats (56). 55–57 may be thought of as a large upbeat to the melody, whose repetitions grow closer together as the register rises and the dynamics build. Four-measure phrases in the flute are set over continuous development in the piano, bringing the piece to the climactic level and leading directly into the recapitulation.

RECAPITULATION Comparison of the restatement of the first theme with its initial version shows that Hindemith carries the momentum of the development forward by insisting on the piano's motive, phasing it out only after the restatement is well under way. As compared to the exposition, the entrances of the theme are reversed and dovetailed. The flute now starts; the piano does not wait for the phrase to end before starting its version. The bridge idea (piano) of the exposition is not used in the recapitulation. Instead the first theme is expanded. The piano concentrates on the theme's first motive, starting in 75, while the flute first mentions the second motive, then takes up its own bridge motive from the exposition. This is picked up by the piano in 84. The two instruments engage in dialogue, using the motive material described above and leading into the second theme.

Looking back, we remember that in the expositon the first theme was in B♭, the second in G♯, a whole step lower. In the recapitulation the first theme is, again, in B♭ and the second in C, a whole step higher. Hindemith has replaced the tonic-dominant relationship with another, stepwise relationship that provides a tonal framework for the sonata-allegro movement. The large tonal movement is completed by the return to B♭, which will be the function of the coda. The second theme is just as it was in the exposition, but it is not answered, as before, by the three cheery measures. We expect them, and Hindemith plays on that expectation, delaying the return until the very end of the movement. While the key of B♭ is not reached until close to the end, the note B♭ in the flute ends the second theme. A quiet coda builds on the sec-

ond motive of the first theme. An eight-measure phrase in the piano is taken up in the flute and leads to a modest climax. The phrase ends with the short idea we were expecting earlier, imitated closely in the piano, repeated an octave higher in the flute and answered again, thickened with 3rds, in the piano.

RELATION TO EARLIER MUSIC Both in its scope and its interplay between the instruments, this piece is much like a Classical sonata movement. The use of the instruments, too, is more like that of the eighteenth century than the nineteenth—that is, the music is abstract in the sense that the emphasis is on the lines and little of it grows from the nature of the instruments or from their coloristic possibilities. The music is unpretentious and straightforward, accessible to players and listeners alike.

For further study

In listening to Classical sonata-allegro movements, go beyond first movements and observe how the form is used in second and fourth movements as well as in overtures. If you have not heard all the Beethoven symphonies, this is a good time to remedy that omission. Be sure to include in your listening at least one classical piano concerto. Where in a symphony or sonata the repeat signs indicate a literal repetition of the exposition, in a concerto there are two expositions. The first is for orchestra alone, the second for the solo instrument and orchestra. Particularly in Mozart piano concertos the second exposition takes on unusual and fascinating aspects.

Listen to nineteenth-century symphonies such as Mendelssohn's *Italian*, Schumann's *Fourth*, Brahms's *Second* or *Fourth*, and Tchaikovsky's *Sixth*. In a general way, how much Classical procedure can you identify in each, and in what ways do they differ from the Classical norms? Listen to at least one symphony each by Bruckner and Mahler, and find any connections you can between those works and Classical symphonies.

Listen to the symphony *Mathis der Maler*, by Hindemith. What is the role of the slow introduction? Listen to Bartók's *String Quartet No. 4* and *String Quartet No. 5,* paying particular attention to the first movements. Try to discover the large tonal organization of each. The string quartets of Debussy and Ravel have first movements that are clear examples of the application of extended tonality to sonata-allegro form.

A late 19th-century cartoon with the caption "General Bass is attacked and overcome by Liszt."

PART FIFTEEN
CHROMATICISM 2

92

Chromatic Motions 1: Prolonging Motions

MOTION WITHIN A CHORD Let us imagine an A-minor triad elaborated with the familiar SP, first diatonically, then chromatically.

Now look closely at ⟦143⟧. The chromatic top line is projected over a tonic pedal point, firmly anchoring the prolongation. Top line and inner voices form a series of $^6_3$-position triads and other passing chords. The tonic thus takes up three measures of the antecedent phrase, followed by a connecting II⁶ and I$^6_4$–V;. The consequent phrase varies the top line with N̂Ts and follows the tonic with I$^6_4$–V⁷–I.

The dominant is prolonged in ⟦159⟧, 24 , the purpose being to sum up the energy of the phrase, which spills out into a six-measure group. Tension grows from the contrary motion in half steps between the baritone (bass line) and the alto. Once again the diminished 7th plays a role in a chro-matic prolongation not as a leading tone chord, but as a passing chord.

The two previous examples began by stating the chord that was to be embellished. But the prolongation may begin with an embellishing note, so that the listener must wait, perhaps to the last sound in the group, before hearing the main chord. This technique may be seen in two excerpts by Wagner. The first simply precedes the V⁷ with a chromatic N̂T. It functions as a leading tone and resolves at once. The same N̂T first steps down in ⟦167C⟧, delaying the move to its goal with two more chromatic PTs. An inner voice in contrary motion adds density to the move.

⟦167D⟧

A minor V⁷

107

D minor: VI$_2^{4\sharp}$ E♭: V$_5^6$

The sketch of 167C shows that the first chord has a "wrong" note, F. It functions as E♯, the leading tone of F♯. The motion is elaborated with voice exchange. Two voices move, two sustain their notes. The main chord is reached only at the fourth sound. The second chord is expanded in the same way. When the dominant, F♯, is reached, it includes both a 9th and a suspended 4th, B. Both demand resolution, which is deferred as long as possible. The dissonant chord is stretched out with a series of contrapuntal chords which demonstrate the seemingly infinite possibilities of generating such sounds. B moves to F♯, G to E, E to C♯, and C♯ to A♯, all constituting motion within the chord. Since almost every move is chromatic, the chords that result are related to the key not through their roots (if one can determine what they are), but through the voice leading within the chord.

In such a situation, chords that had a certain function in earlier music are used without reference to that function. The ear has learned to accept them, and they are simply contrapuntal connecting or prolonging chords. Thus the first sound in the second measure of the sketch 167C above once functioned as V^6 of E♭ or possibly as an augmented 6th (VI$^{6\sharp}$) in D. Here it has no such meaning. In the third measure of the sketch, the second sound once was VII^7 of C♯ major or II^7 of B♭ minor; in this music the chord has no connection with those keys. The link between that half-diminished 7th and B minor is to be found in the chord being pro-

longed and the pedal point. Such use of contrapuntal chromatic chords expanded the tonal system enormously, but also brought it to the breaking point. Once composers learned how to use chords without regard to their original meaning, it became possible to connect them in a purely linear way on the basis of their sonority. This was one of the great lessons that Debussy learned from Wagner.

PROLONGING CHORDS A single NT can prolong a note or decorate a chord. A group of NTs can become a neighbor chord, prolonging another, more fundamentally structural chord. A simple example is in the first measure of 130B, where three NTs (two of which are chromatic) move over a stationary bass to create a diminished-7th chord—not a leading-tone chord, but a neighbor chord—which prolongs I. The same operation in 5 prolongs VI with an augmented 6th that is purely linear and has nothing to do with any dominant. In the second half of the piece I and V are prolonged by motion in 3rds, but we are probably more inclined to hear NTs than a neighbor chord.

Diminished-7th chord as sum of NTs

The dramatic chord in 149, 9, is an augmented triad. It is generated by a NT, D♯, which is emphasized by doubling, indeed, tripling, together with an accent. Another NT in the next measure helps create what sounds like a V^2, but has no such function. It is a neighbor chord, elaborating the E-minor triad. The same music is soon repeated a minor 3rd higher with the same contrapuntal chord.

NTs in 149

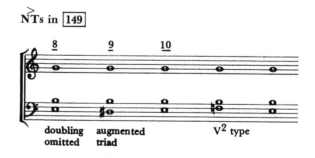

doubling   augmented   V^2 type
omitted   triad

The familiar melodic prolonging motion of a DN may also be used to generate prolonging chords. A partly chromatic version of this opens the aria 158. The string parts show the basic counterpoint most clearly while the voice sings a poly-

108

phonic melody, using notes from three levels. The DN moves in 3rds, generating IV⁶ and a diminished 7th.

Melody and chords in 158

The neighboring and passing motions just studied took place in the upper and inner voices, but they may be heard in the bass as well. The passionate phrase that climaxes the last scene of the first act of Verdi's *Otello,* 160, is built over a chromatic version of **PS**. The phrase begins with I⁶, whose progress to V⁷ is spun out by a series of linear chords, all dissonant. The bass moves down by half steps from 5 of E major to 3 of E minor. The top line centers around 5 and its NT 6, the latter in both major and minor versions. The linear chords that grow out of this oblique motion are dominant 7ths, diminished 7ths, and half-diminished 7ths, highly expressive sounds that inflect and intensify the melody. These chromatic chords, in turn, are further intensified by N̄Ts in the melody. The sketch below shows the chords in four parts.

160: reduction

153 is a study in chord prolongations. The rate of chord change that we perceive is one, two, even three chords to a measure. But the structural chords move quite slowly, and it is their elaborations that keep the surface of the piece active. Thus the I chord controls the first three and one-half measures; within that, the chromatic neighbor chord, identical with the one in 130B, creates a sense of change. V⁷ is elaborated diatonically in the next measure and a half, again using neighbor and passing chords.

After the modulation to the dominant, the second part of the song begins in 14. For two measures the outer voices have a pedal note while the inner voices start from G major, generate two linear chords that clash sharply with the held G, and return to G. The melody uses inner-voice notes. The next two measures continue the prolongation of G. The top line, in the piano, moves through a chromatic SP, more related to G minor than G major. As F♯ gives way to F, G resumes its role as dominant of C. But Brahms moves through C to F. V⁷ of IV occupies 18–20. In the second half of both 18 and 19, the V⁷ is elaborated with a neighbor chord in exactly the way in which I was elaborated in the initial phrase of the song. Indeed, the diminished-7th chord is the same in both cases. A third and final appearance of the same sound is in 27, where it is heard fleetingly, again as a neighbor chord to V⁷ of IV. And, looking back at 15, we see that the same operation yielded a neighbor chord to I of G major, disguised by the pedal tones. The number of structural chords is indeed quite small; but each is elaborated with linear motions that produce linear chords, heavily colored with mode mixture, so that the forward motion pushes on to the very end.

SUMMARY Chromatic prolongations of a chord have the same purposes as diatonic ones—they extend the function of the basic chord. Prolongations of I mean stability; of V, activity and probably drive toward the tonic. We see this most clearly in such Classical pieces as 133 and 134. In both, the dominant prolongations are enhanced with mode mixture. But the same procedures are used in such Romantic works as Chopin's 148. The long dominant at the end of the second section serves the same purpose as in the two earlier pieces—that is, it prepares the restatement in the tonic. However, dissonance is relative, and instead of being the most dissonant part, the dominant prolongation in Chopin calms the agitation of the middle section by being (relatively) less active. Thus it makes a transition between the highest level of activity and the stable restatement that is the third section. The prolongations may venture far from the basic chords, so that their scope increases considerably;

most of $\boxed{160}$ is involved with getting from I_4^6 to V^7. This shows an increase in the time scale of music that is part of the nineteenth-century view.

☞ Worksheet 49

93

Chromatic Motions 2: From I to V

The motion from I to V characterizes many phrases in tonal music; it may follow a chromatic route as well as a diatonic one. The chromatic motion is often heard in the bass alone, but it may also occur in the soprano or in both bass and soprano.

CHROMATIC BASS Each of the three short excerpts from Beethoven piano sonatas, $\boxed{142}$, is built over a bass that descends in half steps from tonic to dominant. Each is different.

In $\boxed{142A}$, the bass does not stop in $\underline{5}$ but pushes on to an accented 4, then circles around to return to the dominant. The soprano travels in contrary motion. A series of contrapuntal chords is developed, including a German 6th that precedes the dominant. There is a melodic accent on the second beat from the first measure on so that the heavier accent in 6 sounds like the natural culmination of the smaller accents that led up to it. Observe that the stress falls on the neighboring IV rather than on the dominant. Beethoven may be emphatic, but he is not obvious.

$\boxed{142B}$ is the opening of a sonata, and the move from I to V is spacious, implying that much more is to come. C, B, B♭, and A are each heard in the bass for two measures. Then A♭ and G alternate closer and closer until the energy explodes into an arpeggiated I that is a neighbor chord within the dominant prolongation. The long phrase is built in units of four, four, and five measures. The first unit moves from I to V⁶ through the latter's V². The same progression is repeated a whole step lower in the next unit. From that point on, the dominant

prolongation is in control. Mode mixture comes in as early as $\underline{5}$, and it is to permeate the entire movement. We also observe that while the left hand stays in the low register, the right-hand part extends for over three octaves in an arching gesture that helps launch the long movement to come.

Where $\boxed{142B}$ ended with the dominant, telling us that more music was on the way, $\boxed{142A}$ and $\boxed{142C}$ both end on the tonic. Each of these is a single, self-contained phrase, whose tonal movement is from I to V, followed by a cadence on I. $\boxed{142A}$ is the theme of a set of variations. $\boxed{142C}$ is the first part of a slow introduction to a fast finale.

The phrase of $\boxed{142C}$ is particularly interesting. We may observe at once that the bass moves down chromatically from the tonic to the dominant, realizing that the first sound is as low as Beethoven's piano could go and that the composer then moved up an octave. But what about the top line? The melody covers over two octaves and has many skips. Where are the lines behind the melody?

Melody of $\boxed{142C}$

Clearly, this is a polyphonic melody. But some notes are missing. The lines can only be fully discovered if all the voices are set forth.

Voice leading of 142C **reduced to one register**

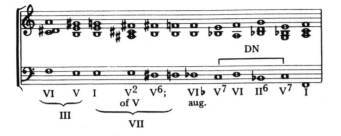

With the aid of the reduction we discover that the outer voices move in parallel 10ths. These are concealed by voice crossing and octave displacement. Even though they are not readily heard, they provide the solid framework for the polyphony of the phrase.

The chord vocabulary is quite rich for so short a phrase. In addition to major and minor triads in various inversions, Beethoven uses dominant 7ths, a diminished triad, and two augmented-6th chords. Stable and unstable chords alternate, although even as stable a sound as the minor triad in root position has something active about it because of its unexpected placement at the beginning of 3. An opening two-measure group with an internal rest ends with a breathing space. The repetition is rhythmically identical, but varied in pitch. The third group carries over where the internal rest had been, providing the one SUS in the phrase. Then the latter half of the unit is expanded into a three-measure group that closes the phrase. The spacious quality of the nine-measure phrase owes something of its character to the rests, which are placed in a remarkable way.

The motion proceeds quite steadily until the dominant is reached. Observe that once the bass touches C, the chromaticism gives way to diatonic sounds. After the dominant is stabilized, one tonic is sufficient to end the thought.

Although the technique of 142B and 142C is much the same, the musical effect is quite different. In the first excerpt, the rhythmic energy of the eighth notes drives the music to a very temporary goal, a dramatic gesture that starts an entire movement. But 142C ends with a feeling of closure that needs nothing else and is quite self-contained.

The bass in 166, 6–8, is not completely chromatic, nor is the soprano; but the two together add up to a highly chromatic texture. The outer voices move in parallel tritones, embellished by PT and SUS. The chords generated include half-diminished 7ths, both minor (7, first beat) and major (7, third beat). Try playing the first-violin part

by itself. You will hear how much the melody needs the accompaniment to give it meaning.

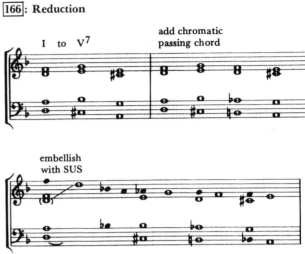

If we extend the notion of moving from tonic to dominant so as to include the I^6 as a possible point of departure, we see the large tonal movement that underlies the Chopin prelude 144B. In 10, the dominant is reached; up to that point everything has been movement, activity, dissonance. The chromatic lines generate one chromatic chord after another, all guided by the motion from the tonic to the dominant. The interaction of chord and line must be studied in detail.

The bass has the most influence, starting from 3 and moving down to 5 in half steps with one whole step from 8 to 9. Its steady progress, mostly one half step to a measure, is counterpointed against a top line that moves very slowly, creating oblique motion for the most part. The tenor follows the bass in 3rds, once pushing the lower voice along with a SUS, in 5–6, once lagging behind, in 10, thus becoming the dissonant voice in another SUS. Alto and bass move in 6ths and 7ths, with SUSs adding their dissonances at every opportunity.

These chromatic lines generate a great variety of chromatic chords—indeed, the piece is a veritable storehouse of such chords. Because of the slow tempo, there is time for every passing and neighbor motion to be heard as a simultaneity. The chord vocabulary includes, in addition to triads, dominant-7th chords, diminished-7th chords, half-diminished-7th chords both major and minor (both in 6), minor-7th chords, and other simultaneities, formed by SUS, which defy categorization. The single major triad is used to telling effect, prolonging the final dominant over a NT in the bass.

Continuous chromaticism makes for continuous phrase structure. Within the first twelve-measure phrase, punctuation is very light. The dominant that ends the first phrase resolves to the I^6 that starts the second phrase so that while there is a breathing space, there is no pause. The thirteen measures of the second phrase include a moment of silence; but that does not end the thought. The cadence then follows. Comparing the tonal structures of the two phrases that comprise the piece, the first is taken up with the motion from I to V^7, then with a three-measure prolongation of the dominant; the second arrives at V more quickly and prolongs it from the middle of 18 to the last tonic.

CHROMATIC SOPRANO Less often than the bass, a chromatic top line may help direct the motion from 1 to 5 and from I to V. 153 includes such a move. It is the guiding force in the modulation to a cadence in V that defines the end of the song's first section. Starting in 6 the top line is literally in the uppermost notes of the piano part, arriving at its goal in 11 . The melody in the voice part starts with top-line notes, skips to inner-voice notes displaced up an octave, and ends by taking over the top line after the piano has reached the G. The bass is in contrary motion. The soprano forces it to get moving with its dissonant and unexpected Db, the first note of its chromatic ascent. The contrary motion generates a variety of dissonant chords related to C major only as part of a directed motion from I to V in that key. As in the Chopin *Prelude in E Minor,* the deliberate

speed of the music allows the chromatic changes to make their full effect felt. It also increases the time scale of a single gesture, such as the move from I to V. Only the very clear direction of the top line unifies the diverse chords of this phrase.

In 149, starting in 17 , a descending chromatic motion in the soprano controls the latter part of the section's tonal movement. The tonal movement has gone from C# minor up to G minor. The return trip begins with the bass and inner voices gradually forming a Gb-major triad under the melody's Bb. From that point the soprano leads the way down by half steps to F#. Each soprano note is the third of a major triad. Parallel 5ths are avoided simply by alternating root position and first inversion. The melody's F# holds for three measures, changing color as it changes from the third of a (prolonged) Neapolitan 6th to the root of a (prolonged) VI^6 and then to the seventh of a V^7.

Two longer chromatic top lines are discernible in 162, 182–198, and in the opening of the prelude to *Tristan,* by Wagner, 167D. The chord progressions are shown in the sketches below.

The Beethoven example, drawn from the recapitulation, demonstrates how the effect of much activity is created in the bridge without modulation. The vocabulary consists of only two chords, V^7 and the triad to which it resolves, so that consonance and dissonance alternate. The motion from I to V is expanded in musical space to fill an octave and a 5th. Each degree of the scale is tonicized by its own dominant. In the major, VII is a diminished triad, thus not suitable for tonicization. But we know that major and minor are never

Two chromatic top lines

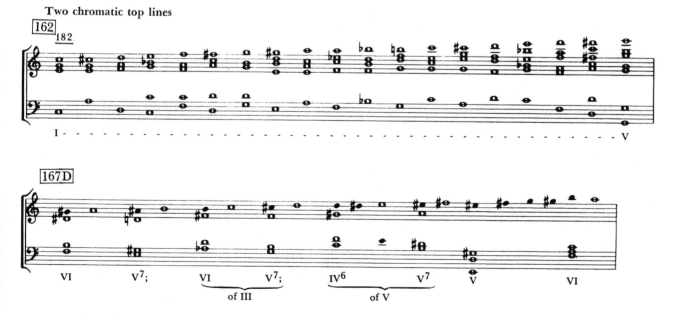

far apart, and the VII of C minor that is used in the progression sounds as natural as the other triads.

The Wagner excerpt is from the opening of the opera, and the original should be compared with the sketch above. The only consonant sound in the section is, possibly, an A-minor triad implied by the first three notes. All other sounds are dissonant. The main chords are French 6ths and dominant 7ths. Where the V^7 was the more active chord in the Beethoven example, it is the less ac-

tive chord in the Wagner. In the latter the more active chords are the augmented 6ths and the half-diminished 7ths formed by the $\overset{>}{P}$Ts. These examples show us again how relative the usages of dissonance are—a chord (V^7) that was the more dissonant in one context is the least active in another. While studying the Wagner illustration we should also observe how the chord progression is elaborated by the exchange of notes between soprano and tenor in the first two pairs of chords, similar to the exchanges of 167C, the *Parsifal* excerpt.

94

Chromatic Motions 3: Other Connecting Motions

PARALLEL 10THS If the bass descends chromatically, the top line (soprano) may counterpoint it with contrary motion, oblique motion, or parallel motion. An interesting use of parallel motion involves 10ths.

One example is in 144H. The first four measures move from I to III, and the next step is to connect III to V. The initial bass move was up a 3rd from 1 to 3, with I and III preceded by their dominants. Another rise of a 3rd would quickly bring the bass to its goal. But by aiming at 5 in a lower octave, Chopin opens up the space of a 6th. This space is filled in the next four measures with half steps reaching the dominant in 8. This bass descent is identical to the one in the *E-Minor Prelude*.

The top line is embellished with NTs and an inner-voice note. Reduced to diatonic form, the basic polyphony is:

The chords that fill in the polyphony are half-diminished 7ths, dominant 7ths, and diminished 7ths, all dissonant. We see here a particularly clear example of a series of linear chords held together not by root connections or even tonal functions, but by directed motion from one point (III) to another (V).

Another progression is parallel 10ths is found in 142C, which should be reviewed now. The top line is concealed by octave displacement at some points, but the parallel 10ths can be heard guiding the motion from I to V. (See the sketch on page 111.)

BASS PROGRESSION IN 5THS The diatonic progression of descending 5ths in the bass is a commonplace of eighteenth-century music. A chromatic version of the same progression, sometimes coupled with a chromatic top line, may be found in Romantic works. It seems that Mozart knew about this progression, too. 135, the minuet from the *D-Minor Quartet*, moves to V at the outset of the middle section, and in 21–22 seems poised for V^7–I. V^7 resolves not to its I, but to a new dominant. V does not become the temporary tonic we expected, but immediately regains its role of dominant. That dominant is prolonged for the next

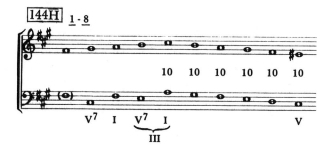

144H 1-8

10 10 10 10 10 10

V^7 I V^7 I   V

III

six measures by a bass motion in 5ths combined with parallel tritones in the two violins. Each chord is the dominant of the next until the bass has moved through all seven notes of the minor scale, bounded by E and B♭. Then the B♭ on which the sequence ends steps down to A to complete the prolonging motion.

In the Mozart example, the chords, heard over the progression in 5ths, are all dominant 7ths and are not embellished. The same progression is heard in 149, once in 33–35 and again in 36–38. Here, the chords include V⁹, and they are embellished with chromatic NTs and SUSs. The level of dissonance is higher in this Romantic piece than in the Classical piece.

With chromaticism obscuring the tonal center to the point where control by any note is in doubt, the song by Alban Berg, 169, clings to the progression in 5ths as one of its last links to tonality. Assuming that the key is E♭, the bass starts with 5 and moves through seven notes a 5th apart, going from B♭ to E. The top line descends chromatically from E (F♭) to B♭, and all the chords are French 6ths in sound but not in function. The sketch below shows the outer voices in 1–4.

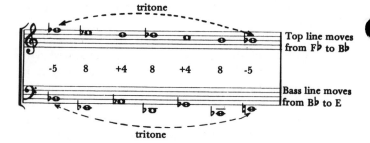

5th motion in 169

At the center of the song, in 11–12, the bass describes 5–1, then descends stepwise, partly chromatically, to 5 (15), and skips to the 1 to pick up the move of the song's opening. The first measures are then recapitulated in shorter note values and redirected toward the concluding E♭. Thus the two motions over descending 5ths in the bass serve as a framework for the entire song and give it most of whatever tonal orientation it has. The descent from E♭ to B♭ in 12–15 conveys little sense of a motion from tonic to dominant because the upper voices do not contribute confirming evidence that we are dealing with chords designed to lead us in that direction.

☞ Worksheet 50

95

Chromatic Motions 4: Modulations and Tonicizations

Chromatic modulations, like diatonic ones, usually depend on pivot chords to link one tonal center with another. The possibilities are almost infinite. A few particularly interesting ones are examined here.

DIMINISHED 7TH Since all inversions of the diminished-7th chord sound alike, this chord may slip in and out of a key with the greatest of ease. Any of its notes may be heard as a leading tone not only to a tonic, but also to any other scale degree that can support a major or minor triad. Given the twelve pitch classes of Western music, there are only three diminished-7th chords with mutually exclusive pitch content. But with the many possibilities of interpretation, the uses to which those three chords can be put is quite impressive. Enharmonic change is frequently necessary. The following is a reading of one diminished-7th chord in twelve keys:

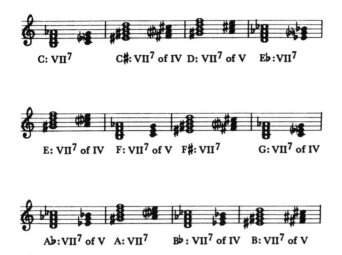

C: VII⁷   C♯: VII⁷ of IV D: VII⁷ of V E♭: VII⁷

E: VII⁷ of IV F: VII⁷ of V F♯: VII⁷ G: VII⁷ of IV

A♭: VII⁷ of V A: VII⁷ B♭: VII⁷ of IV B: VII⁷ of V

But this list does not exhaust the possible interpretations of even the one chord because it deals with I, IV, and V only as goals of the chord. Other triads may be used as well, of course. The list does show ways in which the chord can be used as a pivot, since it can connect any two keys.

[163] is the only chromatic page in a work that is largely diatonic. The reason is to be found in the text. As in many recitatives, no sooner is one tonal center stabilized than a move to another begins. Two moves in this remarkable piece of music use diminished-7th chords as pivots. 5 ends in G minor; 6 utilizes a diminished 7th whose function in G minor is VII⁴₂. But Handel, in 7, looking for a more expressive setting of "broken His heart," interprets that sound as VII⁷ of V in E minor and moves to a cadence on E. Is it E major or the dominant of A? The motion continues without a full stop. 11–13 have all the earmarks of an approach to a cadence in D; we hear the Neapolitan 6th, VII⁷ of V, and I⁶₄–V, but no I. The A in the bass does not fall (or rise) to D. It moves up a half step to A♯, creating a diminished-7th chord whose function in D minor is VII⁴₃, if you hear the bass note as B♭, which is what it would sound like in D minor. But A♯ is taken as the leading tone of B, the diminished 7th as VII⁷ of B minor, and that is the key in which the recitative ends.

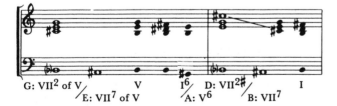

G: VII² of V   V   I⁶   D: VII²♯   I
   E: VII⁷ of V   A: V⁶   B: VII⁷

Again, a slow tempo makes it possible for the abrupt chromatic changes to register on the ear.

And once more we see the need for enharmonic spelling to show the function, which Handel always spells in terms of where he is going, not where he has been.

AUGMENTED 6TH AND DOMINANT 7TH

The German 6th and the dominant 7th sound alike. In isolation, you could not tell one from the other. But chords cannot be studied in isolation. In a musical context, the two function quite differently. A♭–C–E♭–G♭ is V⁷ of D♭, while A♭–C–E♭–F♯ (enharmonic change again) is the German 6th of C. Since the chord may be interpreted in two ways, it is potentially a pivot chord, which may move the tonal center by a half step to a remote key.

The lyric second phrase of the Franck symphony, [166], comes to a cadence on V⁷ in 8 . Taking advantage of the two possible interpretations of that sound, Franck resolves it as an augmented 6th, to I⁶₄ of D♭. The move constitutes a fresh start for a phrase.

The play of dominant-7th and German-6th chords may be seen in [164]. The key is A minor. The oboe melody is built on 3rds, rising to a high point on F. The inner voice of the first violins has been hinting at F since 208 . So that when the melodic high point F is reached and the cellos join in with the A that has been prolonged since the beginning of the phrase, we get a strong sense of the augmented 6th of A minor. But at the same time, the violas play not D♯, but E♭. This is a visual clue to what is about to happen; the listener has no warning. The augmented 6th is interpreted as the dominant of the Neapolitan chord, which follows in root position. Rapid chromatic moves (in slow tempo) steer the tonal direction through B♭ minor to its VI, then its V, at the start of 218 . The V⁷ of B♭ minor then changes back into the augmented 6th of A minor, as the enharmonic change in the first-violin part of 218 and 219 shows. In retrospect, we realize that B♭ was tonicized in the middle of the phrase, the augmented 6th–V⁷ switch being the point of entry and the point of return as well. Mode mixture added to the chromaticism, too, for what Schubert used was not simply the Neapolitan 6th of A minor, which is B♭ major, but its parallel minor. In a most imaginative way Schubert has played with the possibilities of resolving the same dissonant chord in two different ways—first, to move out of A minor, then to move back into it.

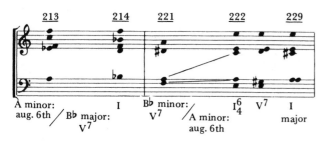

A minor: / I   Bb minor: / I$_4^6$ V^7 I
aug. 6th / Bb major: V^7 / A minor: major
V^7 aug. 6th

In Chopin's *G-Minor Prelude*, 144G, there is a headlong rush in the first sixteen-measure unit to an open-ended move through IV, tonicized briefly in 15–16 with I$_4^6$–augmented 6th. It is the merest suggestion of a tonicization and leaves the tonal direction of the phrase ending in doubt. The bass drives on to Db. 17 starts with a *ff* Db-major triad. What is Db doing in G minor? As always, the meaning of a chord depends on its context. Where did the Db triad come from? The augmented 6th of 16, respelled with a Gb in place of F#, proves to have been a dominant 7th, the dominant of Db. The Db triad, in turn, becomes the IV of a progression tonicizing the Neapolitan 6th: IV–V–I

of Neapolitan 6th.

The open-ended motion into 16 and beyond kept the continuity going; the sudden appearance (al-

beit prepared) of Db gives the second large phrase of the piece a fresh impetus.

From 144G

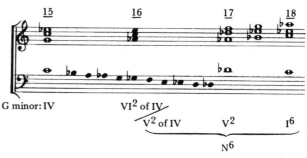

G minor: IV   VI^2 of IV /
                     V^2 of IV   V^2 I^6
                          N^6

HALF-DIMINISHED 7TH   As a pivot chord, the half-diminished 7th is less often used than any of the other chromatic chords studied. Nevertheless, it is susceptible to many interpretations. Probably the most celebrated use of the chord is in Wagner's *Tristan*. Associated with the ideas of love and death that permeate the opera, the chord almost achieves the status of a motive. Six of the ways in which Wagner interpreted the half-diminished 7th are listed on page 74.

96

Mode Mixture 2: Motions in 3rds

As the minor mode penetrated increasingly into major-mode music, motions from 1 to 3 attracted the interest of composers. Both the use of the minor mode's III in the major, and the possibility of using major triads on III and VI in the major mode appealed to the musicians who were searching for the new tonal relationships. In the first

movement of Beethoven's *Piano Sonata* Op. 53, the tonal direction of the bridge is not from I to V but from I to III. Although the piece is in C major, the key of the second theme is E major. In the recapitulation, the same theme begins in A major. Other works of Beethoven, Schubert, and Schumann show similar tendencies.

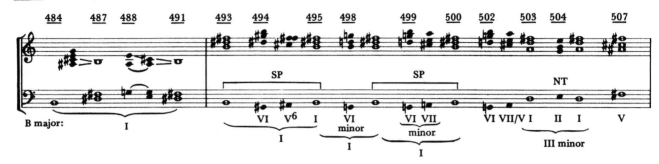

I–III–V (PARALLEL MINOR'S III) The motion I–III–V–I is common in the minor, much less so in the major. The Reicha *Scherzo in G Major*, 137, is an unusual example in major of modulation to a cadence in III. Mode mixture makes available the use of the parallel minor's III in a major piece. This move is the basis of the tonal structure of 130E. The first eight-measure phrase may be heard as a harmonic prolongation of F major. In the middle of the second phrase, the flavor changes from major to minor, and a move to III is confirmed with a cadence. The third phrase prolongs A♭. Then V⁷ leads the fourth phrase from III to V and I. More harmonic prolongation brings the waltz to its conclusion.

165B is a short section that serves as a link between the end of the preceding allegro and the calm last pages of the overture. The melody associated with the love of Romeo and Juliet, first heard as in 165A, now sounds distorted. Below it, a tonic pedal provides stability. Starting in 493 there is a hymnlike texture, with block chords in the winds. The first five measures are built on a contrapuntal prolongation of I. The bass has a SP; the top line keeps within the tonic triad. The chord progression is I–VI–V–I. The parallel 5ths in the clarinets have been part of the phrase since the beginning of the piece, suggestive of the chanting of Friar Laurence's colleagues. Starting with the upbeat to 498, the next move prolongs I in another way, using the minor version of VI as an alternative to the major VI and connecting it to I with the passing chord VII minor in 499. The same move seems to start again. But at the point where VII had stepped back to I, in 502, it changes function. Tchaikovsky interprets the A-major sound as dominant of III minor and resolves it to that chord in 503. D major is then prolonged briefly with a neighbor chord. Very softly, III minor is arpeggiated into a higher register and then is followed by V and a crescendo that will culminate in I. The tonal plan is the same as in

the Schubert waltz 130E, but the approach to the minor's III by way of its own dominant is an original and striking touch.

ANOTHER USE OF III MINOR In 141, Brahms takes good advantage of the rich color that the minor's III in a major context has to offer without following the same tonal plan as the previous examples. 25 ends the third phrase of the movement with the dominant of B minor. In contrast to the dense texture of the first phrases, the clarinet plays a two-measure solo interlude, prolonging the dominant. But the F♯ that starts 27 is not heard as the root of V or even as the fifth of I. Instead it is heard as the third of a D-major triad, III minor in B major.

The phrase that starts so beautifully with the sound of III minor might easily find its way back to V–I. But after having moved to the D-major sound so quickly, Brahms takes his time in returning. Three $\frac{6}{3}$-position triads are heard in succession—on D major, C major, and finally B minor. They are connected with V² chords, so that in 30 the dominant of B minor is followed by the tonic. But both are in inversion, the phrase is still flowing, and the return to the tonic is not emphasized. In 31, the I⁶ leads into an augmented 6th, which functions as a neighbor chord to the tonic that begins the next phrase in 32. No strong dominant has been heard, yet the return to B minor from VI minor is smooth and convincing.

Tonal movement of 141, 27–32

117

III BECOMES A MAJOR TRIAD In another version of I–III–V–I, also in the major mode, the diatonic minor III is replaced by a major triad. This is a chromatic chord since it includes one note that is not diatonic. Such a move may involve only a few chords in a progression. But it may also be part of the tonal plan of a section or of an entire piece.

The Chopin prelude 144D includes both III minor and the major version of III. They have different functions in the piece. The major III is the goal of motion for the second phrase. III minor is a detail in the third phrase, part of a motion from I to V. To see the role of each, review the sketch on page 80. The two usages are shown below.

Two III chords in 144D

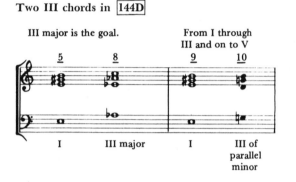

III major is the goal. | From I through III and on to V

I   III major   I   III of parallel minor

VI AND III MINOR BECOME MINOR TRIADS Most frequently it is the minor mode that invades the major to produce the chromaticism characteristic of mixture. But there is mixture in the minor, and it can go beyond the leading tone and the Picardy 3rd. One example is in the short piano piece by Liszt, 149, in C♯ minor. Mixture operates both in the detail and in the tonal structure. In the very first progression, I–VI–II⁷–V⁹–I, the diatonic major triad VI is replaced by a minor triad. In the repetition of the phrase this VI/IV minor in a modulation to E, which would normally be major. But the expected G♯ never materializes. G♮ is heard instead at the upbeat to 9. In E minor, VI becomes a minor triad again. The same modulation brings the tonal center to E minor's III in the form of G minor. Two moves of a minor 3rd have brought the piece to an intermediary tonic that is a tritone from the starting point. Then the soprano guides the motion back to V to conclude the first half of the piece.

DIVISION OF THE OCTAVE IN 3RDS Had Liszt continued the motion in minor 3rds, his

piece would have regained the tonic in two more moves. The Wagner excerpt 167A does follow through a motion in minor 3rds until it reaches the tonic again. Thus the octave is divided symmetrically into minor 3rds. Each triad along the way is tonicized just long enough to create some degree of stability. Then it is undermined either by a change in mode or by a shift to another triad that points to the next stop in the trip. The lack of any strong punctuation and the continuous nature of the accompaniment suggest that the eight measures constitute one long phrase with a single tonal movement. The sketch below shows the main chords and their connections.

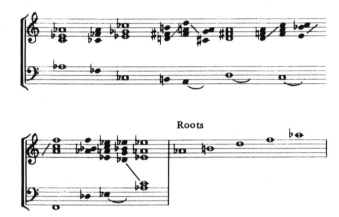

Roots

The same progression, in the same key, begins the *Liebestod*, 168. Comparison of the two passages shows how far Wagner had developed the techniques of chromaticism in a decade. The intermediary goals represented by root-position triads in *Lohengrin* are dissonant $\frac{6}{4}$-position triads in *Tristan*. The result is that in the latter, the dissonance is almost continuous. In the *Lohengrin* excerpt the phrase corresponds to the motion through the octave, both agreeing on eight measures duration. In the *Liebestod* the motion continues beyond the octave, and the phrase surges on beyond the eight-measure format.

168: Polyphony reduced to a single register

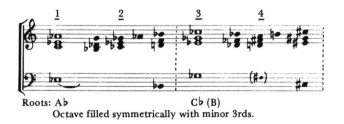

Roots: A♭   C♭ (B)
Octave filled symmetrically with minor 3rds.

Both the *Lohengrin* and *Tristan* examples divide the octave equally into minor 3rds. An unusual instance of dividing the octave into major 3rds is also found in the music of *Die Walküre*, 167B.

The excerpt as a whole is in E major. An opening thought ends on V⁷; in 9. The next measures move into E minor, ending in 16 on V; of VI. Starting from this deliberately veiled point, the motion through the octave begins. Each two measures brings a new major triad whose root is a major 3rd lower (minor 6th higher!) than the previous one.

167B : Polyphony

Examining the polyphony, we find contrary motion. A chromatic soprano line descends against a rising bass line. The soprano simply fills in all the half steps in each major-3rd descent. The bass does not literally move down in major 3rds; it rises in minor 6ths. Its line is a combination of skips and steps in contrast to the stepwise motion of the so-

prano. The contrary motion brings the outer voices together in the middle register: in 17 , they are three octaves and a 3rd apart; by the end of 24 they are but an octave and a half apart. As for the linear chords that evolve by means of the polyphonic process, they are more consonant than dissonant. Their activity and color comes from the unexpected ways in which they are juxtaposed rather than from their own qualities.

Summary project in tonal composition

In Romantic style, write a ternary piano piece or a song. Include as much as you can of the chromatic chord vocabulary. Contrasts between sections should be made in a number of ways, which should be planned in advance. If you set a poem, before writing down any music study it carefully to determine its character, any musical shape that might be suggested by the text, and important details that call for musical expression.

For further study

As always, familiarity with a large amount of music is essential to your development as a musician. Knowledge of specific works can be augmented with the study of writings by theorists. A few suggestions follow.

Richard Goldman's *Harmony in Western Music* contains many insights about chromaticism and tonality, particularly in reference to the music of Wagner.

A detailed analysis of the tonal structure of the prelude to *Tristan*, by William Mitchell, is in *The Music Forum*, I.

The last three chapters of Walter Piston's *Harmony* deal with some of the issues taken up in the present book, but from a somewhat different point of view.

Chromatic excerpts from the music of Beethoven, Schubert, Chopin, Wagner, Fauré, and Scriabin are analyzed in the concluding section of Salzer and Schachter's *Counterpoint in Composition*.

97

Toward Continuous Dissonance

An overview of the music we have studied shows a gradual movement from a consonant vocabulary to a dissonant one. Renaissance music had a limited chord vocabulary, almost entirely consonant. Those stable sounds were embellished and connected with single dissonant tones, occasionally even more than one, all clearly dependent on consonances for their meaning. These same processes led to the growth of dissonant chords in the period we call Baroque. In time, human hearing came to accept simple dissonant chords, such as V^7, as independent sounds, which could themselves be elaborated with more powerful dissonances. Moreover, the time scale in which the interplay of dissonance and consonance functioned became larger. It was necessary for Haydn to resolve each dissonance almost immediately, as the quartet movements [147] show. But in the Chopin *Preludes,* the resolution of a dissonance may be delayed considerably. In the *E-Minor Prelude,* even the few consonances that are used are not the most stable. The single exception is the final consonance, which is why it is the last. Most of the piece is made of dissonant chords.

The restlessness and striving for the ideal that marks the aesthetic of Romanticism found expression in a musical vocabulary that was active and dissonant. The *Liebestod,* [168], contains hardly a consonant sound from beginning to end. The I_4^6 chord, considered a strong dissonance in the context of earlier music, is now, by contrast, almost stable. And after I_4^6–V^7 there is almost anything but I. Our observation that any chord may be heard after the dominant is as true here as in any other music. The final tonic, here, too, takes on greater stability because it is one of the few such sounds in the piece.

By the first decade of the twentieth century, consonance had lost its pre-eminent place on the musical scene, and Schoenberg was to speak of the "emancipation of the dissonance." By this he meant that dissonance was freed from the necessity of resolving to consonance. Such a statement announces the existence of a musical language in which there are no completely stable sounds, but rather a range of unstable sounds. A piece such as Berg's song, [169], has but few vestiges of tonality, as we shall see on page 122; it is no coincidence that there is not one completely stable sound in the piece, even the last tonic being clouded with a tritone and a 7th.

ELISION How does one dissonant chord resolve to another? By skipping a step; the consonant chord which would have come between two dissonant ones is omitted or partially incorporated in the dissonance. To discover the short cut, mentally restore the missing chord. The simplest example has one dominant 7th resolving to another. The sketch below shows the chords of [135], 22–27, with the elided notes restored. Compare the sketch with the music and observe the difference between the alternation of dissonance and consonance in the sketch with the continuous dissonance of the piece.

☞ Worksheet 51

120

98

The Decline of Tonality as a Unifying Force

When we listen to the song by Hugo Wolf, 156, the constant dissonance and chromaticism makes the tonality puzzling. When we know the song better, we may ask the questions: What is it about the piece that makes the center of tonality so difficult to identify? What role does the notion of key center play in this music?

Anyone whose only clue to the key of a piece is the key signature is likely to be mystified, for the two flats mean very little. The piece starts in Ab and ends on a D-major triad. The search for prolonged chords is not very rewarding for the music seems to be moving constantly from one point to another. Two things make the tonal structure problematical: the rapid rate of chromatic chord change and the absence of strong dominant functions. We know that the piece is coming to an end when, starting in 53, D is finally prolonged and the first descent to the lower register occurs.

Indeed, one of the most effective means of expression in the piece is chord change. The melody, mostly shared by piano and voice, is actually the top line of a chord progression rather than an independent tune. Try singing the voice part without its supporting chords. The melody hardly survives by itself, unlike most of Schubert's or Brahms's melodies. In the absence of textural and registral change, the composer has concentrated on the way in which one chord succeeds another.

Considering the song as a whole, Wolf has aimed for the most expressive effect in each detail, sacrificing tonal unity in the process. This is not a value judgment. But it does mean that tonality is losing its central position as the unifying force in music. What can take its place? What do we hear? The melody is held together by a three-note motive. The piano plays it in the first measure, and from then on it is varied and developed in many ways, always remaining in our consciousness. In this song, to a certain extent, motivic unity has partially replaced tonal unity.

Even when tonal centers are more prolonged, movement through many tonicized points weakens the overall tonal unity. We have seen how the song 157 is made of short fragments, each of which is part of a conversation that leads to a gripping climax. As the mood swings wildly back and forth, the keys do the same. F♯ major and minor, A major and minor—all seem equally strong. Tonal unity is put in the background as the composer projects a series of arresting moments.

As in the Wolf song, the dominant does not play a very large role. All kinds of neighbor and passing chords are used to provide the dissonant (and consonant) chord vocabulary used to convey the emotions of the miniature drama. And although the dominant is hardly heard, the tonic is prolonged time after time—but now one tonic, now another. Within those prolongations, chord change is used as an important means of expression, coloring the vocal line and providing a great deal of the musical substance of the song. The melody is not a tune that has a life of its own. It grows out of speech, and the musical line is a heightened version of the poem as it would be declaimed aloud. No one musical motive predominates, but the "Lullaby" melodic fragment, always in A minor, takes on the character of a motive or perhaps a refrain; it is a unifying element in the song.

In studying the Wolf song 156 we found that motivic organization had taken over some of the role of providing musical coherence previously assumed by tonal structure. The music moved rapidly from one tonal area to another, those areas connected by measures in which no clear key could be ascertained. Another piece in the tradition of the German lied is 169, written in the first years of the twentieth century.

What unifies this piece? The tonal direction which we have found in earlier pieces? There are but few vestigial remnants. Yet we sense that the piece does have unity and coherence. What factors create that sense? One thing that strikes the ear is that many of the sounds seem to have something in common. There are many types of chords in the piece, but one interval stands out from the

121

others. The major 3rd is everywhere. The French-6th chords of the first and last phrases are made of two major 3rds a whole step apart. The voice line soon fills in the interval of the major 3rd with whole steps. As simultaneous sound and as succession, the interval of the major 3rd (and its inversion) is the basic building block. The sketch below shows the uses of that interval in the first three measures.

Major 3rds (and minor 6ths) in the first three measures of 169

The filled-in 3rd in the voice part of 2 is picked up by the piano in 4 . This is turned into a motive, the main idea of the piano interlude, 5–8 . There are other motives as well, chiefly the de-scending line of the voice in 9 , which is taken up by the piano in the next measure, and again in 12 and 15 . But the major 3rd continues to play a vital role in the piece. We begin to think that the interval itself has an important status, independent of chord or motive—all of which suggests that when we look at music whose key center is not clear or strong, we would do well to see whether there is an interval or a group of intervals on which the piece is built in some way. It is no accident that "interval music" is another way of describing non-tonal music.

☞ Worksheet 52

Project in tonal composition

Write a short song for voice and piano. Study the poem very carefully before writing any music. Suggestion: recite the first line of the poem aloud and invent a motive based on the rhythmic features of the poem.

PART SIXTEEN
THE EXTENSION OF TRADITIONAL TONALITY

99

Background

With tonal chromaticism pushed to its limits, composers found it impossible simply to continue the evolution that had begun in the Middle Ages. Since the last decade of the nineteenth century, music has faced a crisis that has not been entirely resolved to this day. Different composers have responded to the issues in different ways. If we look at the music of the first fifteen years of the twentieth century we find a growing diversity of styles and languages, suggesting that no one clear direction was accepted by all. The main trends may be defined, but it must be understood that they overlapped and that other tendencies were in the air at the same time. And there are composers who don't fit into any category at all.

To take a broad view of the 1900–25 musical picture, we may say that one group of composers (Schoenberg, Berg, Webern, Varèse) took chro-

maticism as their guiding force, with the consequence that tonality ceased to exist in their music. Other composers (Ravel, Debussy, Bartók, Stravinsky, Hindemith) reinterpreted and, in a sense, *extended tonality* at the expense of chromaticism. The latter group influenced a number of American composers in the period between the two world wars (Copland, Schuman, Harris, Thomson), while other Americans (Sessions, Babbitt, Perle, Carter, Weisgall) have found starting points in the early atonalists.

To begin this study, we ask how the "new" approach to tonality differs from the "old" approach. Most obviously, the dominant function begins to disappear, enduring longest in the works of Ravel and Poulenc. This means that harmonic progression and harmonic prolongation can no longer be relied on for musical punctuation. Other, more

Picasso and Stravinsky: a drawing by Jean Cocteau. Reproduced with the permission of Farrar, Straus & Giroux, Inc. from *Stravinsky in the Theatre*, edited by Minna Lederman, © 1949 by the Dance Index-Ballet Caravan, Inc.

linear impulses take their place. How, then, is tonality established? This question and others that are generated from it are discussed in subsequent sections. We shall look for the ways in which tonal coherence is achieved, and we shall see how phrase structure and form are projected in works using extended tonality.

100

Tonal Structure 1

HOW IS THE KEY ESTABLISHED? We may begin with two observations about 170–179. First, tonal centers are usually quite clear, more so than in some late nineteenth-century music. Second, the dominant function exists only in the earlier of these works—i.e., 170–172—and even in 170–172 it is handled in a somewhat different manner than in previously discussed works.

One of the simplest ways of defining a key is by means of a pedal note. The piano piece 171 relies heavily on that technique. C♯ is heard in one register or another for most of the first twenty-eight measures, relieved only by G♯ in 15–16. F♯ sounds from 29–36. Then A gains control, 37–59; C♯ returns in 60–66; and the tonic, F♯, is in the bass in 67–76. Relatively few measures of the piece are without a pedal note. Chord changes of great diversity are heard over the pedal notes, giving a special mixture of stable and unstable elements that is one of the characteristics of Debussy's language.

Pedal notes or chords used as pedals are in the background of the entire piece 174B. After the opening B major, a D-minor triad is heard with the B, the tonic, included. In 28, a G-major chord sounds; but at the end of 30, B major returns and remains until the end. The sustained triads have quite a different tone color from the melodies since the chords are played as harmonics.

Another simple way of establishing a tonal center and gaining coherence is by repeating a short figure or motive literally. This technique is known as *ostinato*. One example is in 173. On the third line the C-major chord marked *pp* seems to form a group with the subsequent chords, but actually the unit that comprises the ostinato begins with the next sound. Four chords are repeated literally.

The ostinato almost completes four statements, but the final chord is varied. Each of the four chords has tonal implications, although none of them agrees. Indeed, the piece has strong suggestions of many keys, but none organizes the whole. The beginning of the song, the ostinato, and the end all feature the note E; and if any tone is the center, it is E.

A different kind of ostinato organizes parts of 174C. The left hand begins with a chord built on two 4ths and a neighbor chord, both arpeggiated. The one-measure figure establishes G as center, a G that has more in common with the Mixolydian mode than with either G major or G minor. As long as the figure is used as an ostinato, the tonal center is G. The ostinato is over by 15, when changes are introduced. In this piece, the ostinato functions as a tonic prolongation.

175, 56–63, is an example of one of several ostinatos in *The Rite of Spring*. The lower part reiterates four notes, the two lowest of which define B as tonic by means of a 5th. The other two notes are neighbors. In the upper part, B major-minor is the framework of a progression within which a series of linear chords unfolds.

As long as music is tonal, the interval of a perfect 5th will probably have an important role to play—i.e., as long as the 5th is the interval on which musical structure is based, tonality may continue to operate. The 5th that defines the key is as clear in 170 – 172 as in music of earlier centuries. One reason that the tonality of 173 is so difficult to pin down is the absence of a 5th over what seems to be the tonic note, E. Each of the Bartók pieces, 174, has a tonal center of one kind or another. 174A and 174E are the clearest tonally because the 5th is most readily apparent. The section of 175 with the strongest sense of key is the very opening, where the 5th in the bass tells us that **D** is the tonic. Other sections are less specific in their tonal centers, but the section built on an ostinato, starting in 56, is firmly anchored in B by the 5th in the lowest part. The music of 177 relies heavily on the 5th as melodic interval and as simultaneity to establish its various tonal centers. Here, the 5ths are often replaced by 4ths. But the dissonant quality of that interval has been overpowered by stonger dissonances, and the 4th is treated virtually as a consonance. Again, whether a sound functions as a dissonance or a consonance depends on the context; we continue to study sounds in operation, not in isolation. The same remarks apply to 179, which sounds tonal and yet is hard to pin down in any key. What we have here is a constant shift of tonal centers, in which the 5th (and 4th) can play an important role.

101

Tonal Structure 2

If there is a center of tonality in a piece, we should be able to find motion of one kind or another around that center—this is to say, the tonic is prolonged. If there is a dominant, that is probably prolonged, too. The question is, as always, how?

The early Debussy song 170 begins with a dominant prolongation eight measures long. The chord is V⁹; the first measure elaborates it with G♯ as a N͞T to F♯. In 7–8, the main chord is elaborated again, this time with a linear chord that looks like V⁷ of VI but that has no relation to VI. This is an early example of a technique Debussy was to use often—a chord with which we are familiar in a certain context is used out of context as an elaborative sound for its own value as color. V⁹ does resolve to I, in 9.

172 also opens with a dominant prolongation that is very beautifully elaborated. The first chord is the dominant of the dominant, in a form that includes both a diminished and an augmented 5th plus a minor 9th. The dominant itself is V⁹. Neighbor chords continue the embellishment of V⁹ in 4, expanding it in time. Then, in an imaginative move, the E♯–B♯ of 4 turns into F–C in 5 and frames an F-minor triad that is a colorful detail within the large dominant prolongation. In 7, the F resumes its role as E♯ but not its spelling. By the end of 9, F♯ is reinstated, the neighbor note E♯ having held sway for almost four measures within the dominant prolongation.

We have already seen how, in 174C, the left hand establishes and prolongs the tonic G with its ostinato. At the same time, the right hand is in a different key. A pentatonic scale, corresponding to the black notes on the piano, is prolonged without any one tone emerging as center. In 15, a new motion begins, seen most clearly in the lowest voice of the left hand. The octave G–G is filled chromatically. The figure heard in the first measures of the piece is transposed down as the bass descends. The completion of the octave is heard only at the beginning of 24, which starts the second section of the piece. 1–24 may be viewed as a tonic prolongation in two moves. The first runs to the downbeat of 15, the second to 24 and on.

One of the few slow sections of *The Rite of Spring* is illustrated in 175. The seeming immobility of the music stems in part from the remarkable

: Octave displacement in the melody

The polyphonic melody

way in which the first sonority is maintained for fourteen measures. The lowest parts prolong **D minor** by sustaining it in alternation with a very few neighbor chords. The upper parts play D's two chromatic neighbor triads, E♭ (D♯) and C♯. To these, A♯ minor and E minor are added in <u>2</u>. Only very gradually are other triads added to the vocabulary of the piece.

Debussy showed composers how to use a chord for its own sonority without regard for its original tonal context. In <u>24</u>, Stravinsky uses that technique, prolonging what would have once been thought of as a V² in E♭ major. There is no hint of E♭ major in the piece. The melody is in the nature of a *cantus firmus*, which, having just been heard, is now repeated in a different setting. The linear chords that are evolved in <u>24–26</u> are dominant 7ths and half-diminished 7ths major. The line that runs against the progression is simply one of the notes of the prolonged chord, F, and its upper neighbor, sounded in several registers so as to cross the chordal motion. After one measure, which anticipates the next thought, the first two chords of <u>24</u> are heard in reverse order, but with the addition of F's neighbor note, G♭. Finally, the section ends with an open-ended version of <u>24–26</u>, transposed half a step higher. This means that the G♭, now F♯, is the note on which the neighbor motion in eighth notes is based. The linear chords are now a dominant 7th and a minor triad.

<u>176</u> begins with a polyphonic melody that serves, initially, to prolong C minor and then moves to G. There is an affinity, readily observed, between this melody and the opening of Bach's *Art of Fugue*. The melody may be thought of as two

3rds with the leading tone transposed up an octave (see above).

Since the first four notes of the melody are used repeatedly in the movement, their stable quality leads to a tonic prolongation at each repetition. Thus E♭ minor is stabilized at the choral entrance in <u>29</u> and again for a moment in <u>47</u>; B♭ minor is prolonged in <u>61</u>; G minor in <u>66</u> and again in <u>71</u>; other scale degrees fleetingly in the next measures; and E♭ minor-major from <u>84</u> to the end.

Among the several prolonging motions in <u>177</u> we may take a closer look at two. The opening defines B♭, as we have seen, with its emphasis on the 5th. At the same time we should observe the bass line, which fills a descending octave with a B♭-minor scale. Major and minor modes are mixed in the right-hand part; tonality is clear. The octave descent seems to start again in <u>5</u> as the flute enters; but that is a false start, and the second full descent runs through <u>7–8</u>. The end of the prolonging motion does not mark the end of the phrase, as it did in <u>4</u>, and the bass line runs through the B♭ and on toward the next tonal center.

This proves to be A, prolonged contrapuntally by means of oblique motion. The top line prolongs E, while two lower voices in 3rds move away from the tonic sonority, then back to it, filling a 3rd.

<u>177</u>: **Prolongation of A,** <u>18–21</u>

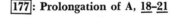
oblique motion

102

Vocabulary

While the rich chord vocabulary of the nineteenth century did not disappear overnight, composers in the early years of the twentieth century found some of the sounds they had inherited far more useful than others. Chords involved in the dominant function and/or the leading-tone tendency fell out of favor before long. Either they were used without regard for their original function or combined with other sounds. The V^9 was much favored by French composers, less by others. The same is true of the half-diminished 7th. The major-7th chord was treated as a consonance by the French composers, as illustrated in 170, 11 .

The major-minor dominant-7th chord has already been mentioned in 175. A version of it appears in 34 , in the lower part. The 5th of the chord is diminished, so that F♭ is heard instead of the diatonic F. That note is reinstated in 38 , where the chord has its normal form.

Added-note chords are triads to which a PT or NT has become attached. They are sounds that would have once been considered dissonant, but that seem relatively consonant in the present context. In 170, 20 , we find the best known of those chords, the added 6th. C♯ is part of the chord, and the sound is not an inversion of the VI chord. From this we learn that all chords do not have to be built in 3rds, for here is one that is made by adding a 2nd to a triad. Another example, also by Debussy, is 171, 38 . From the bass up, there is a 5th, A–E, to which a 2nd and a 4th are added above the root, A. The resulting chord functions as a tonic, and the main note is clearly A, but the mode is undetermined.

A luminous chord ends the ·movement of *Symphony of Psalms*, 176, 88 . The root is E♭, the triad major. To that are added both a 6th and a 2nd. Against the chord, played by the winds, the chorus sings a unison E♭.

In a similar way, added-note chords are used in 52, which should be reviewed at this point. Other aspects of that piece, including the tonal structure, should be more apparent now than when the piece was first discussed.

Since the number of linear chords that can be generated is very great, we have limited this discussion to the types most frequently encountered. A close study of 170–179 will reveal any number of other sounds, all linear in origin. It is worthwhile to play slowly through 179, observing how the sonorities begin with a unison, increase to two parts, then to three, and finally to four. The sounds are mostly diatonic, and the chord types can be described in familiar terms.

Since it is not necessary to build chords only in 3rds, it would seem that many intervals could be used for the purpose. In fact, the only interval that has been used widely to build chords is the 4th. The origin of the sound in an unresolved dissonance is not hard to find.

Origins of the 4th chord

Origin aside, the chord is used as a linear sound in any number of pieces. We have already seen it as a tonic sonority in 171, 38 , where it may be thought of as an inversion of B–E–A–D. The three-note chord that begins 172, 17 , is part of the prolongation of V^9. We also saw how a 4th chord is the tonic sonority in 174C, and how it is transposed to various levels as the piece runs its course. A particularly beautiful use of the chord is in 176, 52 , where C–F–B♭–E♭–A♭ is so arranged that B♭ is in the bass, suggesting the dominant of E♭. Perhaps the chord grows out of the 4th that begins the chorus' melody, the interval that is presented in close imitation at this point.

The composer most often associated with 4th chords is Hindemith. The pages of 177 are filled with such sounds. The melody begins with a 4th, a 2nd, and a 4th, and those intervals make up a good part of the vocabulary of the piece. When triads appear, they are a fresh sound and quite effective.

Ravel's chord vocabulary has a flavor of its own, spiced by 7ths and 9ths. The following progression from the first of the *Valses nobles et sentimentales* is an extended prolongation of the dominant of G. The bass moves in 5ths. Chord types are indicated below.

Discussion of chord vocabulary does not account for all the new sounds in the group of works we are studying. Scales, too, are an important element. The traditional designations of major and minor no longer constitute an adequate frame of reference. For one thing, we realize that the mode mixture we saw with increasing frequency in nineteenth-century music had reached a point in some works of Bartók and Hindemith where we must speak of a major-minor mode. The same is true of the Schuman piece, 179, where a sense of key is always present, but where mode shifts or is indeterminate.

Another scale that came into use in the early years of the twentieth century is the *whole-tone scale*. A notational problem arises with the use of this scale. It is hard to think of D♯–F as a whole tone—or, as we more often say, a whole step. But it is the enharmonic equivalent of a whole step and must serve the purpose. 171 illustrates how the whole-tone scale was used in the music of Debussy, the composer whose name is most often associated with it. Like the pentatonic scale, which corre-

sponds to the black keys of the piano, the whole-tone scale has no leading tone. Indeed, since the scale is generated by a single interval, there is no way to distinguish one scale degree's function from another. The result is that whatever order exists in music built on this scale must be imposed on it since it does not grow out of the structure of the scale. 171, 23–28, has tonal focus because one note, C♯, is repeated in a rhythm that has already been impressed upon the listener's mind as an important feature of the piece. And C♯ itself, from the first measure, has already been established as a focal note.

Looking for the "harmony" in those six measures of Debussy might be a perplexing task until one realizes that any notes of the whole-tone scale may be heard together with any other notes. The scale is the chord. Thus there is no sense of progression in the pitches, although there is in the rhythm. A single sonority, the six notes of the whole-tone scale, is prolonged for the entire passage.

For further study

Examine carefully the piano prelude *Voiles*, by Debussy. The first and third sections use the whole-tone scale. What is heard in the middle section? Aside from the different scales, what means does the composer use to differentiate the sections of the piece?

V^9 · major-minor V^7 · V^7 with major and minor 7th · minor 7th · major-minor V^7 · V^7 with major and minor 7th · minor 7th · major-minor V^7 · V^7 with major and minor 7th · minor 7th · major-minor V^7 with flat 5th · the same · neighbors to V^7 · I

103

Chord as Line

We have long known that two lines in parallel 5ths or octaves tend to be a reflection of each other. They lack the independence that is aesthetically demanded in traditional tonality, and they may also interfere with the sense of key. What, then, are we to make of a passage such as [171], 17–20 ?

There is no question that the parallelism eliminates the independence of the parts. The four notes of the right hand are, therefore, not four real parts. They are one part. The notes in the left hand with stems up are included in that part. Thus, in spite of the fact that there are seven notes heard at once, there are but two parts or lines. One is the parallel chord group, the other the pedal C♯.

Within the chord group, there is no individuality of line, for the parallel motion has eliminated that. But the chord is treated as if it were a line—a line thickened out into more than one register, yet still a single line. This technique was anticipated in the late nineteenth century, but Debussy was the first to use it as a standard procedure. Ravel, Bartók, and Stravinsky, among others, saw the possibilities of the technique and put it to their own uses.

Further examples within [171] show additional ways in which a chord is used in a linear way. The move that started in 17 begins again in 29 , transposed up a 4th. Now it becomes part of a small arch, whose melodic beginning is the F♯ of 29 and whose end is the F♯ of 35–36 . For four measures the chords are all V⁷—or what used to be V⁷ when it had a dominant function. When the line reaches its peak in 33 , the chord type changes to major and minor triads with one augmented triad in 34 . At the same time, the texture expands to three voices: the stream of chords, the familiar rhythmic figure, and the pedal note.

Yet another instance of parallel chords begins in 78 . This is a simple use of major and minor triads, diatonic chords in F♯ major. More chromatic connections are heard in 109–112 , where the triads are arpeggiated but nonetheless parallel. In effect, this passage is in one part.

A striking use of a dominant-7th chord in a linear way is in [172], 18 . The right hand arrives at the V⁹ chord, missing only the B which the left hand had in the previous measure. But the left hand embellishes the B and the chord built on it with a neighbor chord, a dominant 7th built on B♭. The clash of the two neighbor chords is softened only slightly by the G♯ in the right hand, a NT to the F♯. The resolution of all dissonant elements but the 7th and 9th of the dominant leads to the next phrase.

Since Bartók used a root-position triad *sff* to start the harmonics ringing in [174B], the eventual arrival of a line made of a succession of such triads seems quite natural. But it comes only gradually. Another strong triad, D minor, starts the second harmonic chord in 12 ; two more chords are pounded out in 19 ; the two-chord group is heard again in 24 ; 29–30 bring the triad to the upper register; and the march of parallel triads becomes the main element from 31 on. Many of these triads clash with the held sounds, creating much of the piece's tension. The end is something of a question, as the D-minor 7th chord reiterates its disagreement with the sustained B-major triad.

The parallel minor triads of the opening of [175] form one strand in a three-part texture. Initially, there are but two triads a step apart, alternating. They are E♭ minor and C♯ minor, with enharmonic spelling disguising the identity of the first chord. At the end of the second measure, two more chords are added—A♯ minor and E minor. The stream of triads begins to move registrally in 4 , but no new chords are added, and the two heard at the end of 2 only reappear in 6 . 7 adds an F-minor triad and an A-minor triad. At the end of 11 , a G-minor triad and a G♯-minor triad connect two previously heard sounds, then disappear for several measures. Keeping to the practice of introducing new triads in pairs, Stravinsky introduces C minor and F♯ minor in <u>17</u> , but D minor appears alone in <u>19</u> , and B minor in <u>20</u> . At this point all twelve different minor triads are in circulation. In any given measure, however, the composer uses as few different triads as possible, always in parallel motion.

For study

Review ☐53. How many real parts are there? What kind of motion do you hear between those parts? Is there one tonal center that controls the **entire** excerpt?

Review ☐54. How are parallel triads used in this piece? What is the overall tonal center?

104

Tonal Structure 3

We now go beyond individual prolonging motions, which we found to be similar in principle to those of earlier music, to the tonal structure of an entire piece. A close look at the early Debussy song ☐170 (see below) reveals a language that still **relies** on the tonic-dominant polarity of the nineteenth century, but pushes the older practice into new paths.

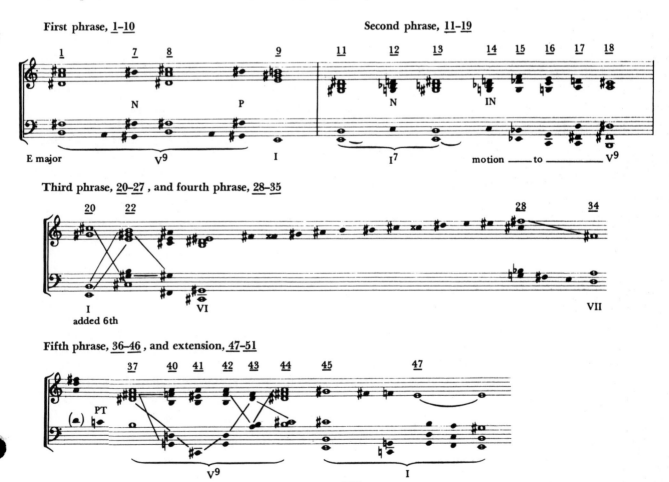

FIRST PHRASE, 1–10 The opening tonic prolongation, in the form of V⁹–I. A linear chord on G♯ embellishes the V⁹. All registers of the piano are opened up. The dominant sounds for eight measures, the tonic for two. Observe the melodic importance of 6.

SECOND PHRASE, 11–19 Motion from a prolonged tonic to the dominant. The tonic takes the form of I⁷. The dominant is, again, V⁹. The neighbor chord that prolongs the tonic in 12 is an inversion of a V⁹, a purely linear chord. The top three voices move as a unit, becoming a single line, but also divide up and regain their individual identities. The same is true of the lower two voices. Observe the different chord types in the passing motion.

THIRD PHRASE, 20–27, AND FOURTH PHRASE, 28–35 The third and fourth phrases are closely linked. Together they constitute a motion from E to D or from I to VII minor. While there is rather little chord change, there is much linear activity. The top line arrives at its goal, F♯, in 28 over a half-diminished 7th major. The other voices reach their goals in the D-major triad in 34. The voice part circles around F♯ in the fourth phrase. The D-major triad sounds particularly stable in this context. How to move back to B, the dominant?

FIFTH PHRASE, 36–46, AND EXTENSION, 47–51 Debussy returns to the dominant effortlessly. A PT in the bass, C, links the D-major triad with the V⁷. The dominant is then prolonged through most of the phrase in a remarkable way. A and B persist through the prolongation, and F is heard also in most measures. A line that starts on D♯ travels through the registers and generates most of the sense of chord change which is, to some extent, an illusion. Follow that line: D♯, D, C♯, D, up an octave, to the C♯ in the V⁹ and the tonic, which includes the added 6th.

In this song, 6 has played a rather important role. It has served both as the 9th of V⁹ and the 6th of the added 6th. Perhaps the prevalence of that scale degree is one of the reasons that Debussy's tonality sounds unlike anybody else's.

Few composers have invented a musical style as personal as Debussy's. The temptation to imitate it seems hard to resist for it is so attractive. Yet most attempts to use his music as a model have not been successful. The principles he discovered, however, have had great influence on the composers of the generation that came to maturity in the early years of the twentieth century. We may summarize those as follows:

1. Polyphony is simplified, often to one or two parts.
2. The sonority is enriched by thickening lines into triads and other chords.
3. The last traces of the S.A.T.B. format, still to be found in Brahms and Wagner, are gone.
4. Although Debussy's chord vocabulary is much the same as Wagner's, the sounds are different because they are connected and juxtaposed in nonfunctional ways.
5. This is to say that chords are used for their own sound value, without always relating them to the key and function of their origin. Their origin is often strictly linear.

One composer whose very concept of tonality owes much to Debussy's innovations in Béla Bartók. In his music, stepwise motion is everywhere, bass motion in 5ths is rare. Passing and neighbor chords, sometimes in parallel motion, prolong the tonic and connect it with other points. The flavor of the music is distinctly Hungarian. But Bartók took the principles of folk song as his guide, not folk material itself. The short pieces of the *Mikrokosmos* illustrate the composer's approach succinctly. The tonal structure of each piece can be readily identified and gives us further insights into the operations of extended tonality.

174A is organized around the A-minor triad. The motion first stabilizes that sound, then is directed to III and V. It returns to I at the end of the first half of the piece. The second half, starting with the upbeat to 11, follows a similar route. But mode mixture turns III into C minor. Taking the new note, E♭, as a cue, Bartók moves up another minor 3rd to E♭ minor, a tritone from the tonic. The trip back to A could mean the end of the piece, but an extension echoes the move from E♭ to A, creating a satisfying sense of completeness.

The melody clearly reflects the tonal structure. It takes the opening skip of a 6th and gradually makes it part of a polyphonic melody; near the end, both implied lines are made explicit, and a three-part texture results. The melody helps establish the tonality by circling around the tonic without the use of a leading tone.

Indeed, the melody has control of the tonal

movement. The lower part moves down chromatically in the first phrase, descending from 5 not quite to 1. This has the effect of an open-ended phrase, an antecedent. A similar motion occupies the bass line of the second phrase. Observe that phrase endings in the two parts coincide only at cadential points; in other places, they overlap. Such a coming together occurs at the end of the third phrase. Within that phrase, the bass has taken up the melody's ascending skip of a 6th, giving it an almost motivic significance.

In contrast to the first part, the left hand has the melody in the second half. The right-hand part is not the same as the left was in the first half, however. Above the melody we hear a countermelody that starts with the rising 6th and moves against the tune mostly in contrary motion. In the final phrase, the right-hand part concentrates on the rising 6th, and its top line descends to reach the 5th that meets the melody's tonic and defines the concluding triad.

Directed motion shapes the piece. All motion is linear—that is, by step—and there is no harmonic progression. The bass has lost its commanding position as the most important voice in the tonal movement. This means that the bass-soprano framework does not necessarily guide the motion. In this piece, the melody implies the entire tonal structure regardless of the register in which it sounds.

The division of labor between the hands is intended to give each hand, in turn, practice in playing the melody and the accompanying part. At the same time, this alternation of roles provides a means of creating contrast between the two halves of the piece.

174A : Comparison of the two sections

first section (1–10)	*second section* (11–24)
three phrases	three phrases plus one
right-hand melody	left-hand melody
beats: 5 + 5 + 3	beats: 5 + 5 + 3
5 + 5 + 3	5 + 5 + 3
5 + 5 + 5 + 3	5 + 5 + 5 + 3
	5 + 5 + 5 + 1
little mode mixture	more mode mixture and chromaticism
reaches high point in the third phrase	reaches high point in the third phrase, but then echoes the third phrase in a quiet fourth phrase
middle register	middle register

In 174C , we saw that the tonic was prolonged in the first fourteen measures. A closer look shows that two motions are heard. The first uses an ostinato to stabilize G and the chord in 4ths built on that note; the second starts in 14 and leads to the end of the section. This motion fills the octave. What happens next may also be understood in terms of directed motion. But why does the first half of the piece sound as if it needs continuation? After all, there is no cadence on V;. What the composer uses to open the end of the section is linear, not chordal. The bass motion is left incomplete at the end of the section. It reaches A, then shifts up an octave to A♭. This note is now within reach of the right hand, which picks it up to start the second half of the piece. The octave move is completed, but by that time the second half of the piece is under way. The two parts are thus linked into one large whole.

As in 174A , the upper and lower parts are interchanged in the second half of the piece, but only for a few measures. The left hand soon gravitates toward G again, but the right hand evokes G♯ minor. In 34 , the G♯ proves to be the A♭ that functions as a leading tone from above, as it did in 23–24 . The rest of the piece recycles the opening ideas, ending with a G–major-minor triad.

The tonal structure of the piece, then, is based on G as center, a white-note scale starting on G, and chords using that scale built on 4ths. Yet tonal structure does not answer all the questions about the piece. What became of *bitonality*—the concept that a piece may have two tonic centers rather than one? It is apparent to the ear that G is tonic and that the pentatonic notes are not strongly defined tonally. One may ask whether the ear can follow more than one tonic in a piece or whether one of the "keys" will not predominate. Rather than bitonality, the concept we suggest is that of opposing sonorities. In this case, the pitch content of each sonority excludes any notes of the other; but this need not always be true. The point is that there is a polyphony of two streams of sound, differentiated in scale, which flow side by side independently and yet are related.

The first page of 175 shows two techniques that Stravinsky learned from Debussy: the long pedal points, and the parallel triads. More important, perhaps, is the concept of opposing sonorities, which Debussy had invented in (among other works) the first piano prelude of Book II and which Bartók used any number of times. The sustained D-minor sound is one key and one tone color; the moving triads are another stream of sounds; and the sustained high notes that gradually evolve into a melody are a third level.

To say that the section moves from D minor to F♯ minor is true, but not as important as such a statement might have been for earlier music. The fact of the opposing sonorities, each with its characteristic timbre, is perhaps a more decisive factor. A listener who tries to pick out the most salient characteristic of the piece will probably decide on the tone color, and this depends more on the opposition of the pitch groups (keys?) and the placing of the orchestral masses than on tonal movement.

Another element that assumes considerable significance is a single interval, the tritone. The first two minor triads, E♭ and C♯, are neighbors and could easily have been arranged so that the top line would be A♯ (B♭)–G♯. But Stravinsky chose another line, A♯–E. That tritone is picked up later and serves as a linking element. It frames the top line in the short prolongation of a dominant-7th chord in 24–26 . In the duet that begins in 30 , B♭ is the starting note of the upper voice, E the last and lowest note of the lower. In 34 , the bass' comment to the other parts is B♭–F♭, which recurs throughout the section. The neighbor chord first heard on the last beat of 34 includes the same tritone. It operates neither as a motive nor in connection with tonal structure, but independently, as a unifying element.

105

Formal Aspects of 170 – 179

What kinds of phrase structure and musical form lend themselves to the approach we have called extended tonality? What kinds of shapes grow out of such a tonal usage? To what extent are the forms of the earlier language of tonality applicable to the expanded type?

Debussy's phrases are apt to fall into balanced units, particularly in his early works. The song 170 is organized largely in two- and four-measure units. The piano introduction is two measures long. The first line in the voice is three measures, but the third measure is also the first measure of the piano's next two. Such an overlap is Debussy's way of disguising the regularity of the groupings. The voice's second group is in 6–9 ; once again, it does not coincide with the piano's phrase rhythm. Both are in agreement in the two two-measure groups that comprise 11–14 , and seem to be in the next four measures. But 18 is both the end of one unit and the beginning of another two-measure group, the same one that began the song. 24–27 arrive at the dominant

in both voice and piano. The prolongation is six measures long (four plus two). But tonal movement is counterpointed against phrase rhythm; the dominant does not match the six-measure phrase exactly, but begins before it, somewhat blurring the regular four-measure unit within the phrase. Three more two-measure groups complete the piece, the last extended just a bit on paper. But the sound is meant to continue until the downbeat of 40 , so that the two-measure unit prevails after all.

Throughout the piece, phrase endings elide into upcoming phrases so that contrast and punctuation are minimized in favor of continuity. This is particularly true of the flow from the triad to the fourth phrase. The phrase structure is as regular as in a song of Brahms or Fauré.

While two-measure groups are still to be found in the later 171, Debussy also includes longer groupings. The first idea, 7–14 , is an indivisible phrase. It is followed by two-measure units. It is difficult to say that these units are phrases or even

measure	section	description	key
1–6	introduction	ostinato rhythm	V of F♯
7–16	first idea	Moorish tune with ostinato	F♯ minor
17–32	interludes	parallel V⁷ chords; whole-tone scale	F♯–C♯
33–37	end of section	parallel triads	move to A
38–41	introduction	ostinato rhythm persists	A
42–49	second idea	ƒ melody with chords	A major
50–60	continuation	melody moves to inner voice; C♯ ostinato returns near end	A
61–66	interlude	whole-tone scale again	
67–77	third idea	habanera rhythm, ƒ	F♯ major
78–91	continuation	rhythm of whole-tone interlude adapted to style and tonality of third idea	F♯ major
92–97	interludes	parallel V⁷ chords again; parallel triads	F♯
98–108	second idea	now surrounded with accompaniment	A major
109–121	interludes	mandolin chords;	C major
		snatch of second idea;	F♯ major
		mandolin chords;	A major
		snatch of second idea	V of F♯
122–127	first idea	with ostinato above, chords below	F♯ minor
128–136	continuation and conclusion	uses rhythm of V⁷ idea; ostinato persists to end	F♯ major

that they group into phrases. The second melody of the piece, related to the first, starts with the upbeat to 42 and is another eight-measure phrase with no interior punctuation. Like the first phrase, this unit is built on a pedal note, which provides a strong unifying element. A third melody, 67–77, is extended to eleven measures. Thus the piece contains a mix of long, not-too-regular phrases and two-measure groups, often repeated literally.

The overall form of the piece is unique. The music suggests a series of impressions of Spain, loosely connected on the surface, tightly connected in structure: The tonality of the piece is the basis of the form. We may think of the piece's shape as being a series of sections, each with its own material, connected with short interludes.

Whether the traditional procedure of dividing a piece into sections is applicable here is a serious question. The piece has a kaleidoscopic effect, in many cases one idea following another without transition. Long areas of stability, built over pedal points, are interrupted by others without warning. Textures, tempos, and registers change just as drastically. Some of the ideas are fairly long, but others are too short to be considered sections. The piece is a series of aural images, confronting each other as much as they connect with each other. The concept of form in this and similar works of Debussy is quite different from most procedures of the nineteenth century and points toward usages that have been explored more fully in the first half of the twentieth century.

Pieces such as *La Soirée dans Grenade* are often labeled "impressionistic," a tag whose application to music did not satisfy Debussy and which we must question. The painters who are grouped under the heading of Impressionism were a generation earlier than Debussy. The connection between those painters and Debussy's music supposedly rests on the use of color as an important constructive element. But to equate color in painting so literally with color in music is a dubious proposition. No doubt the basic impulses that underlie artistic endeavors of all kinds have much in common within any given period, but to demonstrate this in detail is a difficult undertaking. Perhaps we should say, in the most general way, that late nineteenth-century painters and composers grew out of the final stages of Romanticism, bringing that movement to a conclusion in a creative and fruitful burst of energy while opening new pathways that would be of great value to succeeding generations.

The five pieces from Bartók's *Mikrokosmos*, 174, show in miniature the same techniques that the Hungarian composer used in his larger works. Like the Bach inventions and Chopin's and Debussy's *études*, these pieces are not only highly useful as piano exercises, but also have particular value as demonstrations of important compositional procedures on a small scale. We should observe the way in which the form of the pieces grows out of the musical material, often approximating a traditional form but never bound to it literally. The melodic idea, sometimes folklike and sometimes not, is one point of departure for these pieces. Another is the opposition between two sonorities.

The tonal structure of 174A was discussed on page 132. The pedagogical purpose is to have the pianist's hands exchange roles and play melody and countermelody by turns. This shapes the form of the piece into two sections. The second half of the piece is not a carbon copy of the first half. Rather it is a heightened version, with more chromaticism brought about by mode mixture. Since the second part is more intense than the first, it needs more time to return to the quiet level of beginning and end, which is why it is longer than the first part.

The form of 174B is unique. It grows out of the way in which three ideas unfold and interact. All three start with the triad. One is the sustained sound, heard as the piano's harmonics. The second is the staccato triad. At first, its function is simply to punctuate and activate the harmonics. But gradually it takes on a life of its own and becomes a separate voice. The third idea is the single-line melody, which begins by outlining the triad and gradually departs from it. The conversation between the three ideas, each so different in sonority, the carefully calculated dynamics, the many changes of tempo and register, all are the shaping forces of the piece. The phrase structure and form grow out of their interaction. The B that sounds throughout the piece is another unifying element, but the listener is probably more aware of the short snatches of melody, rhythm, and color that give the piece its improvisatory character and make it, indeed, a miniature world.

The gravitation of all the notes in 174C. toward G is interesting to study as a manifestation of one kind of twentieth-century tonality. Beyond that, the opposition of the black-note collection of notes and the white-note collection of notes is found in some form in almost every measure of the piece. Again, the hands exchange roles in the middle of the piece, but in 35 they resume their original positions. A formal element of importance in this piece is the motivic development, based on the first four notes of the melody. Three of them are also the first three notes of the accompaniment so that the melodic material is highly unified. Observe how two ritardandos usher in large phrases, and how much the rallentando adds to the ending. The form may suggest rounded binary, but in fact it corresponds to nothing but the way in which the composer worked out his musical ideas.

While Bartók's procedures owe much to traditional tonality, they also explore newer ways of or-

ganizing sounds. 174D has two main elements: the 2nds of the title, and a sound, G–B–F, that is a frame for the directed motion. But is it a tonic? Not as we have defined a tonic, for all the notes in the piece are not related to that sound in a way that we can define. Yet the motion starts and ends with that sound—it is a point of reference. We see Bartók working in what we might call a gray area between tonality and atonality; no one note emerges as tonic, yet one sound is more important than the others.

Since the melody is in the left-hand part, we look at that line first in a search for coherent melodic motion. We find that the notes fill in the space from B up to G, the 6th, which is the outer interval of the reference sound as heard in the first measure. The basic sound, then, is prolonged by linear motion that stays within its bounds. We move our search for other motions to the right-hand part.

The right hand plays two-note sounds and three-note sounds. Is there any significance to that? Some kind of stepwise motion is present; the line reaches a high point and falls back; and we suspect the existence of PTs and NTs, even though they are expressed as simultaneous 2nds. The two-note groups are a bit more stable, the three-note groups more unstable. A sketch of the right-hand part shows the following:

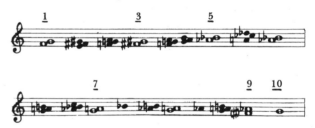

The major 2nds, which the right hand plays as simultaneities, are played by the left hand successively. The major 2nds in the melody, however, are half a step apart so that the line has a chromatic element. At the same time, the two-note groups in the left hand cross the triple meter to provide rhythmic variety.

This piece, too, is in two large sections. Again, the two hands change roles at the mid point, providing an obvious change of texture; and, again, the second half seems to go on with the ideas rather than restate them. Both voices reach a high point in 15, which, in its muted way, is the climax of the piece. The right-hand part reaches F♯ in 17, the left settles on B two measures later. Each of those tones is prolonged with the motivic material of the previous measures. The right hand's *tri-*

chord F♯–G♯–A♯ resolves (if that is the word) at the very end to G–B, heard so many times before. The left hand holds its B to the end, finds and loses the E♯, and reaffirms it to meet the G–B in the last measures. The shape is closed with the reference sound F (E♯)–G–B. The form of the piece not only depends on directed motion rising and falling in reference to a basic sound, but also on motivic development and, within a very limited range, registral rise and fall closely linked with dynamic shadings.

In 174E, a larger form evolves from a tonal plan that divides the octave into major 3rds. This provides four points of stability—B♭, D, F♯, and, again, B♭. They are clearly recognizable as main areas because the main musical idea of the piece appears in each. Each, in turn, is followed by a contrasting idea, whose tonal center is half a step higher. The tonal plan of the piece is as follows:

The tonal structure of the piece is only one of its aspects. What about the "reflection" of the title? This refers to what is called *mirror writing*, in which each line is the inversion of the other. In the first part of the piece, both hands play simultaneously. Small rests begin to appear, then grow more frequent. At 23, the right hand is an eighth

note ahead of the left, which means that we hear a canon at the distance of half a beat. Another canon, at the distance of a whole beat (quarter note), begins at 63, after which the parts draw closer together but do not coincide completely until the last measure. The texture is controlled largely by the consistent use of inversion.

In this piece we hear very clearly the change from one phrase or group to another. What tells us of those changes? Register, density, tempo, articulation, and dynamics. The outline below shows how a large number of elements impose on the piece its very convincing shape.

It is instructive to compare the four presentations of the main idea, each of which is different. The tempos are fairly constant, the dynamics loud, and the register stays in or near the middle. But the melody is varied by extension and contraction, which shows in the changing meters. Most interesting is the final section, which does double duty as restatement and coda. The canonic lines overlap to make a continuous thought through 73. Then, as if to continue the motion of the tonal plan, B becomes the center of the upper part, but the lower part stubbornly resists and clings to B♭. The clash of those two notes is more than just an arresting dissonance; it pits the activity of the B against the stability of the B♭, and when both lines agree on the B♭ the piece is over.

The first movement of William Schuman's *Third Symphony* bears the title *Passacaglia*. The excerpt

174E: Outline

	measure	tempo	dynamics	register	articulation	tonal center	meter
	1–14	allegro	f; $p < f$	middle	legato	B♭	$\frac{2}{4}$ with $\frac{5}{8}$ and $\frac{3}{8}$
	15–22	faster	alternating p and f	higher middle	legato, with accented notes	B	$\frac{2}{4}$
	23–29	tempo I	$mf < f$	spreading out around middle	legato	D	$\frac{3}{4}$, then $\frac{2}{4}$
	30–39	fastest	p	close around middle	legato, with accented notes	E♭	$\frac{2}{4}$
Main idea	40–46	a bit faster than tempo I	f	starts low middle, moves to high middle	legato	F♯	mixed, with $\frac{5}{8}, \frac{3}{8}, \frac{2}{4}, \frac{3}{8}, \frac{7}{8}$
	47–62	fastest	p, then $< mf$	high and middle, spreading to very high, very low	legato	G	$\frac{2}{4}$
	63–82	tempo I, then faster	f, then louder	middle, then higher, through middle to low, then middle	legato	B♭, then B and B♭, finally B♭	$\frac{2}{4}$, then mixed, then $\frac{2}{4}$

[179] is written in canon. There are four real parts, with much doubling. Each voice enters one half step higher than the previous entry, as follows:

[179]: Outline

measure	instruments	starting note
1	viola	E
7	violin 2	F
14	cello	F♯
21	violin 1	G
28	bass clarinet, bassoon, viola, bass	A♭
35	horn, violin 2	A
42	piccolo, flute, oboe, English horn, clarinet	B♭

Thus the 5th relationship, which guided imitation in Renaissance and Baroque canons, is replaced by a stepwise order. The melodic line, however, favors 5ths and, even more, 4ths. These lend the impression that the music is prevailingly diatonic, even though chromatic motion is used, too. The melodies do not stabilize any one point for more than a fleeting moment, yet they seem to be tonal rather than atonal.

Simultaneities of many types are heard in these measures, but 5ths and triads appear at most of the crucial points. The first *dyad* (two-pitch simultaneities) is a 5th, under the violin 2 on F. 9 is a C-minor triad, and the simultaneous sounds of 10–11 have much to do with the D–major-minor triad in the melody. Not all of the sounds can be related so directly to triads, but many can. Yet no one triad predominates, so that the question of key center is not resolved in favor of any one. Rather there is a succession of points that are stabilized so briefly that we soon become accustomed to the constant shift and expect no overall tonic. That the ear receives the effect of tonality is undeniable, yet it might better be described as many tonalities in constant circulation.

For further study

An advanced stage of Ravel's piano style may be seen in *Gaspard de la nuit* and in a deliberately stylized form in *Le Tombeau de Couperin*. A good piece to analyze after studying [171] is Debussy's *La Puerta del Vino,* in the second book of piano preludes, after which the orchestral *Iberia* should be heard. A structural analysis of the same composer's *Bruyères* and of the first section of *Prelude to "The Afternoon of a Faun"* are to be found in *Structural Hearing.* The same book also includes insightful analyses of music by Bartók, Hindemith, and Stravinsky.

Further study of the adaptation of sonata-allegro form to the usages of extended tonality may be found in *String Quartet No. 4* and *String Quartet No. 5,* by Bartók, as well as in his larger works, such as *Sonata for Two Pianos and Percussion.*

Listen to the complete *Rite of Spring* and *Symphony of Psalms.* Other Stravinsky works that should be heard include, at least, *The Story of the Soldier, Octet for Winds, Concerto for Piano and Winds, Oedipus Rex,* and the opera *The Rake's Progress.*

106

Comprehensive Analysis of *Nature, the Gentlest Mother*, by Aaron Copland, [180]

The song [180] is the first in a cycle of twelve on the poems of Emily Dickinson. The poem is a quiet tribute to nature, personal and intimate. The music admirably expresses the serene lines of the poem. In the music, as in the poem, simplicity masks artfulness.

If we begin by listening for sounds that define a key, we first hear a B♭-major triad, elaborated at some length. Is it the tonic? What about the bit of melody in E♭? As the voice starts, E♭ steals in and seems to take precedence over the B♭. The 5th E♭–B♭ now seems definitive. Then what is the role of B♭? Possibly the dominant of E♭. But "dominant function" does not correspond to what we hear in this music. It may be closer to the mark to say that there is one large sonority that is exposed gradually in the first five lines of the song. This sound combines B♭-major and E♭-major triads in what we can call a *polychord*.

E: Tonic polychord

We start with the tonal structure, then discuss each phrase in a comprehensive way, ending with comments on the style of the music.

Tonal structure of 180

The tonic is elaborated by the means we have seen before—arpeggiation and PTs. A new technique consists of adding 3rds above and below the tonic sonority. This creates momentary polychords, the first, in 5 , built on B♭, the second, in 17 , on A♭. All of these polychords have overlapping pitch content, and there is no sense of chord progression from one to another. Rather, there is a tonic prolongation, twenty measures long.

Motion away from the tonic starts in 21 . The slow-moving bass circles around F through 26 . Over that we hear first a 6/3-position D♭-major triad with a strong E♭ NT. From that point on, the chords are 7/3 position, and it sometimes seems as if the 7th will resolve to the 6th. But even if it does,

the 7th returns as the main note, and a gentle level of dissonance results.

The circling motion in the bass breaks off in 27 , and a long descent to the climax of the piece begins. The 7/3 chord persists as the basic sonority until the goal of C♭ is reached (40). Over this is the most dissonant chord in the song, which superimposes a 6/3 F-minor triad over a 5th whose lower note is a tritone from F, namely, C♭.

The tonal structure of the last part of the piece is a condensed version of the first, larger part. The tonic polychord is set forth again in 44–52 , paralleling the first twenty measures. The bass starts forth from F once more (53) under the 7/3 chords, but reaches only as far as D. This is then absorbed into the final statement of the tonic polychord.

One additional observation: in listening to the song, you may have noticed how the widely spaced, long-held B♭s, first heard in 8 , act as phrase starters. They initiate a gesture in 8 and again in 20 . They do the same for the similar phrases, starting in 44 and 51 . Their final appearance, in 65 , begins the last sounding of the tonic and the last phrase.

PHRASE STRUCTURE AND FORM

FIRST PHRASE, 1–7 The lovely piano introduction establishes the mood of the song, sets forth the B♭-major portion of the tonic polychord, and carries the suggestion of the melody which will soon be sung. The texture is two part, but more than two lines are implied. The register might be called high middle—only two notes are below middle C. Despite the *mf* markings, the music is quiet. The meter change and the first of many indications to slow the pace suggest that the approach to rhythm will be flexible. The piano begins with a five-note motive, repeated and varied in the course of this introductory phrase.

The next three phrases are continuous. They might be considered one long phrase subdivided twice, but we prefer separate phrases.

SECOND PHRASE, 8–13 After the tolling B♭s in the piano, the voice begins with a simple line whose first pitches are the lower five of the tonic polychord. The accompaniment is bare and picks up only at the end of the phrase to form a link to the third phrase.

THIRD PHRASE, UPBEAT TO 14–18 This phrase contains the main melodic idea of the song, an upward skip B♭–E♭ followed by a descending scale line.

139

The piano is still centered around the middle register. The phrase ending is marked by arrival at longer notes and "held back."

FOURTH PHRASE, UPBEAT TO <u>19–26</u> The low B♮s start this longer unit in which the bass revolves around F. Activity in the piano gradually increases. It includes a return of the opening motive, which provides the transition to the upcoming phrase. The voice part remains in the middle register; the piano part reaches .out just a bit. The piano writing thickens to three parts. Chromatic changes begin to occur.

The fifth and sixth phrases combine in a larger unit. The end of the fifth phrase is clearly marked in the voice line but the division is concealed by continuous motion in the piano part.

FIFTH PHRASE, UPBEAT TO <u>27–34</u> Sixteenth-note motion in the right hand of the piano part is virtually unbroken. The opening motive is woven into the figuration The inner voice starts to move in eighth notes; it is a polyphonic line. Registrally there is no expansion either in voice or instrument. With this phrase, the bass has left F and is on a long journey back to the tonic.

SIXTH PHRASE, <u>35–43</u> This is the climactic phrase. The rate of change speeds up. The bass, in <u>40</u>, reaches C♮, the neighbor of B♭, and that C♮ is prolonged for four measures plus a long *fermata*. Above the C♮ is the most dissonant chord in the piece. This sound is made up of two perfect 5ths a tritone apart. C♮–G♮ is one 5th; F–C the other, represented as a 4th. C, D♭, and E♮ elaborate the F–C. Interestingly enough, the climax is achieved by intensification of rhythmic activity, chromaticism, and dynamics, but not by registral movement.

The final three phrases are, again, one long unit.

SEVENTH PHRASE, <u>44–50</u> The second and third phrases are combined into one longer phrase, launched by the far-flung B♭s. The piano texture is back to its original thin shape.

EIGHTH PHRASE, UPBEAT TO <u>51–59</u> Starting with the B♭s and the melodic 4th, this long phrase has the same material as the fourth phrase. It is not a literal restatement, but, rather, a shortened one.

NINTH PHRASE, UPBEAT TO <u>60–67</u> In both voice and piano the rhythm slows down to the final *fermata*. With the single exception of C, all pitches are part of the tonic polychord. The phrase is divided as the last line of the poem is repeated. All elements combine to express the mysterious silence of nature.

STYLE Taking its cue from the simple surface of the poem, the composer creates a vocal line that moves much of the time in even notes, eighths or quarters. As a result, the slight displacements and syncopations are particularly telling. Although the range of the voice part is limited, the line moves within that range freely and includes large skips. These combine with stepwise motion to produce what might be called a gentle angularity.

The piano part, too, draws its character from the poem. Nature sounds are suggested in the motive and the figuration. The way in which the piano keeps to its central registers imposes a degree of evenness on the entire song, in keeping with the contemplative style of the words.

The chord vocabulary is distinctly of the twentieth century. Yet the level of dissonance is never very high. The minor 7th imparts its characteristic soft sound to the piece, and the tonic polychord seems positively consonant—or at least stable.

All in all, a carefully selected range of musical materials is used with great poetic effect to produce an eloquent work in which every note has a purpose. Here is an American art song worthy of the great tradition established by the European masters of the past.

Projects in composition

1. Using the vocabulary of Ravel, Debussy, Poulenc, Copland, and/or Milhaud, write a short piano piece or a choral piece.
2. Using the vocabulary of Bartók's *Mikrokosmos*, write short piano pieces, each based on a specific device. Suggestions: opposing sonorities, parallel triads or other chords, mirror writing, one interval as basis, and mode mixture.
3. In a linear style, write a canon, a two-part invention, or a fugue, for available instruments.

POSTLUDE
BEYOND TONALITY

For many centuries it was taken for granted that music had to be tonal. Many people still think so today. Tonal music, as we have defined it, is music in which all the notes in a piece are related to a central note, the tonic. The relationships are many and complex and grew increasingly sophisticated in the last century. But no matter how far-flung the connections were, they always existed and were a controlling factor in the organization of pitches.

The notes most closely related to the tonic are the diatonic ones; the chromatic notes are related more indirectly. For quite a long time the tonal system was able to contain the tendency of the chromatic notes to move away from the tonic, so that tonal moves were expanded but the center of gravity was not lost. By the late nineteenth century —indeed, after *Tristan* (1856)—the chromatic notes became as available as the diatonic ones. Tonality began to lose its power to organize the pitch content of the piece. What could take its place?

The network of relationships that function in tonal music exists independently of any particular piece. E♭ major, the scale, the chord progressions within it, can be thought of without reference to a specific piece in that key. But without such a scale, with no external source of intervallic order, the frame of reference must be created within the piece itself. The term *atonal* tells us that there is no tonic. But music cannot be built on a negative principle. We must also say that each atonal piece has its own internal structure or order, invented systematically or intuitively (probably a combina-

tion of both) by the composer as surely as he or she has invented the piece.

In studying an atonal piece, then, we must first identify the particular intervals that are used in some consistent way. In some works, this is done rather easily; in others, even the most careful study has yielded but a few hints thus far. In either case, we may learn much about the composer's way of thinking.

The music we are now studying has no center of tonality; thus it is atonal. Not only has tonality lost its power as the organizing force of pitch structure, but pitches themselves have lost their place as the center of musical interest. Register, texture, density, dynamics, and timbre were always of some importance in music, but now they may become decisive elements. This may be seen as the latest stage of a long historical development. A page of Renaissance music shows only pitches and their durations, without indications of dynamics or tempo; registral movement and rhythmic changes are minimal. Baroque composers gained considerable control of registral movement and expanded the vocabulary of rhythm. They also ventured into variable levels of dynamics with the use of the echo principle and the contrasting sonorities of the *concerto grosso*. By the late eighteenth century, musicians were beginning to compose with dynamics as well as pitches. This is particularly true of Beethoven, whose crescendos and *sfz*s are an integral part of his musical conception. So are his registral dispositions, his powerful control over the rate of chord change,

Among the participants, one may identify Benjamin Britten (top row, second from right), Karol Rathaus and Roger Sessions (middle row, third and fifth from right), Peggy Glanville Hicks and Béla Bartók (bottom row, first and second on the left).

and his rhythmic intensifications. These newer resources were assimilated only gradually by nineteenth-century composers. But by the beginning of the twentieth century, composers were in command of considerable resources in the nonpitch aspects of music. These began to take over some of the functions previously performed by the tonal system.

An examination of a piece that consists solely of melody, 183, introduces some of the specific concerns of atonal composition.

Is there a tonal center in this music? Searching for a 5th or a 4th that might define such a center, we scan the intervals in the melody. In the first measures we find half steps and whole steps, minor 3rds and a tritone. An occasional 5th does not seem to be decisive. And despite the many semitones, no sense of a leading-tone tendency is forthcoming. Whatever pitch organization underlies this music, it is not one that relates to a tonic. The piece is atonal. The coherence of the music must arise from relationships that are built into it. What are those relationships? How are the intervals used?

The initial short phrase flows into the third measure. The first two intervals deny tonality; there is no major or minor scale that includes F–E–F♯. After the 2nds we hear a perfect 4th, then a tritone. The meaning of these is not yet clear, although we see that the tritone is the boundary for the phrase and that E bisects that tritone. The significance of the tritone becomes more apparent as the second phrase unfolds, from the upbeat to 4 through 5. G–C♯ is still the frame for the music, and the upper half of the tritone, E–G, is explored chromatically. Two phrases have been contained within G–C♯.

The third short phrase starts from the low C♯ in 6. The stabilized tritone is briefly mentioned again and moves above G for the first time. The C that concludes the phrase in 8 does not sound like a resting point. The impulse to go on is satisfied by the very next note, D♭, in which the upward gesture is completed. But that D♭ is the C♯ of the earlier part, respelled and in a higher octave. The initial tritone still prevails.

The fourth phrase, 9–12, features a long crescendo which leads to D. It is the first D of the piece, and it breaks out of the G–C♯ tritone. Immediately we hear D–G♯, another tritone, a half step from the first one. Its reiteration occupies almost two measures. Another tritone, A–D♯, ends the phrase. But a crescendo takes us directly to a concluding thought, with the effect of a partial closure that leads to the next idea. It is expressed as a tritone, B♭–E. This brings the piece to a mo-

mentary halt, which marks the middle of the first section.

The latter part of the first section begins with the first motivic material transposed up a major 7th. The pitches spread out from the initial E, and we look for another tritone. But the outer limits of the phrase 15–17 are D♯–G. No tritone is to be found. Going on to the next phrase, we find that it is comparatively long, 18–23, and that it ends the section. It begins with B, the last of the twelve notes to be introduced. This proves to be the center of a tritone. First the motion is down from B to G♯, then up from B to D. Thus the tritone of 11 is restated as the section ends.

The transition 24–28 is a short lesson in differentiation. It is largely in the low register of the instrument, which has a characteristic sound all its own. It is the only part of the piece to use the key-slapping technique, which also has a special tone color. At the same time, the flowing legato articulation of the first part is replaced by short, detached notes with rests between. All these factors tell us that the initial section is behind us and that something new is on the way.

The something new begins with a vehement ff attack on the highest G (29), presenting the rhythmic motive of the very beginning in diminution. The phrase that runs from 29 to the middle of 32 covers all three registers. First it fills the tritone E–B♭. Then the pitches reach up, moving toward the next point. One of the two climactic areas of the piece follows. It is built on a new interval formation, B–F♯–A (32), and is repeated insistently. Two phrases that form a small group, mid-36–38 and 39–40, bring the dynamic and registral levels down, preparing for the restatement of the opening idea. Those two phrases build up from the C, then reach down to B, never quite extending as far as a tritone, stopping at a major 3rd, B–D♯.

41–45 are more of a reminder of the opening than a restatement and are followed by something quite different. Since the phrase is half a step higher than 1–3, we are not surprised to see that the boundary interval is also half a step higher. The second climactic phrase, 46–mid-50, reaches the highest note in the piece. It is built solely on the minor 3rd that is part of the D–A♭ tritone just heard. That same interval occupies 50. We are still short two tritones out of the six available. In 51, two transitional notes, A and G, lead into a phrase that introduces C–F♯, one of the missing tritones, dwelling upon it and expanding it. The rest of the piece is one long phrase, lightly punctuated in every measure but, as a whole, driving to the end.

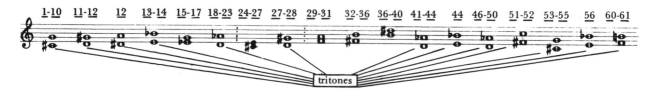

Two tritones are recapitulated, C♯–G in 54–55 and B♭–E in 56. In 58, the final gesture is launched. It starts from the lowest note on the instrument, which has not been heard until the final phrase. The line takes four measures to climb to the last two notes, F (E♯)–B, the last tritone.

In summary, certain observations may be made:

1. There is no tonal center.
2. Pitches are related by the way in which they are kept within certain boundary intervals.
3. Most boundary intervals are tritones.
4. Some, but not all, of the tritones are half a step apart.
5. A rhythmic motive introduced at the outset plays an important role in defining the beginning of a section.
6. There is much repetition of small pitch units two and three notes long. This has the effect of stabilizing the pitches and intervals which are repeated. Rhythmically, however, repetition is not literal.
7. Octave displacement is used frequently to vary the register and expand the pitch material in musical space. One example is the D of 25, which fills in the minor 3rd between the C♯ and E heard an octave lower.
8. The rhythmic shape is constantly changing. The only two measures that have the same rhythm are 1 and 41, in which the rhythmic motive is stated.
9. The music flows through time with little emphasis on the downbeat. Indeed, there is little sense of meter at all. The $\frac{4}{4}$ meter sign is merely a convenience.
10. Register is important in defining the form of the piece. A register is stabilized; then the line breaks out of its confines and moves to a new register. The first half of the piece is in the low and middle registers; the transition is in the low register; the second large section starts high, arrives at two climaxes in the highest register, descends near the end, and summarizes the total space with the last rise.
11. This is interval music. The notes are related to each other by virtue of the interval and interval group they comprise.

Once again, we see that in a fine piece of music a great many elements are used in an integrated way to embody the musical content. Perhaps pitch relationships are at the core of the piece. But they are so closely connected with the motion within registers and from one register to another, with the different ranges of the flute, with the many rhythmic aspects of the piece, with dynamics, and with various modes of articulation, that we can scarcely isolate the effect of any one from any of the others. In this respect, *Density* is no different from a tonal piece, which relies not only on tonality for coherence and expressivity, but also on so many other dimensions of music.

Another work in which each note is weighed for maximum effect is 182. Short as it is, the work has three sections: 1–5, 5–6, and 7–11. Although we shall focus on the pitch relationships in the piece, other elements necessarily make their presence felt. In particular, pitch groupings are combined with special timbres in an unusual and effective way.

The Alpine stillness of the opening is projected by the high register, the use of instruments with little carrying power, the very quiet dynamics, the incorporation of the bells into the chord, and a dissonant sound with six different notes. This fantastic sonority is no mere background; it is an essential part of the piece, much like a motive. In counterpoint to the ever-moving chord, we hear a melody in two phrases. The most conspicuous interval in the melody is the tritone. With all twelve tones equally available, Webern keeps them all in circulation much of the time. The four notes of the melody's first phrase duplicate none of the six heard in the chord. Thus, ten different notes are heard in the first two measures. The remaining two might easily have been used in the next phrase, but Webern does not follow a procedure quite so obvious. The horn's first note, E♭, is indeed one of the missing sounds, but the twelfth note, G, is saved for the second section. The last two notes of the horn's phrase, A♭ and D, are also in the chord, but that sound has ended, suggesting that the opening section is also about to end. The E–F in the harmonium is heard behind the horn's phrase, and a bell sound links the first section with the second.

The middle section, all of two measures long, consists of tiny melodic segments woven together so

Pitch-class content of 182 , register reduced

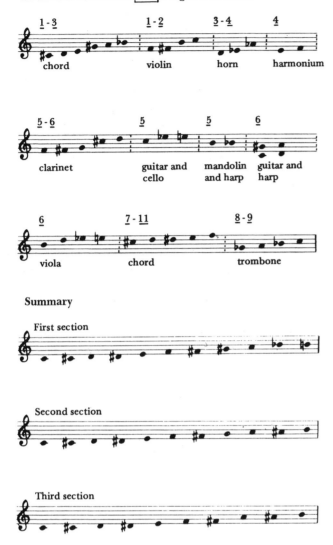

Summary

First section

Second section

Third section

ten different pitch classes are used here. The notes of the chord that is heard throughout the section are, if reduced to a single register, simply a series of half steps. Extension in musical space and choice of timbres give the sound its particular quality.

One thing that makes this music different from tonal music is the absence of the bass-soprano polarity. All lines are equally important in guiding the flow of the music. It is difficult even to speak of top lines or inner voices since many of the lines move through several registers. Along the same line, the concept of melody and accompaniment does not exist; everything is melody.

What principle controls the choice of simultaneities? Aside from the avoidance of triads, we can see that the same intervals that make up the melodies are used in the chords. Almost any chromatic combination seems possible in this music. But we must also keep in mind that Webern rotates the notes of the *total chromatic* (i.e., the entire chromatic scale) in such a way as to emphasize none, and that affects the groupings of notes into simultaneous sounds, too.

The very brevity of the piece commands our attention. If Wagner taught us to grasp a musical gesture longer than any that had been heard before, then Webern has done the very opposite. Now we must listen to every melodic particle as an important component. We must adjust our sense of time to fit the small scale of the piece. If you can hear the trombone's phrases in 8–9 as a complete melodic unit, you are listening with the perspective necessary to hear this piece.

What enables Webern to do so much with so few notes? Perhaps the most striking aspect of the piece is the way in which those notes are placed within musical space, emphasized by the choice of very specific timbres. Although the lower register is hardly mentioned, there is a great sense of depth, within which notes advance and recede. Thus the orchestral dimension is created with only a handful of instruments. The dynamic range is as limited as the other dimensions, but each crescendo and diminuendo has an expressive purpose. The same is true of each accelerando and rallentando, which also help to set off the sections from one another.

If any composer may be said to have "invented" atonality it would be Arnold Schoenberg. True, he disliked the word, but it has become part of musical terminology. Op. 23 marks the last stages in Schoenberg's "free atonal music"; the final piece of the set is the first twelve-tone piece. The first piece, 181, shows many important aspects of the composer's musical thought.

Historically, we saw how motivic connections re-

that none is background; all are foreground. The clarinet has a more clear-cut motive than that heard in the first section—one of the distinguishing features of 5–6. It moves to a high point on the last of the twelve pitch classes to be introduced, G. In counterpoint, a solo cello and guitar play a C–major-minor triad. The melodic line is continued by a viola, while the guitar-harp chord in 6 provides the notes that are not heard in the other parts. Where the first section leisurely unfolded eleven different pitch classes within four measures, all twelve are heard in the two measures of the second section. Thus the rate of change is one more factor in differentiating the sections and in making the second more active than the first.

The third section recapitulates much of the tone color of the first, making a similar aural effect, although scored differently. The melody now has but one phrase, again starting with a tritone. Only

145

placed tonality as the force that can bind together the notes of a piece. In an atonal piece, those relationships must be created anew in each piece. In some atonal music the pitch structures, spelled out in intervals, are the germinal ideas; the rhythms animate them in a variety of ways. If a particular group of intervals is used consistently in a piece, we may refer to it as a *set*. If the set includes all twelve tones, we call it a *twelve-tone set*. The particular pitch classes that represent it are of no great significance, but the intervals that comprise the set are the essential element. Interestingly enough, the rhythmic motive, so important in tonal music, becomes rather unimportant in some atonal music, at least in direct relation to the set. 181 is built on two interval sets, which are heard in a context of chromatic counterpoint that is free and intuitive.

This means that some of the pitches are ordered, some are not. The organized *series* of pitches in the first section is set forth most clearly in the right-hand part, 1–3. It consists of seven notes, six intervals, never transposed in the piece. From that set a *subset* is derived, much as a motive was abstracted from a theme in tonal music. The subset appears in various ways: transposition, retrograde inversion, and octave displacement. Examples from the first five measures show these transformations.

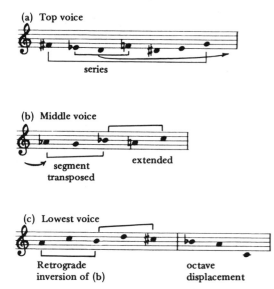

(a) Top voice

series

(b) Middle voice

segment transposed   extended

(c) Lowest voice

Retrograde inversion of (b)   octave displacement

A close look at the series reveals a special feature. The last two intervals are the same as the first two, in reverse order (retrograde) and inverted.

As we hear the first page, we realize that the three-note segment pervades the music. The two lower lines begin with it in two different forms. In each case the third note is also the first of the segment's next statement. Although the three-note seg-

ment is used repeatedly, the complete series is not presented again in the first part of the piece.

New intervals, different textures, changes in articulation, focus on a narrow part of the lower-middle register, and a slower tempo all inform us of a new thought that begins in 13 . An alternation of a major 3rd and a major 7th is a recognizable feature here. But this unit is not a series, for the interval between the 3rd and the 7th is not fixed. Against these soft dyads the series returns as a melody. It starts in 16 in the lowest register and moves rapidly into the highest. Octave shift of the pitch classes makes available this extraordinary expansion of line in musical space.

In a sectional piece, we would expect the second section to bring forth new material, with the third returning us to the familiar ground of the first. But Schoenberg's conception of form is quite different from, shall we say, that of Brahms. True, Brahms often varied his restatements considerably. But even when sectional divisions are blurred, they are decisive in the form of the piece. Schoenberg's thought in Op. 23 No. 1 is to continue the evolution of the first idea even while the second is being developed, and both are important throughout the section. Indeed, it is difficult to say just where the section ends, or if it does end, or whether the piece does not go on without a pause until the end. The traditional organization of pieces in sections may apply here only to the first section. After that, ideas that were to be heard successively in earlier music are now heard simultaneously.

One way to follow the argument of the piece is to trace the appearances of the seven-note series.

Observations:

1. Rhythmically, the series is never presented in the same way more than once.
2. The first appearance of the series is in a single register. The next is spread over all registers. The rest are fairly compact registrally.
3. The series is never transposed.

Three statements of the series are linked, starting in 28 . The last note of the first statement is the first note of the second, retrograde statement. The last note of that retrograde statement is the first note of the next statement. Thus the series is heard continually in the last phrases of the piece.

In the final, modified statement, the first note is postponed until the end of the statement. Two additional notes, C and G, are interposed after the initial D♯.

Together with the complete series, the segment and the 3rd–7th idea comprise the main material of the piece. But by no means do these account for all the notes. Figures in 4ths, fragments of the chromatic scale, and nonordered groups fill a good part of the piece. One might wonder if an interesting aspect of the piece isn't the way in which the ordered elements are imbedded in unordered ones. Apparently, Schoenberg would not have thought so. His line of thought led to the organization of the total chromatic into a series, which he then used in ways growing out of the methods of Op. 23 No. 1.

An entirely different kind of atonal music is exemplified in the song by Charles Ives, 173 . There is no set, a great many notes are used, and the only pattern is an ostinato of four chords, discussed on page 125, beginning at "più moto." An E♭ pedal in the piano introduction has no influence on the upper voices, thus conferring no sense of tonality. Ives also does away with bar lines. The rhythm is unproblematical; it simply is not metrical. In the third line the voice's pulse is expressed as a dotted eighth, while the piano proceeds in quarters; otherwise the rhythmic relationship between the two is quite straightforward.

The chord vocabulary is enormously varied, from major triads to such complex chromatic sounds as the very first. The chords are connected by very free voice leading, difficult to categorize but easily heard. After the opening sonority, the left hand has a two-chord group, joined by changing chords in the right hand. This unifies the piano introduction, and elements of that material continue into the next part of the piece. Each of the chords in the ostinato is taken from tonal music,

but in the context of this music, those sounds have no tonal function.

Heard in isolation, the voice part sounds rather tonal, with E and C taking turns as centers. But this suggestion of key is lost when the voice is heard with the piano part. The notes of the vocal line are included in the piano part with very few exceptions, but rarely in the piano's top line. The voice part is included in the chord progression and is not inflected or colored by the chords as in a tonal song. Nor can we speak of a bass-soprano framework here; all is resonance and sonority.

Finally, to understand why the music is the way it is, we must look at the poem. The piano's first line is meant to set the sunset mood of the entire song. The limited range of the voice part embodies the quiet of the close of day; the descending chromatic line depicts the setting sun. When the poet makes the point that truer beauties lie in memory, the music becomes static, contemplative. The voice circles around within the range of a 4th, rising above B only for the last phrase, while the piano settles into its ostinato and eases out of that, too, just in time for a slight emphasis on the last thought. The entire piece is colored by the use of both the piano's pedals, specified by the composer, giving the instrumental sound a particular shading that helps express the meaning of the words.

The dissolution of tonality and the emergence of atonal music certainly constitute a major turning point in the history of music. It cannot be expected that changes of such magnitude would take place quickly or that they would be absorbed in a few years. The concern felt by the early atonal composers continued to be relevant through the middle of this century, and their explorations still bear fruit in contemporary music. One example is the music of Elliott Carter, whose version of interval music builds on the work of the European atonalists, yet strikes a distinctly American note.

The first of his *Eight Etudes for Woodwind Quartet*, 184A , is based on a working out of two intervals—the major and minor 3rd. The etude opens with a strong introductory phrase of three measures. The first measure and a half fills a minor 3rd chromatically, with typical octave displacement lending registral interest. The particular minor 3rd used, D♯–F♯, recurs in the piece from time to time, but never becomes an organizing element. The balance of the phrase arpeggiates a B-minor triad and a G♯-major triad. These have no tonal function, but are used for their sonority and are connected by the F♯–D♯. In 4 a canon starts. The melody is based largely on minor 3rds. Flute, oboe, and clarinet enter in close succession, the bassoon following in the next measure. The dyads in <u>4</u> are all 3rds, major and minor, except for the last one. The three- and four-note chords in <u>5</u> include many 3rds as well as other intervals. The minor 3rd is also the interval by which the canon is transposed when it starts anew in <u>6</u>. This time the bassoon joins the close imitation, so that the phrase is shorter. But it is also open-ended, leading into the next idea. The bassoon starts <u>8</u> with D♯–F♯, the end of the previous phrase and the beginning of a syncopated line that runs on until <u>10</u>. There, it is handed over to the flute. While the outer lines play quarter notes, one an eighth ahead of the other, the inner lines double on sustained notes. These are heard off the beat at every opportunity, and their arrival on the first beat of <u>15</u> is the composer's way of telling the listener that the thought is ending.

The balance of the piece uses the idea of the introductory phrase, which is continued rather than repeated. Again, the quartet is divided into two pairs. The flute and oboe, a 3rd apart after the first two unisons, are counterpointed against the clarinet and bassoon, in 3rds and 5ths. As the piece draws to a close, B emerges as a goal of motion, but not as a tonal center.

One interesting stylistic aspect of this music is that while it deals with many of the same issues that we found in the works of Schoenberg and Webern, it sounds quite unlike those pieces. Part of the reason lies in the choice of intervals, 3rds being as conspicuous in the Carter work as tritones were in the Webern. Another difference is in the rhythm, which, in the etude, is far more steady and closer to the pulse than in the earlier works. Changes in dynamics and tempo, too, are less frequent in the etude. No doubt the fact that one group of pieces comes from Central Europe and another work comes from the United States is an important factor, but one that is difficult to analyze.

The listener who wants a tune to whistle will be as frustrated as the analyst who is sure that there is a tonal structure in every piece by the seventh etude of the set, 184B. There is only one pitch class, G, and it is heard in only one register from the beginning of the piece to the end. If the pitch does not change, what does?

TONE-COLOR MELODY In the third of his orchestra pieces, Op. 16, Schoenberg began with a chord that was immediately repeated in a different scoring. The entire piece uses the device of unchanging pitches/changing tone color. The change

of color itself is intriguing to the ear and has something of the effect of a melodic change even though the pitch does not move. The technique of creating a quasi-melodic effect by changing timbre on a given note is known as *tone-color melody*, a translation of the German *Klangfarbenmelodie*.

The Carter etude 184B is a study in tone-color melody. The single note is presented in as many ways as possible. Observe for example, the many fluctuations in dynamic level. But it is no empty exercise. The piece builds from a quiet opening to a climactic point at the beginning of <u>19</u>, and the tension is maintained by means of dynamics into <u>21</u>. From there the level diminishes to the soft ending played by the same instrument that began the piece, the clarinet.

Earlier, on page 141, we pointed out that in the twentieth century pitch lost its position as music's main ingredient as composers began to explore register, rhythm, dynamics, and tone color. 184B is a case in point. The use of pitch is minimal. All our attention is focused on tone color, reinforced by dynamic levels. To those who say "but this isn't music," we can only answer "True, it isn't what music was, but it's what music is."

The desire to exercise complete control of the pitch content of chromatic music led to a method of organizing the twelve notes into a set or series or *row*, which provided the basic intervals for an entire piece. While the pitches that comprise a series may be transposed so as to start with any pitch class, the intervals are not changed. Thus the very term *twelve-tone series* must be understood to mean a series actually consisting of eleven intervals.

One logical conclusion of the method used by Schoenberg in such a piece as Op. 23 No. 1 is to invent a series that includes all the pitch classes. In this way a specific kind of order is imposed upon the total chromatic, and no notes are unaccounted for. While the series may be transposed, inverted, or reversed, its intervals do not change. In this way composers worked out a structure for pitches that was autonomous in the sense that it did not refer to anything outside of the piece, such as a scale. Each piece has its own series, which may emphasize certain intervals and perhaps omit others completely. The choice of intervals for a series is a crucial one for the composer.

Most twelve-tone pieces begin with a statement of the series. Broadly speaking, this may take two forms. The series may be identical to the pitches of the melody, as in many pieces by Schoenberg, including 186. Or the row may permeate the entire texture through all or some of the registers.

Rather than write out the set with pitches, which suggests that one form is more "original" than others, we show the series in a chart called a *matrix* (see below). This indicates all possible transformations of the row.

P is the prime form of the row, read from left to right. R is the retrograde, read from right to left. I is the inversion, read from top to bottom. RI is the retrograde inversion, read from bottom to top.

The twelve transpositions of each form are listed by their upward distance from the first note, Eb, measured in semitones. Those half steps are indicated by the numbers that run across the top of the matrix and the numbers that run down the left side. Any transformation of the set may be found, in any transposition, by combining the form with the appropriate transposition number. For example, the voice part of 185A begins with the pitches F–B–C. Reading from left to right, from top to bottom, and from bottom to top, these pitch classes do not begin any series; but reading from right to left, we identify them as R^4, the retrograde of the row four semitones above the original. The second song, 185B, begins with G♯–A–G in the voice part, which is readily found if we remember enharmonic spelling: it is P^5. The opening of the vocal line in the third song, 185C, resembles the instrumental opening of the first, F–B–C, and we are not surprised to find R^4.

The composer is in no way bound to use all the possible transformations of a set. In a relatively short piece, such as the *Goethe Songs*, that would be difficult and unnecessary. But in a longer work many of the transformations may be needed in the interest of variety and of helping to differentiate one section from another.

Since the series is, by definition, an ordering of the twelve pitch classes into which we divide the octave, no pitch class can appear more than once. In making a piece out of a row, naturally, the composer may repeat a note as many times as he chooses. This does not affect the series in any way. For a series is not so much a set of pitches as it is a set of intervals, which is why transposition does not change it in the slightest.

Before examining some of the ways in which the series is used, we should study the intervals that comprise it. There are three half steps, three whole steps, two tritones, two perfect 4ths, and one minor 3rd. Octave displacement makes the inversion of all these intervals available, so that the only intervals not included are the major 3rd and the minor 6th. The choice of intervals determines much of the particular sound and color of the music.

While the matrix shows the vocabulary of the piece, it gives no clue about the way in which the intervals are to be used. For that we must study the music.

Matrix for song cycle 185

↓ **I** ↓

	0	1	11	9	3	8	6	7	2	5	4	10	
0	Eb	E	D	C	F#	B	A	Bb	F	Ab	G	Db	
11	D	Eb	C#	B	F	Bb	Ab	A	E	G	F#	C	
1	E	F	Eb	C#	G	C	Bb	B	F#	A	Ab	D	
3	F#	G	F	Eb	A	D	C	Db	Ab	B	Bb	E	
9	C	Db	B	A	Eb	Ab	F#	G	D	F	E	Bb	
→ 4	G	Ab	F#	E	Bb	Eb	Db	D	A	C	B	F	← R
→ 6	A	Bb	Ab	F#	C	F	Eb	E	B	D	Db	G	←
5	Ab	A	G	F	B	E	D	Eb	Bb	Db	C	F#	
10	Db	D	C	Bb	E	A	G	Ab	Eb	F#	F	B	
7	Bb	B	A	G	Db	F#	E	F	C	Eb	D	Ab	
8	B	C	Bb	Ab	D	G	F	F#	Db	E	Eb	A	
2	F	F#	E	D	Ab	Db	B	C	G	Bb	A	Eb	

P (left) ... R (right)

↑ **RI** ↑

149

We said earlier that the use of the series might take place in two dimensions. One is exemplified in the first four measures of the instrumental part of 185A ; the fourth measure is an overlap with the next form, R⁷. The P⁰ form provides all the pitches for the instruments in these measures. Is the listener supposed to hear this as an exposition of the row? Not very likely, with the intervals dispersed among the three clarinets. Here the row is a unifying element whose shape is perceived only as the piece progresses and the same groups of intervals are recognized. Observe how each of the three instruments has four notes of the row, and how they are elaborated, even repeated; the composer is exploring the possible relationships between the notes of the row.

The other way of setting forth the set is seen in the voice part. Here the notes are indeed heard as a series; the series is the melody. The voice sings R⁴, accompanied—or, better, partnered—by R⁷. Again the clarinets divide up the row among them, which may lead us to ask about the simultaneities and what controls them. Of course, they will include the intervals of the row, given the way in which the composer is using his series at this point. Other guidelines include the avoidance of triads and octaves, both of which would sound incongruous in this chromatic context. Perhaps even more important are reasons of aesthetic preference, the same kinds of reasons that made the Carter piece sound so different from the Schoenberg.

Complete forms of the series are used throughout the first nine measures. But as the words "you may bedeck your form with magic" begin, the composer disguises the series by breaking it into three-note units, which occupy both voice and instrumental parts throughout the phrase. When the poet asserts that he can see through his beloved's disguise, the composer brings back the series in its entirety. In 13–17 , each of the four lines has its own version of the series. Then the last interval of the series, the tritone, is echoed in the final measures, as if the thought of the loved one will not go away—a striking touch.

One of the fascinating aspects of this music is the independence of the lines and the rhythmic freedom. The pulse is elusive, the rhythmic impression much more like that of prose than poetry. Notes enter just before or (more often) just after the beat and the meter shifts frequently. When the instruments do play together it is a significant event, and the effectiveness of the end owes much to just such an agreement. The groupings of sixteenth notes

shift from three to four with great flexibility. To this the composer adds triplets in sixteenths, eighths, and quarters to produce a rich vocabulary of durations and units. The changes of register and the meticulously indicated dynamics add to the subtle coloration of the sound, always in the service of the poem.

The second song, 185B , is based on P⁵, I⁶, and their retrogrades. The piece is a two-part canon at the unison. The voice sings eight and one half measures, imitated by the soprano clarinet. But while the clarinet is playing what the voice has sung, the voice sings the retrograde of its first eight and one half measures. This means that the soprano part reads the same from beginning to middle as from end to middle, including pitches and durations.

The elegant layout of the canon is no mere trick. It is inspired by the poetic image, the riddle of the sun that embraces the moon. As in many songs, close reading of the words gives many a clue as to why the music goes the way it does. Dallapiccola has expressed the meaning of Goethe's words on more than one level, and the music fits the words perfectly.

The ways in which composers have explored the possibilities of twelve-tone sets are limitless. One technique that has engaged the attention of some musicians is to subdivide the row into segments, which may gain a special identity as motives. In 185C , the fourth song of the cycle, the first three notes of P⁷ are used as a unit. Each of the instruments starts with an accented statement of three notes, and the opening soprano clarinet gets to play another three while the clarinet is finishing its third note. The intervals played by each instrument consist of a whole step and a half step; they are the first two intervals of the series. The first twelve notes of the piece are as follows:

We have a new series derived from the basic one by the same operations that were performed on the series itself in the course of the first pieces. Such a *derived row* (Milton Babbitt's term) can be the basis of a phrase or a section. In this song it is not used throughout, but is one of several ways of segmenting the row. The next overlaps with the opening series, in 3 . The second segment used consists of the last three notes (i.e., two intervals) of the series. The tritone and half step usually involve a

150

trill on the latter interval, giving this segment its own character. Discovery of the various segments used in this song is a fairly simple matter; but we must also discover the imaginative ways in which these are set out in musical space, the fluency of the rhythm, and the varied tonal colorings that Dallapiccola gets from the three clarinets.

That most difficult of compositional problems, the ending, is resolved by the statement of another row derived from the first three pitch classes of the original. The last four measures sum up the pitch operations, the octave shifts, the dynamic level, and the intensity of the entire song. The voice, having given expression to what seems like a hopeless declaration of love, can find no more words and bursts into an exclamation that blends with the instruments in the final crescendo.

We must pause to distinguish between two different uses of the term *inversion*. In tonal music we speak of the inversion of a melody, meaning that ascending intervals have been replaced by descending ones of the same size. Whatever went up, goes down; this is *contour inversion*. The same kind of inversion can also take place in atonal music. But the inversion of a set does not usually lead to contour inversion because the set has no implication of contour. Is the second note of the Dallapiccola set higher or lower in the P form? The question is meaningless not only for the P form, but for any form. The set is a list of pitch classes that define one version of a group of intervals. The inversion of a row is derived from the original form by inverting the intervals; but that tells us nothing about how those intervals will be deployed in musical space.

The *Goethe Songs* represent a rather straightforward approach to twelve-tone music. They show how much can be done with relatively simple means. Yet the issues in that piece are much the same as in longer and more complex works. What is the function of the series in establishing musical coherence? What, besides pitch relationship, must be used? How can variety be achieved with the use of a single row? What principles can be developed to control simultaneity? Such questions are central to the language of *dodecaphonic* (twelve-tone) *music*. We may pursue our investigation a step further with the study of another piece based on a row, 186 .

The series on which the entire quartet is based is stated in the first violin part, 1–6 . Fill in the matrix for the piece, as follows:

1. Write the pitch classes of the row across the top line. This is P0.

2. Write the pitch classes of the inversion down the first column, starting with the D of P0.
3. Complete the row form for each line, either from left to right (P) or from top to bottom (I).
4. Indicate transposition levels for each P form, counting semitones up from D.
5. Indicate transposition levels for each I form, counting semitones up from D.

Matrix for 186

The statement of the series is quite clear: it is the melody. But what about the chords that accompany the melody? They add up to no form of the row, yet they grow out of it. What Schoenberg has done is to divide the row into four three-note segments. Each segment is used as a simultaneity. This extension of the serial principle has been called by George Perle the "verticalization of adjacencies," a forbidding-looking phrase which, however, means exactly what it says. The row thus becomes a resource not only for melody, but also for simultaneity. Some writers have used the term *trichord* to distinguish a three-note atonal sound from a tonal one, particularly from a triad. If we agree that triads are built in 3rds, the word *chord* can be applied to atonal music without confusion.

Trichords in 186

From P 0

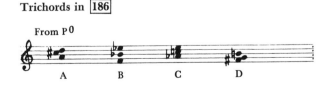

A　　　　B　　　　C　　　　D

151

The four trichords used in this excerpt are labeled A, B, C, and D. They are worth a close look. The first and the fourth prove to be inversions of what we used to call a major-7th chord, with the sharp clash of a semitone or major 7th. Trichord B is a chord built on perfect 4ths. Trichord C is an augmented triad, a sound Schoenberg favored in some of his early works and now finds a place for in the new scheme of things. The variety in the make-up of these sounds, needless to say, is built in quite deliberately. The quality of the chords is not altered by inversion, and, in fact, D is the inversion of A.

Since we can speak of melody and accompaniment in this music, we may ask about the relationship between them. This leads to another look at the question of simultaneity in twelve-tone music. The first consideration is that there be no duplication of notes, which means that the octave is not used as a simultaneous sound. For example, while the melody in $\underline{1}$ uses the first two pitch classes of P^0, the accompaniment uses the last nine. The principle of avoiding octaves is followed consistently throughout the piece.

But there is more to the matter of simultaneity than merely avoiding octaves. Schoenberg also evolved a method of combining two different forms of a set, both heard at the same time. Referring to the matrix, we see that the first *hexachord* (six notes) of P^0 and the first hexachord of I^5 have twelve different notes. This means, at the least, that those hexachords may be played together without producing repetition of pitch class. More important, the combination yields another way of circulating the twelve tones in a controlled way. The principle of combining row forms in this and other ways is known as *combinatoriality*.

The overall layout of the excerpt shows that Schoenberg is still writing in phrases and using change of texture and register to articulate the phrase changes. Each phrase brings a different row form, too, or a different treatment of the row.

The following is an outline of 186 .

First phrase, $\underline{1-6}$:
  violin 1 P^0
  violin 2 ⎫
  viola   ⎬ trichords from P^0
  cello   ⎭

Second phrase, $\underline{6-9}$:
  violin 2 I^5
  violin 1 ⎫
  viola   ⎬ trichords from I^5
  cello   ⎭

Third phrase, upbeat to $\underline{10-16}$:
  violin 1 R^0 plus first three notes of P^0
  violin 2 ⎫
  viola   ⎬ trichords from P^0
  cello   ⎭

Fourth phrase, upbeat to $\underline{17-21}$:
  cello
  violin 1 ⎫
  violin 2 ⎬ trichords from I^5
  viola   ⎭

Fifth phrase, $\underline{21-24}$:
  After the end of the previous phrase, which spills over into the beginning of $\underline{21}$, all instruments play I^5 in close imitation. The three-note segmentation that yielded the trichords is now heard melodically. Segments of the row are repeated for musical emphasis, which does not change the structure of the row in any way.

Sixth phrase, $\underline{25}$–mid-$\underline{31}$ (introduction, $\underline{25-26}$):
  In $\underline{25}$, the division of the row between two instruments, characteristic of this phrase, is introduced. Violin 2 and viola share the pitch classes of P^0. The same instruments continue into $\underline{26}$, where they play I^5. These two forms of the series having been presented separately, they are now combined in the rest of the phrase. The combinations are:

The first hexachord of P^0 is combined with the first hexachord of I^5. The second hexachords are combined similarly. In each half measure we hear a new unit of twelve different pitch classes, made up of one hexachord from each version of the series. This unit is called an *aggregate*. The pitches are notated here in the register in which they occur in the piece. But they are the same forms that are on the matrix; change of register does not affect pitch relationships. Also, note that two pitches of the series are often presented simultaneously; again, the verticalization of adjacencies.

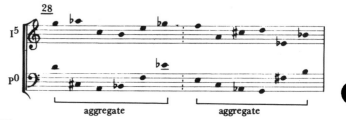

152

The instrument pairs reverse roles. The violins play I⁵; the lower instruments share P⁰.

Violins 1 and 2 play the retrograde of the prime form; viola and cello play the retrograde of I⁵. The aggregates formed are identical to the ones in the previous measures, but in reverse order. The order of the last two notes in the first hexachord of R⁰ is reversed. The same is true of the last two notes in the second hexachord of RI⁵. As the phrase builds to a climax, short segments of the series are repeated, making this statement of the row longer than the previous ones. Again, such repetition does not affect the structure of the row, but does emphasize the notes being repeated.

This is the reverse of the previous arrangement. The rhythm brings out the three-note segmentation of the series.

This survey of the opening of Schoenberg's *Fourth String Quartet* illustrates the main lines of the composer's thought. The musical material grows out of the series, its various transformations, and their combinations. The principle form of the row is presented in a complete phrase as a melody. Each of the other row forms is also set forth clearly before any two are combined. Thus the first four phrases are expository, with one instrument playing the melody and the other three accompanying with chords drawn from the four trichords that result from dividing the series into four units. At 21, the series is broken up for the first time, in a straightforward pattern of imitation.

Before combining different forms of the series, Schoenberg reminds us of them by having two measures, 25 and 26, in which only a single form is heard, divided between two instruments in a manner that will continue through the rest of the

phrase. Then we hear the prime and inversion combined. The combination generates twelve-note groups called aggregates, made up of the respective hexachords of each row form being combined.

Schoenberg is concerned about keeping the twelve notes of the total chromatic in circulation at all times, stabilizing rather little. The rate of chord change, or simply of change in pitch, is carefully controlled. The first phrase begins the piece with three chords to the measure, twelve notes to four beats on the average. The punctuation at the end of the first phrase is particularly clear partly because the rate of change slows; three chords are spread out over almost three measures. A rapid increase in the rate of change begins in 21, a transitional phrase. The second beat has three different pitch classes, the third beat six, the fourth beat nine, and the first beat of 22 all twelve. From there on, the rate of change slows, and in 25 it takes all four beats to run through the twelve pitches.

Rhythm is partly independent, partly associated with the pitch organization. The opening two-measure rhythmic motive is rarely repeated literally, but variants of it function as a unifying element in the melody. At the same time, triplet rhythms tie in with the three-note groupings within the series. This is the case in the eighth-note triplets that start on the second beat of 21 and the quarter-note triplets first heard in the viola, in 24, and taken up by violin 1 in 30.

Since this is only the beginning of the quartet, you should follow up this preliminary investigation by hearing the entire work.

Clearly there is more to twelve-tone music than running through the series over and over. The possibilities of the procedure invented by Schoenberg have been explored by any number of composers in both Europe and the United States. The results are too diverse to be categorized—at least from the present perspective. One example, which shows an approach that has been followed up fruitfully in recent years, is a short piano work by Milton Babbitt, 187. A set of variations, it calls to mind other examples of this form that have been studied, and comparisons with those may be valuable.

As with any set of variations, we begin by looking for the theme. But the theme is not stated here, any more than it is in many sets of variations by Renaissance and Baroque composers. The basic material is the twelve-tone row rather than a theme. Does this mean that a piece called *variations*, if it uses the twelve-tone procedure, must not have a theme? Not at all. Schoenberg's *Variations for Orchestra* have a clear-cut theme, followed by the variations. But then Schoenberg often made a mel-

↓ **I** ↓

	0	8	1	10	9	11	5	3	4	7	2	6	
0	Bb	F#	B	Ab	G	A	Eb	Db	D	F	C	E	
4	D	Bb	D#	C	B	C#	G	F	F#	A	E	G#	
11	A	F	Bb	G	F#	G#	D	C	C#	E	B	Eb	
2	C	Ab	C#	Bb	A	B	F	Eb	E	G	D	F#	
3	C#	A	D	B	A#	C	F#	E	F	G#	D#	G	
→ 1	B	G	C	A	G#	A#	E	D	D#	F#	C#	F	←
P													**R**
→ 7	F	C#	F#	D#	D	E	A#	G#	A	C	G	B	←
9	G	D#	G#	F	E	F#	C	A#	B	D	A	C#	
8	F#	D	G	E	D#	F	B	A	A#	C#	G#	C	
5	D#	B	E	C#	C	D	G#	F#	G	A#	F	A	
10	G#	E	A	F#	F	G	C#	B	C	D#	A#	D	
6	E	C	F	D	C#	D#	A	G	G#	B	F#	A#	

↑ **RI** ↑

ody out of his row. Webern's *Piano Variations* have no "theme," but begin at once to work out the possibilities of the row. In this respect, the Babbitt variations follow Webern's example. There are six variations.

We would expect that the variations would be differentiated by means of rhythm, texture, and dynamics. These aspects of music are in play whether there is a tonal center or not. Since the most obvious way in which this piece differs from earlier variations studied is in the pitch structure, we begin with that.

The row is stated in the highest voice, in 1–12. What about the other notes? Following them in sequence yields nothing that resembles a form of the row. If we listen closely to the first measures, we may hear a lowest voice—not a bass line, but a line nevertheless. C#–F–C–Eb–E–D separate themselves from the rest of the sounds. The matrix shows those notes to be the first hexachord of I³.

Since we have a top line and a bottom line, we look for other lines as well. One line, D–E–Eb–C–F–Db, is the line next to the top. The matrix shows this as the first hexachord of I³ in retrograde order. It is also the retrograde of the bottom line.

The remaining line, next to the bottom, is A–G–Ab–B–Gb–Bb. If these pitches seem familiar, it is because they belong to P⁰, whose first hexachord consists of those pitches in retrograde.

The same principles show the row forms in the second variation. In the sketch below, each row form is shown on a separate line. All pitches are notated in a single register. All notes are natural unless marked sharp or flat.

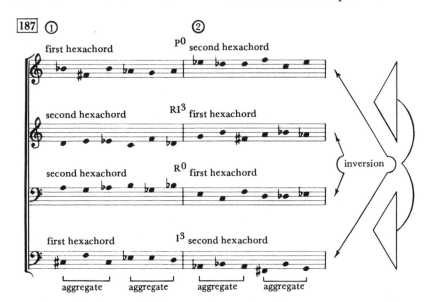

187 ① ②

From the sketch, we may make several observations:

1. The outer voices are in an inversional relationship to each other.
2. The same is true of the inner voices.
3. Combining these observations, we see that the upper and lower pairs of voices are in an inversional relationship to each other.
4. The first hexachord of any row form is, by definition, combinatorial with the second hexachord—that is, they have no notes in common.
5. P⁰ and I³ are combined here—their first hexachords are combinatorial, as are their second.
6. The row is partitioned into hexachords; the hexachords are partitioned into trichords. Combining the first trichord in P⁰ with the first trichords of the other three parts gives an aggregate of all twelve pitch classes, once each. The same is true of all the other trichords.
7. The hexachords of any two adjacent voices have mutually exclusive pitch content. Another way of saying this is that the hexachords of any two adjacent lines form an aggregate.

From all this, it is apparent that it is not the entire row that is being used as a unit, but the hexachord. The content of the first hexachord determines the content of the second. The order of the hexachords may be reversed; the row has changed but the hexachord has not. Thus we may consider that the composer is using the hexachord rather than the entire row as the basic series.

How is it possible to invent a row that is combinatorial? If the goal is to set up two hexachords with no notes in common, we can see what we are aiming for by listing the pitch content. This list, which is not the row, is a *source set*. The row is made from it.

Source set for any hexachord that combines with P⁰

Source set for first hexachord of P⁰

What can we learn by comparing the sketch of the first two variations on page 154 with the music?

The division of musical space among the four lines is closely adhered to. But these lines do not correspond to S.A.T.B., as we can see from the different registers occupied by the two variations.

The prime form of the row stands out most

clearly, being played legato while all other voices are staccato. Moreover, it is played in a more continuous manner than the other lines.

These introductory observations on the pitch structure may now be complemented with comments on other aspects of the piece.

Range of each variation

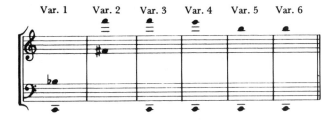

The use of register as a compositional factor in the first three variations is particularly clear. The first variation stretches down from B♭ below middle C; its range is one octave and a minor 7th. The second variation extends from F♯ above middle C for one octave and a major 7th. The third variation combines the registers of the first two. In the last three variations, the upper limit comes down somewhat while the lower limit stays fixed on low C.

A factor that sets the third variation somewhat apart from the others is the sudden appearance of three-note simultaneities. These form three chord types: (a) perfect 4th plus major 6th; (b) minor 3rd plus perfect 5th (up or down); (c) three adjacent semitones. Octave shifts make possible different spacings of those types, so that the vocabulary seems larger than three chords.

The rhythm of the piece has its own interest. In the first variation, we see at once that every measure has a different rhythm. But closer examination also shows that every beat has its own rhythm, too. Using the sixteenth note as the smallest unit, the beat is filled in every possible way.

There being nothing in the way of a rhythmic motive, the music moves through time in an unpredictable way. Although the downbeat is never emphasized, the effect is often much like syncopation. The only long notes appear in the second variation; elsewhere, the effect is of maximum activity.

The rhythm follows a pattern of 3–2–3–3–2–3 beats in each variation. These pulses are expressed as quarter notes in every variation except the fourth, where they are heard as half notes. This means that the fourth variation is twice as long as any of the others since each of its measures is twice as large as the measures in the other variations.

One more factor making for differentiation between variations is the treatment of dynamics. No variation remains at one dynamic level throughout, but each variation has its own plan. The first variation is quiet, fitting in with the low register; the second is loud, matching the high register. The prevailing level in the third is soft, and the longer fourth variation is even softer. The fifth variation opens with a *f*, gradually falling off to a quiet level which is interrupted by the *fff* that starts the last (sixth) variation. Here, changing dynamics lead down to a quiet close.

On the whole, the piece is in the great tradition of variation forms. While there is no tonal structure, the set serves as the unifying element in the pitch organization. Over this basic structure, the imagination of the composer finds many ways to activate the pitches rhythmically and with dynamics, to expand them in musical space, and to integrate all the elements into a musical whole. The underlying principles of variation form are embodied in modern terms.

For further study

George Perle's *Serial Composition and Atonality* is an excellent study of the concerns and the methods of posttonal music, focusing mainly on the music of Schoenberg, Berg, and Webern. Some of the techniques introduced in the previous pages are investigated more fully in Milton Babbitt's article "Some Aspects of Twelve-Tone Composition," *The Score* (June, 1955). A detailed discussion of the *Semi-Simple Variations* is to be found in an article by Elaine Barkin entitled "A Simple Approach to Milton Babbitt's *Semi-Simple Variations*," *The Music Review* (Nov., 1967). A collection of articles published under the title *Perspectives on Contemporary Music Theory* takes up many of the issues of atonal music on an advanced level.

Studies in atonal composition

1. Write a piece for solo wind instrument. Use two pitch classes only, one interval and its inversion. Set this forth in every register of the instrument, using rhythm, dynamics, various modes of articulation, and special means of tone production (such as *flutter-tonguing*) to gain variety and musical interest.
2. Compose a piece for solo string instrument. Use one interval only, which may be transposed to any pitch class. The interval may be sounded as a simultaneity, using a *double-stop*. Again, use all nonpitch elements to vary the statement of the interval.
3. Write a duet for a wind and a string instrument. Each has one interval, which may be transposed. The instruments may also exchange intervals during the piece.
4. Write a study for ensemble, band, or orchestra, whose pitch material consists entirely of setting forth the twelve tones. Determine the pitch order in advance. Notes may overlap so that any number may be heard at the same time. Use tone-color melody to elaborate pitches. For a longer study, reverse the order of the pitches after they have been exposed once so that the last note is the same as the first. Plan the general shape of the dynamics and textures before writing.
5. Base a short piano piece on a cell of three or four notes. The cell may be heard as a line or a simultaneity; it may be inverted, played in retrograde, and transposed. All pitches in the piece may be based on the cell, or they may coexist with other, unordered material.

CODA

To instill the habit of thinking about music; to present specific information about musical procedures—these have been the general aims of *Gradus*. To that end you have studied principles rather than rules, and application of those principles should make it possible for you to approach a new piece, no matter what the style, in an intelligent manner. But the general is useless to you without the concrete. Thus you have also studied a great many pieces in detail in a technical way. All along the way, the effort has been made to show the specific in a large conceptual context.

Throughout this book we have stressed a comprehensive approach to the study of music. Melody, counterpoint, harmony, texture and register, timbre, rhythm, and the interaction of all make a piece what it is. Form has been studied as the sum total of all musical elements. In the background is the perspective of the history of music, which helps us to locate each individual work and relate it to others as well as to important cultural and historical trends. Your own experience in playing and singing music also indicates the importance of its performance aspect.

It remains to be added that the twentieth century is, as of this writing, three quarters over. There is no excuse for ignorance of this era's musical language and literature on the part of any musician. No doubt much of the music being written today will not last forever; but the same is true of the music of any period. The music of today, however, means something special to us today. It is our music, and if we do not experience it ourselves, we are missing an important part of the musical experience.

One thing is certain. The world will change in your lifetime, and music will change. Many musicians will not understand these changes and will condemn them. One hopes that musicians who are trained to see a whole piece, to look for common elements in all music, and to respect creative effort will be able to teach themselves what they need to know about the music of their own contemporaries. That is one of the purposes of this book. For, in the words of Paul Klapper, "education is preparation for change."

MUSICIANSHIP AT THE KEYBOARD

PART TEN

1. Play all S.A.T.B. chorale settings from score.
2. Play selected S.A.T.B. settings, singing one part and playing the other three.
3. Perform 117 and 120, singing the chorale melody and playing the other parts.

PART ELEVEN Elaborate the following progressions by preceding each chord except the first with:

    (1) its dominant triad in root position;
    (2) its V⁷ in root position;
    (3) its V⁷ in any inversion;
    (4) its leading-tone chord (VII⁷) in any inversion.

At the cadence, use I_4^6–V⁷–I. Play each exercise in a particular meter and tempo. Count aloud if you

find it helpful.

PROGRESSIONS:

    (a) I–II–V–I, in major.
    (b) I–III–IV–V–I, in minor.
    (c) I–VI–IV–V–I, in major and minor.
    (d) I–II–III–IV–V–VI–V–I, in major.

PART TWELVE Improvise a single phrase based on

    (a) tonic prolongation plus cadence;
    (b) tonic prolongation, connecting chord(s), plus cadence.

The purpose of this study is to learn to think at the keyboard. Memorizing a phrase you have written is not improvising. Use simple motivic material, and don't hesitate to repeat it. Practice in as many keys as possible.

Each improvised phrase must have a definite meter, tempo, and musical character. The two examples below show a few of the possibilities.

PART THIRTEEN

1. Connect I and V in as many different ways as you can.

Illustration

160

2. Play from the score [129], [131], and [135].
3. Improvise single phrases. Follow these guidelines:
   (a) prolong I;
   (b) use chromatic connecting chords to V and the cadence.

Illustration

PART FOURTEEN

1. Improvise phrase pairs modeled on the Schubert waltzes, [130].
2. Improvise periods of antecedent and consequent phrases.

   (a) the antecedent phrase ends on a cadence on V; while the consequent phrase ends on a cadence in I;
   (b) the antededent phrase modulates to a cadence in V while the consequent phrase returns and ends with a cadence in I.

Illustrations

3. Play from the score [158], [162] introduction, and [164].

GLOSSARY

Words appearing in SMALL CAPS in the definitions are themselves defined in the glossary.

a bocca chiusa (It.): (sing) with closed mouth, hum.

accelerando (It.) getting faster; abbreviated *accel.* or *acceler.*

adagio (It.): very slow, slower than LARGO in the eighteenth century, not clearly distinguished from LENTO in later times.

added-note chord: a chord, such as a triad, to which a dissonant note has become "frozen." The resulting sound would have had to be resolved in an earlier period, but in the era of EXTENDED TONALITY it is accepted as a stable sound. The best-known example is the added-6th chord.

ad libitum (Lat.): denotes a passage that is to be played with considerable freedom, "at (your) pleasure"; abbreviated *ad lib.*

aggregate: in the TWELVE-TONE SYSTEM, a collection of twelve different pitch classes formed by combining a HEXACHORD from one ROW form with a HEXACHORD from a different ROW form.

allargando (It.): slowing down, broadening.

allmählich (Ger.): gradual, gradually.

alto: (1) the lower female voice; (2) (Fr.) viola.

altus (Lat.): alto.

andante (It.): literally, "walking or going"; a moderately fast tempo in the eighteenth century, taken somewhat slower in the nineteenth century.

andantino (It.): a bit faster than ANDANTE.

appoggiatura (It.): literally, "a leaning note." (1) Some theorists use this term for the NT; (2) the small notes that embellish normal-size notes in eighteenth-century music; the small note takes half the value of the large note.

arco (It.): bow; the indication to the player of a stringed instrument to stop plucking the strings (PIZZICATO) and resume bowing.

a tempo (It.): (return to) the main tempo.

augmentation: the process in which the rhythmic values of a series of notes is increased by a constant factor.

ausdrucksvoll (Ger.): expressive.

avec plus d'abandon (Fr.): with more abandon.

aveu (Fr.): avowal, confession.

bar form: a form that originated in secular medieval song in France and Germany, and that may be outlined AAB.

bassus (Lat.): bass.

belebt (Ger.): lively.

beschleuningend (Ger.): getting faster, same as ACCELERANDO.

bewegt (Ger.): lively.

binary form: a two-part form in which each section is repeated.

bitonality: the use of two keys simultaneously.

breve (It.): short.

brevissimo (It.): very short.

cabaletta (It.): in nineteenth-century Italian opera, a fast aria with emphatic or vigorous rhythm, or a section that concludes a slow aria with a contrasting fast tempo.

calando (It.): DIMINUENDO and RITARDANDO.

cambiata (It.): in Renaissance music, a group of four notes in which the first, on a strong beat, is consonant, the second is a step lower and dissonant, the third note, a 3rd down from the second, is consonant (one of the few cases of a leap from a dissonant note), and the fourth, a step up, is consonant.

canon: literally, "rule"; a musical procedure in which IMITATION is carried out exactly for an entire piece or section. The term is also used for a piece so written.

162

cantata: literally, a sung piece as opposed to a played piece (sonata). Deriving its forms from opera, the cantata uses choral and/or solo singers, with instrumental accompaniment; there are usually several movements.

cantus (Lat.): (1) soprano; (2) melody, what the soprano sings.

canzona (It.): an instrumental piece of the late Renaissance and early Baroque, derived from the French CHANSON. There are several sections, in different tempos, each beginning with imitative entrances of a salient motive.

canzonet: the English version of the French CHANSON.

carezzando (It.): in a caressing manner.

cavatina (It.): a type of aria less formal than the DA CAPO ARIA, or an instrumental piece of the same kind.

chanson (Fr.): (1) in Renaissance music, a secular choral piece, often in less than four parts; some are chordal, others quite linear; (2) the French word for "song," although the term for "art song" is *mélodie*.

character variations: the type of variations on a THEME often found in nineteenth-century composition. Each variation has a decided character of its own, somewhat like a separate piece.

chorale: the words and/or music of a congregational hymn associated with Protestant church worship.

coda (It.): literally, "tail"; a concluding section of a composition.

colla voce (It.): direction to instrumentalists to follow the voice part, which may be performed with some liberty.

combinatoriality: in the TWELVE-TONE SYSTEM, the method of combining HEXACHORDS from different ROW forms without duplication of pitch class.

comes (Lat.): literally, "companion"; a name given to the second entrance in a FUGUE, since it is the "companion" to the first.

con amore (It.): with love.

con bravura (It.): to be played brilliantly, with flourish.

con brio (It.): with dash, vigorously.

concerto grosso: a type of Baroque concerto in which there is more than one solo instrument.

con forza (It.): with force.

con fuoco (It.): with fire.

con sordino (It.): played with the mute on.

continuo: short for *basso continuo* (It.); the continuous bass characteristic of Baroque music. The term refers both to the bass line itself, figured or unfigured, and to the instruments that perform it, a keyboard instrument and low strings or winds.

contour inversion: that type of INVERSION in which the melodic shape is literally inverted, interval by interval.

contredanse (Fr.): a country dance, a lively dance popular in the eighteenth century.

corta (It.): short.

countermelody: a second melody that is heard against a given, first melody.

countersubject: in a FUGUE, the melody that is heard in the first voice together with the entrance of the SUBJECT in the second voice.

crescendo (It.): literally, "growing"; getting louder. Abbreviated *cresc.*

da capo aria: a form much used in Baroque opera, less in Classical, in three sections: (1) an opening section; (2) a contrasting middle section, often lightly accompanied; (3) repetition of the first section from the beginning ("da capo") often with embellishment by the singer.

decrescendo (It.): getting softer; abbreviated *decresc.*

derived row: in the TWELVE-TONE SYSTEM, a SERIES of twelve different notes derived from the basic ROW by using a segment of the original ROW, such as three notes, and performing on it such operations as INVERSION and RETROGRADE.

development section: in SONATA-ALLEGRO FORM, the second of the three main sections, in which the emphasis is on the development of motivic ideas set forth in the opening section.

diminuendo (It.): getting softer, same as DECRESCENDO; abbreviated *dim.*

diminution: the process in which the rhythmic values of a series of notes is decreased by a constant factor.

dodecaphonic music: *see* TWELVE-TONE SYSTEM.

dolce (It.): gently, sweetly.

doloroso (It.): sadly.

double counterpoint: a procedure of writing two lines in such a way that even though their positions may be reversed (i.e., the higher is transposed down an OCTAVE and becomes the lower, or vice versa), the dissonant-consonant relationships will still make sense.

double fugue: a FUGUE with two SUBJECTS. There are two types: (1) the first SUBJECT is set forth in an EXPOSITION and at some later point the second SUBJECT is set forth; they are then combined; (2) both SUBJECTS are set forth simultaneously.

double-stop: playing more than one note at a time on a stringed instrument.

dux (Lat.): the leading (first) voice to enter in a FUGUE.

Einleitung (Ger.): PRELUDE, introduction.

en augmentant beaucoup (Fr.): growing much louder.

en dehors (Fr.): bring out (the passage so marked).

enharmonic change: change in spelling a note without changing the sound—e.g., G♭ is F♯ spelled enharmonically.

ensemble: a group of voices or instruments.

episodes: the passages in a FUGUE which connect those sections in which the complete SUBJECT is restated. Episodes may be based on some fragment of the SUBJECT or may have new material.

erste Zeitmass: at the original tempo.

étude (Fr.): a study piece.

exposition (fugal): the first section of a FUGUE, in which the SUBJECT is introduced in IMITATION in all the voices that exist in the piece.

exposition section: in SONATA-ALLEGRO FORM, the first of the three main sections. The basic tonal movement is from I to V or, in the minor mode, from I to III. Each key area may have its own characteristic thematic material. A connection known as the bridge leads from the first key area to the second. A concluding section, the codetta, rounds off the exposition.

extended tonality: a general term for the musical language in which key centers are established by essentially linear terms, without use of the dominant and leading-tone functions, and often fairly diatonic. Much music in the first half of the twentieth century, from Debussy on, utilizes this language.

fantasy or **fantazy:** in seventeenth-century English music, an instrumental piece based on IMITATION, much like the CANZONA. Nineteenth-century composers used the term loosely for piano pieces of a romantic character.

feminine ending: a term borrowed from poetry, meaning that the final chord in a cadence is on a weak beat.

figurated chorale: a CHORALE setting for organ in which at least one part uses a particular figuration consistently.

figure: (1) a melodic idea of two or three notes which can be spun out into a line; (2) a characteristic rhythm and/or pitch pattern in an accompaniment, making an accompaniment figure.

flat (or flatted) 6: a product of mode mixture, the minor mode's 6 is used in the major.

florid counterpoint: a line of counterpoint in which mixed note values (whole notes, half notes, quarters, and eighths) are used; the exercise in which such a line is set against a *cantus firmus.*

flutter-tonguing: a technique of wind- and brass-instrument playing. The sound produced is a rapid TREMOLO.

fore-imitation: anticipatory IMITATION, presenting in smaller notes a melody which will become the leading idea of a phrase.

fugato: a section of a piece that is, in effect, the EXPOSITION of a FUGUE.

fugue: a contrapuntal piece based on a clear-cut SUBJECT that is introduced in IMITATION and that is the main musical idea of the piece.

funeste (It.): mournful.

gesteigend (Ger.): getting faster.

grace note: a decorative note printed in smaller type than the other notes and played either just before the beat or on the beat.

heiter (Ger.): cheerful, cheerfully.

hexachord: (1) in medieval music, a scale of six notes; (2) in the TWELVE-TONE SYSTEM, either half of a twelve-tone ROW.

homophonic: an informal term for a texture that is predominantly chordal.

im Hauptzeitmass (Ger.): in the original tempo, the same as TEMPO PRIMO.

imitation: the procedure in which the same melodic idea is introduced in successive voices.

innig (Ger.): inner.

in rilievo (It.): literally "in relief"; bring out.

inversion: (1) the procedure by which the lower note of a simple interval is raised an OCTAVE or the upper one is lowered an OCTAVE; (2) the positions of a chord in which the bass is not the root—the $\frac{6}{3}$ position of a triad is called the first inversion, the $\frac{6}{4}$ position of a triad is called the second inversion; (3) a transformation of a melody in which all ascending intervals become descending intervals of the same size, and all descending intervals become ascending intervals of the same size; (4) a procedure used in atonal music in which a ROW or SERIES is so transformed that each interval is replaced by its complement, found by subtracting the number of semitones in the interval from 12.

invertible counterpoint: a general term for linear music in which the relation between parts can be inverted and the polyphony will continue to make sense. Reversing the upper-lower relationship between two lines is called DOUBLE COUNTERPOINT; similar INVERSIONS among three lines is TRIPLE COUNTERPOINT; four parts may be written in QUADRUPLE COUNTERPOINT.

key-slapping: a technique of flute playing. As the key is slapped a small amount of air is blown through the instrument, producing a soft, percussive sound. The marking + over a note indicates that the key is to be slapped.

langsam (Ger.): slow.

la prima parte senza replica (It.): (play) the first part without repeats.

largo (It.): broad, slow; not as slow as ADAGIO in the eighteenth century, not consistently distinguished from LENTO or ADAGIO in later times.

legato (It.): smooth, connected.

léger (Fr.): light.

leggiero (It.): light.

Leidenschaft (Ger.): sadness, melancholy.

lento (It.): quite slow but not as slow as GRAVE or ADAGIO until the nineteenth century, when the distinction between these terms became less consistent.

l'istesso tempo or **lo stesso tempo** (It.): the tempo does not change.

lointain (Fr.): far off.

lunga (It.): long.

maestoso (It.): majestic.

major-minor mode: an informal term for a mode that combines notes of both major and minor so consistently that neither mode predominates, although the tonality is not affected.

manual: a keyboard of the organ that is played by the

hands, as opposed to PEDAL, the keyboard played with the feet.

mano dextra (It.): (play with the) right hand; abbreviated *m.d.*

mano sinistra (It.): (play with the) left hand; abbreviated *m.s.*

masculine ending: a term borrowed from poetry, meaning that the final chord in a cadence is on a strong beat.

mässig (Ger.): moderate; same as ANDANTE.

matrix: in the TWELVE-TONE SYSTEM, a chart showing all transformations of the ROW in all transpositions.

mazurka: a Polish dance in triple meter, the tempo moderate to quite fast. There is a characteristic accent on the second beat, and the rhythm is also typical.

meno mosso (It.): less moving.

mezza voce (It.): literally, "half voice"; sung with less than full volume.

minuet, menuet (Fr.), or **minuetto** (It.): a dance in triple meter, the tempo moderately fast. Until about 1760 the minuet is in BINARY FORM; thereafter it is in ROUNDED BINARY FORM.

mirror writing: a relationship between two lines whereby each is the simultaneous INVERSION of the other.

mit Leidenschaft (Ger.): passionately.

modulation: a change of key, meaning that a phrase ends in a different tonic from the one on which it began. Large-scale tonal movement is often described as modulation.

morendo (It.): dying away.

mormorato (It.): murmured.

motet: (1) in medieval music, a piece built on a tenor derived from chant, usually in three voices; each may have a different text; (2) in the Renaissance, a setting of a sacred text for voices, often in imitative style.

mouvement du début (Fr.): TEMPO PRIMO, the tempo of the beginning.

octave: the smallest interval between two different statements of the same pitch class.

opposing sonorities: an informal term for a texture in which at least two different kinds of sound are contrasted either simultaneously or in succession.

ossia (It.): an alternative version.

ostinato (It.): a short motive that is repeated a number of times.

parlando (It.): played or sung in a speechlike manner.

passacaglia (It.): or **passacaille** (Fr.): a Baroque continuous-variation form built on a repeated bass pattern. The distinction between passacaglia and chaconne meant little to musicians of the seventeenth and eighteenth centuries.

pedal: in organ music, that part which is played on the lowest keyboard, by the feet; the lowest keyboard itself.

perdendo or **perdendosi** (It.): dying away.

period: a group of measures that is made up of two or more phrases and that ends with a cadence.

pesante (It.): heavy.

Picardy 3rd: the major mode's 3 appearing in the last triad of a piece in the minor mode.

pizzicato (It.): indicates that the player of a stringed instrument is to pluck the strings with his or her finger rather than to play with the bow; abbreviated *pizz.*

poco a poco (It.): little by little.

polychord: a simultaneity formed by the superimposition of two simple chords, such as triads or 7th chords; they are an element of the language of extended tonality.

prelude (Fr.) or **preludio** (It.): in Baroque music, a short introductory piece often based on a single melodic figuration. While Chopin's *Preludes* are not introductory, they retain the notion of a piece based on a single idea. The term is also used for a short introductory piece in an opera.

presto (It.): very fast.

program music: instrumental music which follows a story line or has a connection with a literary idea.

quadruple counterpoint: a case of INVERTIBLE COUNTERPOINT involving four parts. The parts are so written that they can reverse their positions, with the polyphony still providing satisfactory dissonant-consonant relationships.

rallentando (It.): slowing down; abbreviated *rall.*

real answer: in a FUGUE, when the second voice enters with an exact (diatonic) transposition of the SUBJECT.

recapitulation section: the third section of a movement in SONATA-ALLEGRO FORM. In this part, the material of the EXPOSITION is restated, entirely in the tonic. Literal recapitulation is rare; the best composers find innumerable ways of varying the ideas and maintaining the interest.

reprise (Fr.): restatement.

retenu (Fr.): RITENUTO, held back.

retransition: in TERNARY FORM, the connecting link between the end of the second section and the beginning of the third.

retrograde: a melody that is read backward, starting with the last note and finishing with the first.

ricercare (It.): in the seventeenth and eighteenth centuries, a "learned" piece, often based on IMITATION; a precursor of the FUGUE.

rinforzando (It.): strengthened, louder.

ritardando (It.): slowing. This should be abbreviated *ritard.*, but is often abbreviated *rit.*, in which case it is confused with the abbreviation for RITENUTO.

ritenuto (It.): held back, slower. This should be abbreviated *riten.*, but is often abbreviated *rit.*, in which case it is confused with the abbreviation for RITARDANDO.

ritmico or **ritmato** (It.): rhythmic.

rounded binary form: a form whose tonal structure is in two parts—I–V, V–I—and whose design is in three.

In sketch:

```
        A              B       A
    ||:      :||:   :||:           :||
        I–V          V–      I
```

It should be noted that B is a continuation or development of the material set forth in A.

row or **tone row:** an arrangement of the twelve different pitch classes in a specific order. Another term is *twelve-tone* SERIES. The term *set* is also used, borrowed from mathematics, but it does not include the concept of order.

rubato (It.): indicating that the tempo is flexible rather than strict; sometimes *tempo rubato*.

ruhig (Ger.): calm, quiet.

scherzo (It.): literally, "joke." Haydn and Beethoven wrote MINUETS in faster tempos and with elements of surprise or rustic humor, calling them scherzos. While retaining the form of the MINUET, the character of the scherzo movement was eventually made more serious. Later composers wrote scherzos as character pieces.

schmachtend (Ger.): languishing.

senza ripieno (It.): in a Baroque CONCERTO GROSSO, indication to the large ensemble (the *ripieno*) that only part of the whole ENSEMBLE is to play.

serial music: *see* TWELVE-TONE SYSTEM.

series: *see* ROW.

simile (It.): in the same manner.

smorzando (It.): dying away; abbreviated *smorz.*

sonata-allegro form: a three-part form frequently used in the first movement of an instrumental work such as a sonata or symphony. The three large sections are EXPOSITION, DEVELOPMENT, and RECAPITULATION. A CODA is often added.

sostenuto (It.): sustained.

sotto voce (It.): in an undertone.

staccato (It.): detached, separated (notes).

stentando (It.): holding back each note in a passage; abbreviated *stent.*

stretto (It.): (1) in a FUGUE, bringing in the entrances of the SUBJECT before previous ones are completed, making an overlapping effect that is often part of the FUGUE's climax; (2) in nineteenth-century music, *stretto* is an indication to press the tempo forward.

stretto maestrale: literally "master STRETTO"; in a FUGUE, a STRETTO that involves all the voices.

stringendo (It.): pressing forward.

strophic: a way of setting words to music so that the same music is sung to each verse (strophe) of the poem.

subito (It.): suddenly.

subject (fugal): a THEME used as the basis of a FUGUE.

susurrando (It.): whispering.

tempo giusto (It.): (1) a moderately fast speed; (2) in strict time.

tempo primo (It.): in the original tempo; the same as IM HAUPTZEITMASS. This marking is most often found at the beginning of a restatement, after the tempo has varied from the initial one.

tenore (It.): the tenor voice.

tenuto (It.): held.

ternary form: a three-part form, containing different material in the first two parts and a restatement of the initial section in the third part.

theme: (1) an informal term for the leading melodic idea of a piece, particularly one in SONATA-ALLEGRO FORM; (2) the idea, in the form of a PERIOD, on which a set of variations is based.

theme and variations: a form consisting of a set of variations (modifications) of a musical idea (THEME) which is stated at the outset.

theme transformation: a procedure by which a THEME is altered, keeping some of its characteristics but changing others to create a new but related THEME. In this way two or more THEMES may be of contrasting character but still have common elements.

through-composed: a way of setting a text in which the music changes to express the changing content of the poem; there is little repetition.

tonal answer: in a FUGUE, the entrance of the second voice, with the SUBJECT reshaped in such a way as to reverse the position of 1 and 5 in the melody; other adjustments are usually required to retain the contour of the SUBJECT.

tone-color melody or **Klangfarbenmelodie** (Ger.): a "melody" in which the pitches do not change or change very little while the musical interest is provided by the changing tone colors.

tone row: *see* ROW.

tranquillo (It.): calm.

tre corde (It.): indicates that the pianist is to release the left pedal, ending the muting of the instrument.

tremolo (It.): in string playing, the rapid movement back and forth of the bow across the strings, either measured or as fast as possible; also, the music thus played.

trichord: a three-note chord that is not a triad.

trio: (1) a piece for three performers; (2) the middle section of a MINUET, SCHERZO, or march.

triple counterpoint: a case of INVERTIBLE COUNTERPOINT involving three parts. The parts are so written that any two can reverse their positions, with the polyphony still providing satisfactory consonant-dissonant relationships.

twelve-tone (dodecaphonic) system: a method of composition invented by Arnold Schoenberg utilizing a specific ordering of the twelve notes. The SERIES provides the basis for a composition.

una corda (It.): indicates that the pianist is to mute the instrument by depressing the left pedal.

unison: also known as prime, the intervallic distance of zero.

vivace (It.) or **vivement** (Fr.): lively.

weich (Ger.): weak.

whole-tone scale: one of the two scales made up of six whole tones to the OCTAVE.

wogend (Ger.): surging, fluctuating.

zart (Ger.): sweet; the same as DOLCE.

Zeitmass (Ger.): tempo.

zurückhaltend (Ger.): holding back; the same as RALLENTANDO.

LIST OF BOOKS AND ARTICLES REFERRED TO IN THE TEXT

Babbitt, Milton, "Some Aspects of Twelve-Tone Composition," *The Score,* XII (June, 1955), 53–61.

Bach, Johann Sebastian, *Cantata No. 4,* ed. Gerhard Herz, New York, W. W. Norton, 1967.

—— *Complete Organ Music,* New York, Dover, 1970.

—— *371 Chorales,* ed. Riemenschneider, New York, G. Schirmer, 1941.

Barkin, Elaine, "A Simple Approach to Milton Babbitt's Semi-Simple Variations," *The Music Review,* XXVIII/4 (1967), 316–22.

Berlioz, Hector, *Fantastic Symphony,* ed. Edward T. Cone, New York, W. W. Norton, 1971.

Chopin, Frédéric, *Preludes, Op. 28,* ed. Thomas Higgins, New York, W. W. Norton, 1973.

Davidson, Archibald T., and Willi Apel, eds. *Historical Anthology of Music,* II, Cambridge, Harvard University Press, 1950.

Goldman, Richard Franko, *Harmony in Western Music,* New York, W. W. Norton, 1965.

Grove's Dictionary of Music and Musicians, ed. Eric Blom, 5th ed., New York, St. Martin's Press, 1954.

Hindemith, Paul, *Ludus Tonalis,* Mainz, B. Schotts Söhne, 1943.

Mann, Alfred, *The Study of the Fugue,* New York, W. W. Norton, 1965.

Mitchell, William, "The Tristan Prelude: Techniques and Structure," *The Music Forum,* I (1967), 162–203.

Morley, Thomas, *A Plain and Easy Introduction to Practical Music,* ed. R. A. Harman, New York, W. W. Norton, 1973.

Nelson, Robert, *The Technique of Variation,* University of California Press, 1973.

Perle, George, *Serial Composition and Atonality,* Berkeley, University of California Press, 1962.

Piston, Walter, *Harmony,* 3rd ed., New York, W. W. Norton, 1969.

Salzer, Felix, *Structural Hearing: Tonal Coherence in Music,* 2 vols., New York, Dover, 1952.

Salzer, Felix, and Carl Schachter, *Counterpoint in Composition,* New York, McGraw-Hill, 1969.

Schenker, Heinrich, *Five Graphic Music Analyses,* New York, Dover, 1969.

Sweelinck, Jan P., "Composition Regeln" ("Composition Rules"), *Werken van Jan Pieterszoon Sweelinck,* Leipzig, Breitkopf & Härtel, vol. 10, ed. Hermann Gehrmann, 1943.

WORKSHEETS

Worksheet 24

1. Reduction and synthesis.

2. Write a florid counterpoint above a *cantus firmus* of your choice.

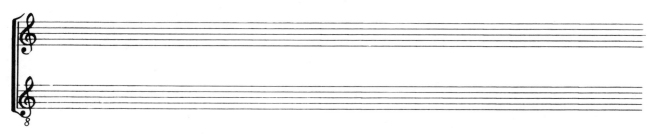

3. Write a florid counterpoint below a *cantus firmus* of your choice.

Worksheet 25

1. Write at least three short imitations in two parts, approximating Renaissance style. Take 100A, 100B, and 100C as models. Use real answers. Imitation may be at the octave, the 4th or 5th above, or the 4th or 5th below. *Dux* should be followed by *comes* quite closely. Vary the modes from one exercise to another.

2. Write short imitations in two, three, and four parts, approximating Baroque style. 100D and 100E may be taken as models. Use both real and tonal answers. Imitation may be at the 4th or 5th above or below. From one exercise to another, vary the distance between imitations so that one has close imitation, another imitation at a longer distance.

3. In any style, write an exercise using imitation by inversion. Imitation may be at any interval.

4. In a different style from the preceding, write an exercise using imitation by augmentation and/or diminution.

5. In any style, write a two-part imitation in invertible counterpoint. Write out both versions.

6. Review 51B and study the imitation. Find other imitative pieces in *Mikrokosmos*, Vols. I, II, and III. Taking such pieces as models, write a short imitative exercise in the language of extended tonality.

Worksheet 26

1. Score ⟨101B⟩, using the staffs below. Analyze the piece completely for dissonance and consonance. Add bar lines.

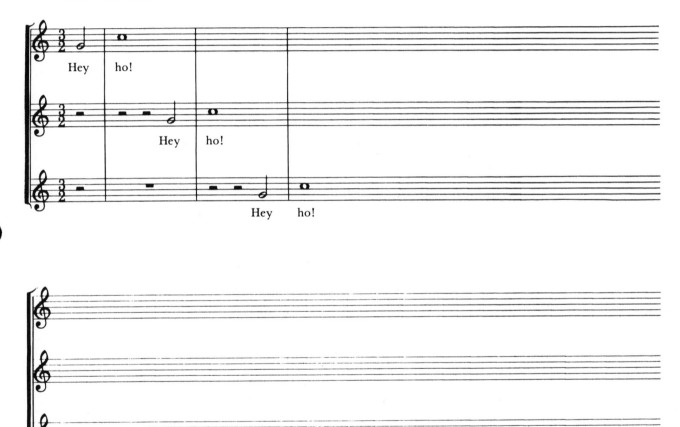

2. Write a two-part canon at the octave in any style. Start in the same way as the previous exercises (i.e., Worksheet 25)—with imitation—but continue the imitation until just before the end. A break in the imitation is needed to conclude the canon in some cases.

3. In Renaissance style, write a two-part canon at the unison or octave.

4. In Baroque style, write a two-part canon at the unison, octave, or 5th.

5. In any style, write a three-part canon, using imitation at the unison or octave.

6. In any style, write a four-part canon at the unison or octave.

7. Review ⟨51C⟩ and ⟨51D⟩. Write a two-part canon in the language of extended tonality.

Worksheet 27

Refer to 106 .

1. In how many different ways does Wilbye fill the four beats of the measure? Write all the different rhythms to be found in the soprano-1 part.

2. Is the first answer real or tonal?

3. Identify all simultaneous intervals in the first five measures. Circle all dissonances, and show their function.

4. The center of tonality in <u>20</u>–<u>25</u> is ————————.

5. The center of tonality in <u>26</u>–<u>32</u> is ————————.

6. Three examples of SUS are in the ———, ———, and ——— measures.

7. In <u>73</u> , why doesn't the first soprano's descent to 1 sound like the end of the piece?

8. What factors contribute to the sense of finality at the end?

Worksheet 28

Refer to 109 .

1. Identify all dissonant usages.

2. Determine the phrases.

3. Determine for each cadence whether it is a cadence *in* or cadence *on*.

4. For each cadence in, explain the modulation by finding the pivot chord and showing its two functions.

5. Indicate all tonicizations, and show functions within each.

6. Identify all prolongations.

7. Figure all chords.

Worksheet 29

Refer to 110.

1. Indicate phrases and cadences.

2. Show modulations and tonicizations.

3. Figure all chords.

4. Compare the first and fourth phrases. Indicate whether each melody note has been set as root, third, fifth, or seventh of a chord.

5. The first phrase is a prolongation of I. Does the setting of the same melodic phrase have the same kind of stability when it is set again? Why?

6. Compare the second and fifth phrases. Indicate whether each melody note has been set as root, third, fifth, or seventh of a chord.

Worksheet 30

1. Write four different settings of the melodic phrase given below following the tonal direction indicated. Figure all chords. If there is a modulation, explain the pivot chord. Suggestions: Be sure that you know whether you are writing a prolongation or a motion from one point to another. Determine the function of each melody note before starting to write. For instance, in melody (a) you find two short moves. The first is an ascent from 1 to 3 and back to 1; the second is taken as motion within I since the instruction keeps the entire exercise within the tonic triad. The simplest solution is to set melody notes B♭, D, and F as part of the I chord. But try other possibilities as well. The second B♭ can also function as third or fifth of a triad without weakening the prolongation since the I chord is so clear a boundary. Melodies (b), (c), and (d) all begin with tonic prolongations, which may extend for three or five notes. Decide how long each tonic will be; then find a way to move to the goal.

2. Set the scale pattern 1–2–3–4–5–4–3–2–1 the following four ways, using quarter notes and half notes:

   a. with the first seven notes prolonging I;

   b. with the inclusion of a tonicization of IV;

   c. with the inclusion of a tonicization of II when set in major, III when set in minor;

   d. repeating the last 2 and ending with II_5^6–V^{8-7}–I.

   Any pitch may be repeated. End with a harmonic cadence. Set each in both major and minor. 2–1 should have the rhythmic placement weak-strong.

3. Set the following melodic phrase two ways:

D major: prolongation of I, V;   B minor: prolongation of I, V;

Worksheet 31

Complete the following setting in the style of the opening:

Worksheet 32

It is not likely that Bach made figurated chorales out of pre-existing S.A.T.B. settings; his familiarity with the tunes and their possibilities in terms of tonal structure enabled him to compose the elaborated version directly. For the student, working from a given setting can be a useful preparatory exercise.

Compare the first two phrases of the chorale prelude and the hypothetical version, which is a reduction of the original. Find where each of the following elaborative techniques is used: polyphonic melody, PT, NT, S, and SUS. These are the same techniques you put to use in the counterpoint exercise in which whole notes were elaborated into quarter notes. The present exercise builds upon the earlier one.

After careful examination of the first two phrases, complete the last three phrases. The cadence at the end of the piece is identical with the one that ends the second phrase; the same material may be used in the lower voices. All of the notes in the hypothetical version must appear in some voice in the figurated version.

Hypothetical version of chorale

Chorale prelude by Bach, from the *Little Organ Book*

Worksheet 33

Identify completely all dissonances in:

a. [129A], violin-1 part.

b. [130D], 1–8 , all parts.

c. [135], 1–3 , all parts.

d. [138], 1–2 , all parts.

e. [139A], 5–8 , outer voices.

f. [144A], complete.

g. [150], 5–10 , between voice and piano.

h. [157], 1–first half of 4 . What triad lies behind these measures? Explain the function of the notes that are not part of that triad.

Worksheet 34

1. Identify the chord type in each of the following:

— — — — — — —

2. Over the given root, write a

V^7 diminished 7th   half-diminished 7th   augmented triad

3. What is the function of each of the following chords in the designated key:

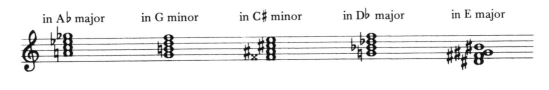

— — — — —

4. In the given key, write:

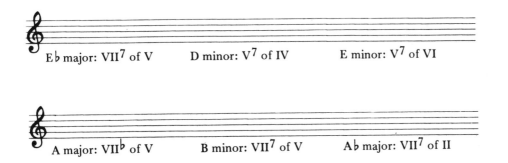

E♭ major: VII⁷ of V   D minor: V⁷ of IV   E minor: V⁷ of VI

A major: VII♭ of V   B minor: VII⁷ of V   A♭ major: VII⁷ of II

Worksheet 35

1. A I_4^6 chord occurs in $\boxed{144A}$, ____ measure.

2. Explain all chords in $\boxed{150}$, $\underline{11}$ and $\underline{37}$.

3. Find all I_4^6 chords in $\boxed{158}$, $\underline{62}$–end.

4. In $\boxed{167B}$, $\underline{14}$, how can the $\frac{6}{4}$-position chord be understood?

5. In a work by Mozart or Haydn not included in this book, find an example of a tonic prolongation that includes IV_4^6 as a neighbor chord.

6. Write three examples of cadences that include I_4^6 as follows:

   a. in the first, the 4th is a $\overset{>}{PT}$;

   b. in the second, the 4th is a SUS;

   c. in the third, the 4th is a NT.

Worksheet 36

1. In $\boxed{115}$ there are several tonic prolongations two measures long. Find one and describe it completely.

2. Describe the prolongations in $\boxed{120}$, $\underline{7}$–first beat of $\underline{8}$, $\underline{14}$–first beat of $\underline{15}$, $\underline{21}$–first beat of $\underline{22}$.

3. In $\boxed{121}$, what is the main chord behind the figuration of $\underline{35}$–$\underline{37}$?

4. In $\boxed{129A}$, how long does the opening tonic prolongation extend? How long does the dominant prolongation that starts after the double bar extend?

5. In $\boxed{130A}$,

    a. figure all chords;

    b. indicate all dissonant usages;

    c. bracket the dominant prolongation;

    d. explain the function of the I_4^6 chord in the prolongation.

6. In $\boxed{162}$, how can $\underline{9}$–$\underline{12}$ be understood as a unit? Explain.

Worksheet 37

In the following, figure the chords within the tonicizations. For example, in ⬚130A⬚ , $\underline{9}$–$\underline{12}$, the figures are $\underbrace{V^7\text{–}I}_{\text{of VI}}$ $\underbrace{V^7\text{–}I}_{\text{of V}}$ (two tonicizations).

a. ⬚130D⬚ , $\underline{8}$, last quarter, and $\underline{9}$. _____

b. ⬚130F⬚ , $\underline{7}$, last quarter, and $\underline{8}$. _____

c. ⬚132⬚ , $\underline{3}$, last quarter, and $\underline{4}$, first quarter. _____

d. ⬚132⬚ , $\underline{9}$, last quarter, and $\underline{10}$, first quarter. _____

e. ⬚132⬚ , $\underline{11}$, last quarter, and $\underline{12}$, first quarter. _____

f. ⬚132⬚ , $\underline{12}$, second and third quarters. _____

g. ⬚134⬚ , $\underline{15}$, and $\underline{16}$, first two quarters. _____

h. ⬚136⬚ , $\underline{74}$, last quarter, and $\underline{75}$, first quarter. _____

i. ⬚138⬚ , $\underline{3}$–$\underline{4}$. _____

j. ⬚144H⬚ , $\underline{3}$–$\underline{4}$. _____

k. ⬚147A⬚ , $\underline{30}$–$\underline{34}$. (What is the key?) _____

l. ⬚158⬚ , $\underline{11}$–$\underline{12}$. _____

m. ⬚158⬚ , $\underline{19}$–$\underline{26}$. _____

n. ⬚162⬚ , $\underline{63}$–$\underline{69}$. (What is the key?) _____

o. ⬚166⬚ , $\underline{3}$–$\underline{4}$. _____

2. In each of the examples below, fill in the empty beats with applied chords, using the following three methods:

   a. dominant-7th chords in root position;

   b. dominant-7th chords in the inversion that produces the smoothest voice leading;

   c. leading-tone chords (diminished-7th chords).

Worksheet 38

Outline the textures of $\boxed{162}$, omitting the introduction. Identify the instruments or groups associated with each texture.

Exposition
Theme 1
<u>13</u>–<u>33</u> *melody in unison strings, chords in winds and horn*

Bridge
<u>34</u>–<u>52</u> *tutti, all registers active, violin-1 melody*

Theme 2
<u>53</u>–<u>68</u>

Continuation
<u>69</u>–<u>77</u>

Continuation
<u>77</u>–<u>87</u>

Ending
<u>88</u>–<u>109</u>

Development
First section
<u>110</u>–<u>121</u>

Second section
<u>122</u>–<u>143</u>

Third section
<u>144</u>–<u>159</u>

Transition
<u>160</u>–<u>177</u>

Recapitulation
First phrase
<u>178</u>–<u>187</u>

Continuation and further development
<u>188</u>–<u>198</u>

Preparation for theme 2
<u>198</u>–<u>205</u>

Theme 2
<u>206</u>–<u>221</u>

Continuation
222–230

Continuation
230–240

Ending
241–259

Coda
First section
259–270

Second section
271–276

Third section
277–297

Worksheet 39

1. Describe the techniques of motivic development in 134 .

2. Is 144A built on a motive or a figure? Why?

3. Define the motive in 144D . How is the rhythm of the motive used throughout the piece? Is the pitch aspect of the motive of any importance? Why?

4. In 144H , what term describes the way in which the motive is used in 5–7 ?

5. How many motives are used in the introduction to 152 ? Does any of this material play a part in the rest of the song?

6. In 147A , what is the motivic connection between 1–2 and 23–24 ?

7. In 169 , compare 1–3 with 15–16 . Also, define the rhythmic motive and trace it through the piece.

Worksheet 40

Using the following plans, write at least three single phrases, each with a complete tonal movement, ending with a harmonic cadence:

a. major mode: the melody begins with 5, prolongs it, and descends quickly at the cadence;

b. minor mode: figuration predominates, bass moves up from 1 to 5;

c. major mode: the structure of the top line is 3–4–5–4–3–2–1;

d. minor mode: the structural chords are I–VII–III–IV–V–I;

e. major mode: the melody is in the bass;

f. minor mode: polyphonic melody;

g. major mode: the melody begins 1–2–3, prolongs 3, descends 3–2–1.

Worksheet 41

The tonal structure for the following two-phrase periods is:

antecedent: I–V; or I–modulation to a cadence in V
consequent: I–V⁷–I

In writing these phrases, use a variety of tempos, meters, textures, and densities.

a. *antecedent:* prolong I with a pedal point, melody prolongs 3 or 5, descends to 2 for cadence.
   consequent: similar, ending with harmonic cadence.

b. prolong I with contrapuntal chords, particularly V⁷ inversions.

c. *antecedent:* brief tonic prolongation, tonicize another scale degree, precede V with its dominant or leading-tone chord. *consequent:* tonicize another scale degree, emphasize the dominant to strengthen cadence.

d. *antecedent:* start with harmonic prolongation of I, go directly to V;. *consequent:* prolong V to the cadence.

e. (minor mode only) *antecedent:* prolong I in any way, move to V;. *consequent:* start with III and prolong it, return to V and emphasize it, cadence.

Worksheet 42

1. Write the following phrase groups. All moves to V may be either to a cadence on V; or modulation to a cadence in V.

   a. *antecedent 1:* prolongation of I, motion to V.
   consequent 1: prolongation of V.
   antecedent 2: similar to antecedent 1, more chromatic.
   consequent 2: through I, V of IV, to cadence.

   b. *antecedent 1:* I, little or no prolongation motion to V.
   consequent 1: prolong VI as neighbor to V return to V.
   antecedent 2: similar to antecedent 1, more figuration.
   consequent 2: emphasize V, small V⁷–I before final V⁷–I.

   c. (minor mode only) *antecedent 1:* prolong I, motion to V.
   consequent 1: start with III, cadence on III's dominant.
   antecedent 2: prolong III.
   consequent 2: move to V and emphasize it, harmonic cadence.

2. Select one of the three phrases given below. For whichever one you choose, write two different continuations, following these instructions:

   a. *antecedent 1:* the phrase as given below.
   consequent 1: modulate to a cadence in V.
   antecedent 2: prolong V.
   consequent 2: similar to antecedent 1, but leading to harmonic cadence, with (optional) extension.

   b. *antecedent 1:* the phrase as given below.
   consequent 1: modulate to a cadence in III.
   antecedent 2: prolong III.
   consequent 2: return to V and cadence.

3. Outline the phrase groupings in [141].

Worksheet 43

Using the progression (major mode) I–VI–II^6–I$^6_4$–V^7–I as a basis, write seven different phrases, described below. Use linear chords to connect or embellish those given. Write each in a particular tempo and character.

a. Include flat 6 as 7th of a chord.

b. Include flat 6 as 5th of a chord.

c. Include flat 6 as 3rd of a chord.

d. Include flat 6 as root of a chord.

e. Include V^9.

f. Include an augmented-6th chord.

g. Include a half-diminished 7th as an applied-leading-tone chord.

Worksheet 44

Refer to 144C .

1. Define the main motive of the piece.

2. Where does the repetition of the first idea begin?

3. How is that repetition different from the original statement?

4. What goal of motion is reached before the repetition?

5. Summarize the tonal movement of the piece with chords written in Roman numerals.

6. Indicate the prolongations of those chords.

7. Figure all chords in the piece.

8. What elements heighten the tension in the middle of the piece?

9. How is the ending stabilized?

Worksheet 45

1. Select one of the four themes given below, and write a set of variations on it. Study the theme carefully before beginning. Determine the structural chords. These should be maintained in the variations. Observe the embellishing and connecting chords. Can you think of alternatives for any of them? Structural notes in the melody can be the basis for many types of elaboration. Some form of arpeggiation can be applied to each of the themes. The themes are fairly limited in register. This gives you the opportunity to expand the material in musical space. Include a pair of variations in opposing modes as a group. Give each variation a definite character.

Themes for variations

(a) Allegretto

(b) Andantino con espressione

(c) Largo molto e mesto

(d) Andante

2. Listen to the chorus *See, the Conquering Hero Comes* from Handel's *Judas Maccabaeus* and compare it with Beethoven's variations on that theme for cello and piano. Then write a set of variations for a melody instrument and piano on the duet *La ci darem la mano* from the first act of Mozart's *Don Giovanni*. In making the arrangement of the duet that will constitute the theme, be sure to include the entire chord content even if registers must be reduced. The repetition of the first phrase may be omitted, and the theme should stop at the cadence before the transition to the coda in $\frac{6}{8}$. This will give a rounded binary form to the theme.

Name . . . . Date . . . .

Worksheet 46

Refer to 147B

1. Where does the reprise of the first idea begin?

2. How is it prepared?

3. How is it different from the original statement?

4. Describe the phrase grouping in the first ten measures.

5. Explain the pivot chord in the modulation to V.

6. What is the surprise element in the first section?

7. What tonal function controls the next twelve measures (11–22)?

8. What makes those measures different from the first ten?

9. Describe the overall melodic shape of those twelve measures.

10. Why is the cello silent for four measures?

11. Describe the phrase grouping in the reprise.

12. What role do dynamics play in this piece?

Worksheet 47

1. Choose one of the minuet beginnings given below, and compose a continuation and conclusion for it.

   a. For minuet a: *first phrase:* the phrase as given below.
   second phrase: prolong V for eight measures.
   third phrase: repeat part of first phrase, then revise so as to end in I or
   optional fourth phrase: another chord leading into a short extension.

   b. For minuet b: *first phrase:* the phrase as given below.
   second phrase: starts in III, prolongs it, leads to V.
   third phrase: restates first, embellished.

(a) For three instruments

(b) For piano

2. Choose one of the piano-piece beginnings given below. Complete the piece, using the motivic material of the beginning.

first phrase: the phrase as given below.
second phrase: modulates to a cadence in V, changes texture.
third phrase: tonicizes VI or flat VI, returns to V.
fourth phrase: restates the first, but prolongation of the dominant leads to a short extension.

3. Write a minuet or scherzo for an available instrumental group. The trio section is optional. Plan the overall tonal structure by deciding (a) whether the first section ends V⁷–I or V; or modulates to a cadence in V, and (b) what happens after the double bar.
4. Write a piano piece in rounded binary form in Romantic style. Use a tonal plan different from the one you employed in exercise 3.

Worksheet 48

1. In what ways does the music of ⟦150⟧ reflect the meaning of the poem? Consider both the vocal line and the piano part.

2. Analyze ⟦151⟧, including the following:

   a. identity of all phrases (are cadences open or closed?);
   b. tonal structure;
   c. modulations;
   d. tonicizations;
   e. prolonging motions;
   f. figuring of all chords;
   g. reduction of the vocal line, 1–15 ;
   h. the function of the following notes: 20 , F♯; 26 , C♯; 34 , C♭;
   i. description of the section from 68 to the end;
   j. interesting aspects of the final cadence;
   k. ways in which the poem has shaped the musical content.

3. Study the antecedent phrase given below. Use the material to complete a four-phrase period.

   antecedent 1: the phrase as given below.
   consequent 1: modulates to a cadence in V.
   antecedent 2: prolongs V, with mode mixture.
   consequent 2: similar to antecedent 1, but ends with a harmonic cadence.

   The phrase is extended by a postlude in the piano, either built on a tonic pedal point, a harmonic prolongation, or an extended cadence.

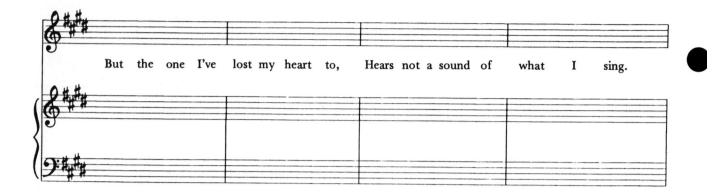

But the one I've lost my heart to, Hears not a sound of what I sing.

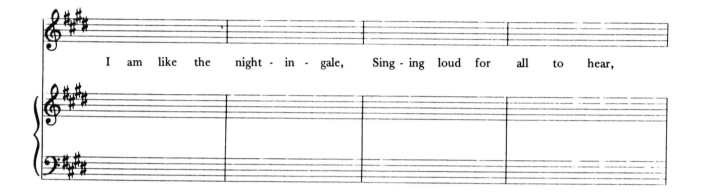

I am like the night - in - gale, Sing - ing loud for all to hear,

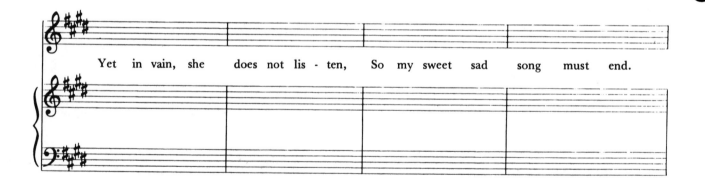

Yet in vain, she does not lis - ten, So my sweet sad song must end.

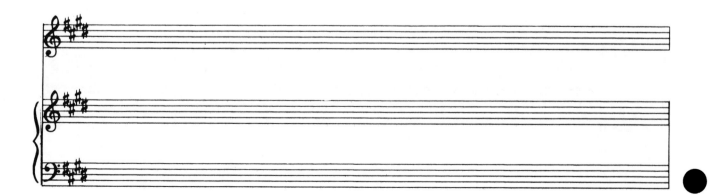

Worksheet 49

1. Explain each of the following prolongations as completely as you can. What is being prolonged? How? What are all the chords?

    a. 139A, 5–6

    b. 150, 26 and 54

    c. 155, 25–30

    d. 157, 23–32

    e. 158, 68–69 (write out on two staffs)

2. Make a piano setting of the following melody:

Worksheet 50

1. Write the following three single phrases. Make each complete in itself. End each with a harmonic cadence.

   a. The bass descends chromatically from 1 to 5, prolongs 5.

   b. The soprano descends chromatically from 5 to 1.

   c. The bass begins on 5, descends chromatically to 3, then ascends chromatically to 5.

2. In three different ways, connect the two chords in each measure (given below) with two (or three) others. Make each cadence different, using chromatic embellishing notes.

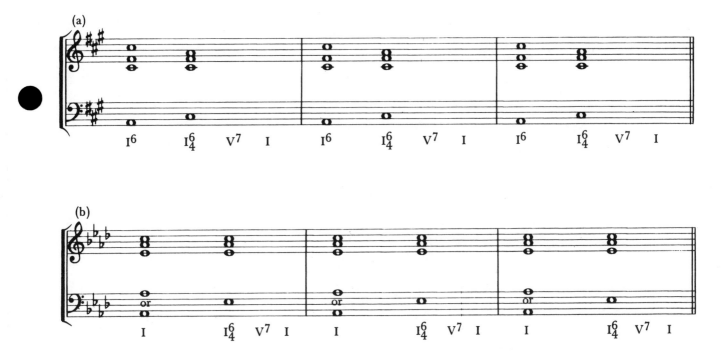

Worksheet 51

Refer to 165A .

1. Make a piano reduction of the excerpt.
2. Explain the modulation from D major to D♭ major.
3. Figure all chords.
4. What is the meaning of B♭♭ in 189?

Worksheet 52

Supply the "missing" chord in the following elisions:

Illustration

A: V⁷   I

(a) 144E , 3-4   (b) 144F , 20   (c) 148 , 32-33   (d) 153 , 17-18

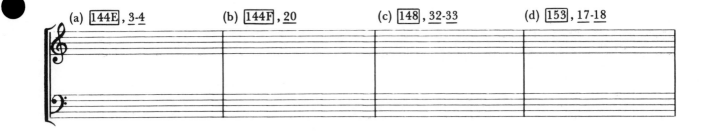